facebook me!

SECOND EDITION

A Guide to Socializing, Sharing, and Promoting on Facebook

DAVE AWL

Peachpit
Press

Facebook Me! A Guide to Socializing, Sharing, and Promoting on Facebook, Second Edition
Dave Awl

Peachpit Press
1249 Eighth Street
Berkeley, CA 94710
(510) 524-2178
(510) 524-2221 (fax)

Find us on the web at www.peachpit.com.
To report errors, send a note to errata@peachpit.com.
Peachpit Press is a division of Pearson Education.

Copyright © 2011 by Dave Awl

Editor: Rebecca Gulick
Production Editor: Myrna Vladic
Development and Copy Editor: Corbin Collins
Proofreader: Suzie Nasol
Compositor: Dave Awl
Indexer: Valerie Haynes Perry
Interior design: Charlene Charles-Will with Danielle Foster
Cover design: Charlene Charles-Will

ISBN-13: 978-0-321-74373-2
ISBN-10: 0-321-74373-3

9 8 7 6 5 4 3 2 1

Printed and bound in the United States of America

Acknowledgments

Getting the chance to write a book about Facebook the first time was an unexpected adventure. Getting to update it with a second edition is an honor and a privilege for which I'm indebted to all the readers who've embraced it (especially everyone who recommended it to their friends, both on and off Facebook).

Toppermost thanks for this edition are due to my ace editorial and production team. Editor Rebecca Gulick did a terrific job of helping me solve problems and calming my occasional eruptions of authorial hysteria. My development editor for this edition was my old friend Corbin Collins, who first started me on the road to becoming a Peachpit author a decade ago. As I just told him in an e-mail, his two cents are always worth at least a Groucho Marx seven-cent nickel. Becky Morgan and Becca Freed were my editors for the first edition, and their invaluable work in helping to shape the structure and style of this book continues to pay off in the current edition.

Thanks to my production editor Myrna Vladic for making sure my layouts were seaworthy; to my proofreader Suzie Nasol for her typo-spotting prowess; to Charlene Charles-Will and Danielle Foster for design; to Sara Todd and Laura Pexton Ross for helping get the word out; and to Nancy Davis, editor in chief, and Nancy Ruenzel, publisher of Peachpit Press. And continued gratitude to Sharon Steuer and Sandee Cohen, who mentored me in the Way of the Peachpit Author.

Part of the *Advertising and Promoting* chapter was originally published in somewhat different form on the CreativePro site as the article "12 Tips for Creative Pros on Facebook." Thanks to CreativePro editor-in-chief Terri Stone for once again giving me a place to develop ideas I used in this book.

Thanks to everyone at Becker Professional Education, especially Yasmeen Schuller, Diana Davis, Sue Burns, Tamika Nurse, and Carla Carry, for helping me learn by putting theory into practice.

Thanks to every single person who gave me permission to use their name and photo in this book (even if I didn't manage to fit you in somewhere); and especially to Matt Solomon, Bill Vanstone, Leah Clue Vanstone, Jill Bernard, Dan Telfer, Robbie Q. Telfer, Pip Lilly, Aaron Smith, Ellie Maybe, Rachel Claff, and various members of the Neo-Futurists for providing or helping me create key shots. Thanks to everyone who gave me useful input, especially Jennifer Senft, Shaina Lyn-Waitsman, Yehudit Hannah Cohn, Ben Frisch, Ian Belknap, Leigh Barrett, John Szymanski, Lola H de Santos, and Jason Katzwinkel.

Thanks to the friends who help me make it through—especially Jim Farruggio, Sara Miller Acosta, Danielle Christoffel, lynne Shotola, Lori Dana, Kevin Spengel, Tim Clue, Kathryn Lake, Tom Doyle, John Hansen, Andy Heaton, Kristin Amondsen Sassi, Lisa Buscani, Diana Slickman, John Pierson, Ayun Halliday, Sandie Stravis, Jorjet Harper, and Dan Loughry, as well as Richard Cooper, Elizabeth Hoffman, Yvonne Studer, Chris Bell, and Janis Van Court of The Kraken, and all the Earthlings. Thanks to my dear friends Tracey Bettermann Wetzstein and Kathy Zant for dragging me onto Facebook in the first place. All of you guys are (still) the reason the Confirm button was invented.

And once again, I'm grateful beyond words for the love and support of my family: my siblings, Jane and Earl, and Stephen and Sarah; my dad, Richard; and most of all, my mom, Charlotte.

Chicago, November 2010

Contents

The Preliminaries

Preface to the Second Edition

Hello, and welcome to the shiny new second edition of *Facebook Me*! And pardon my Swedish, but boy howdy have things changed since I wrote the first edition in the fall of 2008. In those days, people over 35 were just discovering Facebook; these days it's one of the most popular sites on the web. Its tools for sharing content have made it one of the first places people turn for news and info, while its population has rocketed past the half-billion mark.

And all the while, Facebook has been steadily adding new features to its site, and redesigning the old ones. In response, this book has been fully updated and expanded with new content to bring you up to speed on everything that's changed. It responds to the various privacy controversies with more detailed coverage of Facebook's privacy settings and advice for keeping your Facebook experience as secure as possible.

This edition also includes a brand-new chapter (*Advertising and Promoting on Facebook*) that shows you how to apply the principles of social media marketing to Facebook's specific user culture, in order to win new fans and customers and build stronger bonds with existing ones. And because the intersection of the personal and the professional on Facebook remains an area of keen concern, I've pumped up the *Facebook at Work* chapter with more guidance and tips on how to keep your profile professional—and use it as a tool to advance in your career.

Introduction

Life on Facebook is full of surprises. In fact, I'm still surprised that I'm on Facebook at all, let alone writing a book about it.

I was not an early adopter of Facebook, to put it mildly. The truth is, I had to be dragged clicking and screaming into the ranks of its users. Like you—I'm guessing—I joined Facebook when I got an invite from someone I couldn't say no to. Two such people, in fact, on the same afternoon.

In the fall of 2007, members of my old college speech team had started joining Facebook—a large, far-flung group of people I love but had difficulty keeping in touch with in the two decades after I graduated. But within a month of joining Facebook, I felt like my old friends were back in my life. I knew where they lived and who they were married to or dating, had seen pictures of their kids and animal companions—and through the magic of Facebook's News Feed, I knew what they'd done over the weekend, what was making them laugh out loud, and what songs were stuck in their heads on a given morning.

That's the single best argument I can think of for joining Facebook and checking it daily: the fact that it can help you stay connected with, and bring you closer to, the people you miss and wish were more of a presence in your life.

My goal for this book is to give you strategies for using Facebook intelligently and effectively. It's easy enough to sign up and create a profile—but how do you get the most out of your Facebook experience? How do you use it to make fascinating new friends, build new bridges to people you love but have fallen out of touch with, share the latest news with all your friends, effectively spread the word about your band or your graphic design business, and generally become the rich and famous rock star you were always destined to be?

Well, okay, that last one might be a little beyond the scope of this book. But the rest of it is definitely on the menu.

How to Use This Book

The structure of this book is fairly self-explanatory. It starts by covering the basics—how to set up your profile, configure your privacy settings, and so forth; then moves on to explore Facebook's various tools for communicating and interacting; and then wraps up with some more advanced topics like how to promote creative and business projects, and the workplace politics of Facebook.

One caveat: Facebook changes a lot. The folks at Facebook are always tinkering with and fine-tuning its interface. As with the previous edition, during the time I was writing this book, new features were added and controls were changed on an almost daily basis. So by the time this book makes it into your hands, Facebook may have evolved quite a bit from the version I've written about here. Some of the screen shots and specific instructions you see in these pages may not precisely match what you see on your screen when you log in. Some features I talk about may have been renamed, moved, or removed from Facebook altogether. That's one of the occupational hazards of writing a book about a web site—especially one that changes as continuously as Facebook does.

The best advice I can give you is not to get too hung up on the specifics as you read this book. My goal is to familiarize you with the general way Facebook works and the kinds of tools it offers. The screen shots

and instructions presented here are intended as illustrations and exercises to help you figure out the larger principles behind Facebook's various features—how to use its News Feed, Pages, Groups, Events, photos, videos, links, and so forth creatively and effectively. Once you understand what it's possible for you to do on Facebook, and get the basic hang of the place, you should be able to use the visual cues provided by Facebook's interface itself to figure out how to get from point A to point B—even if point B isn't exactly where it was the last time you looked.

Facebook generally offers multiple ways to do the same thing—so in the interests of space and not publishing a book that weighs more than your refrigerator, I've usually chosen to explain one expeditious method for accomplishing each given task, rather than describing all 17 possible workflows—or in some cases, maybe playflows. (Is that a word? Can I coin it?)

In deference to my subject matter, I will end this introduction with a ceremonial use of the Facebook third person:

"Dave Awl has written you a book about Facebook. He hopes you like it."

COLOPHON

This book was written and laid out on an Apple iMac partially covered by layers of indecipherable sticky notes, using Adobe InDesign CS3. Screen shots were taken using Snapz Pro X. The main fonts are Warnock Pro for body copy, and the Serif and the Sans for headings.

ON THE WEB

Visit DaveAwl.com for news and updates related to this book. And look for the official *Facebook Me!* Page on Facebook, to connect with the author and other readers of this book. You can also follow Dave on Twitter at twitter.com/DaveAwl.

The Anatomy of Facebook

Until you actually join Facebook and play with it a little, it can be hard to figure out what's so appealing about it. Some stories in the media make it sound like the hottest hipster fad since the invention of the black turtleneck, while others portray it as a cross between an opium den and a shark-infested lagoon.

So you put off signing up for a while, wondering: What could possess otherwise sane people to sit hunched over their computers all day, posting photos, playing word games, and sending each other imaginary cupcakes or pictures of cute animals? What could possibly make a website so addictive that its members refer to it as "crackbook"?

To me, the answer is simple: Facebook does a better job of connecting you with your friends, and keeping you in touch with each other, than any invention since Alexander Graham Bell first crank-called Watson.

You can think of Facebook as the online dashboard for your social life: a centralized display that gives you up-to-the minute data on what your friends are up to, what's on their minds, and what they're planning for the weekend.

But there are a couple of other levels to its appeal, too. In addition to strengthening social connections, Facebook gives you a set of power-

 Welcome

 News Feed

 Messages

 Events

 Friends

ful and versatile tools for sharing news, information, and ideas—not just with your own friends, but with the larger social network they connect to. In a sense, Facebook is like having your own personal broadcast network. That's the real reason why, with more than half a billion members and still growing, Facebook has rapidly become the new town square—the place where people gather to discuss the news of the day and spread the word about everything from new music, books, and movies to grass-roots political causes.

And finally, Facebook's sharing tools give you an inexpensive yet highly effective way to promote whatever creative, professional, or business projects you may have cooking. If you've got a band, a theater company, a coffeehouse, a graphic design business, or anything else you want to promote, this book will tell you how to set up official Facebook Pages to find fans and customers, and use Facebook's promotional features to get the word out to the kinds of people who are most likely to be interested in what you have to offer.

What Can You Do on Facebook?

What's an Application?

Facebook applications let you do all kinds of fun things, from playing games to sending offbeat greetings to your friends. Often referred to as "apps" for short, applications are simply programs designed to run on Facebook. See the *Applications and Other Add-Ons* chapter for complete info on Facebook's applications—what they are and how to use them.

In upcoming chapters, we'll look at the various ways you can use Facebook:

- Reconnecting with old friends and making brand new ones
- Keeping track of what your friends are saying, thinking, and doing
- Sharing info with friends by posting notes, links, photos, and videos
- Using applications to play games with friends around the world; spread the word about charities and political causes; recommend books, movies, and music; and much more
- Inviting your friends to parties, performances, book groups, meetings, and any other kind of get-together you can dream up
- Creating Groups and Pages to connect with others who have similar interests—and spread the word about creative projects and business endeavors

I'll also give you tips and strategies for dealing with common problems and concerns about Facebook:

TIP: See the *Privacy and Security* chapter for lots of tips and info on how to make your Facebook experience safe and secure.

- How to protect your privacy and enjoy Facebook safely
- How to evaluate friend requests from complete strangers
- How to decide which apps are trustworthy and which ones to give the brush-off
- How to avoid unintentionally annoying the bejabbers out of your Facebook friends

- How to reduce the chances that your Facebook obsession will get you in hot water at work

But for now, let's start at the beginning, with a guided tour of Facebook's most prominent features.

The Blue Bar

Running across the top of every page on Facebook is the same bright blue bar, cleverly known as "the blue bar." It will be your faithful companion for all your journeys on Facebook, more loyal than Tonto, Robin, or even Dr. Bunsen Honeydew's faithful lab assistant, Beaker.

The left side of the blue bar

The right side of the blue bar

The links in the blue bar help you navigate your way around Facebook.

- **Facebook** and **Home** take you to your Home page on Facebook.
- Click on the **Friend Requests icon** to open a pop-up menu that shows you the most recent friend requests and friend suggestions you've received.
- Click on the **Messages icon** to open a pop-up menu that shows you summaries of the newest messages you've received in your Inbox.
- Click on the **Notifications icon** to see your latest notifications—short messages that let you know when something has happened that Facebook thinks you should know about, such as a friend writing on your Wall or commenting on something you've posted.
- Toward the middle of the blue bar is Facebook's **search field**. You can use this to find all sorts of things on Facebook: people, Groups, Events, Pages, apps, and more. You can even use it to search for results on the web.
- **Profile** takes you to your Profile page.
- Clicking on **Account** opens a menu that lets you access your account settings, privacy settings, and other account management tools. It's also where you'll find the command to log out of Facebook when you need to.

TIP: If you use a shared computer, it's important to make sure you're logged into Facebook as yourself before you start posting—rather than the last person to use the computer, who may have forgotten to log out. One quick way to check that from any page on Facebook is by clicking Account in the blue bar, which will show you the name and profile pic of the person who's currently logged in.

The three icons in the blue bar, from left to right: Friend Requests, Messages, and Notifications. All three light up with numbers in little red balloons to let you know how many new friend requests, messages, or notifications you've received since the last time you checked. Click on them to open their pop-up menus for more details.

A Brief History of Facebook

Facebook's rise to prominence on the Internet has been meteoric. At the time of this writing, Facebook has more than 500 million members around the world and is still growing by leaps and bounds.

Launched in February 2004 by Mark Zuckerberg, then a student at Harvard University, Facebook took its name from the printed directories known as "face books" that students were given to help match their classmates' names with their faces. (The various controversies about Facebook's beginnings, and ensuing court battles, have been covered thoroughly by other books and at least one blockbuster film, so I won't rehash those here.)

The original idea for Facebook was to build an online, interactive version of a traditional face book, which would allow students to create, personalize, and update their own profiles.

Another key idea was that Facebook's members would use their real names, and their identities would be verified by virtue of the fact that their profiles were linked to school-issued e-mail addresses. Unlike MySpace and other popular networking Web sites, no pseudonyms, aliases, or fake names would be allowed on Facebook, thus making its members accountable for how they behaved.

Facebook's membership was originally limited to Harvard, but the site proved so popular there that it was quickly expanded to other universities and colleges, and then high schools, and then workplaces.

The biggest turning point, however, came in September 2006 when Facebook dropped the requirement for a school- or work-issued e-mail account, effectively opening its doors to anyone older than 13 with a working e-mail address. By July 2007, nearly half of Facebook's users were 35 and older, as parents and grandparents joined teenagers and college kids on its rolls. These days, according to Internet marketing research company comScore, Facebook has the most site traffic of any social media site in the world.

Facebook © 2010 · English (US)   About · Advertising · Developers · Careers · Privacy · Terms · Help

Facebook's footer

The Footer

| Afrikaans |
| Azərbaycan dili |
| Bahasa Indonesia |
| Bahasa Melayu |
| Bosanski |
| Català |
| Čeština |
| Cymraeg |
| Dansk |
| Deutsch |
| Eesti |
| English (US) ▼ |

A few of the many choices in the Language dialog. Click the triangle next to English to reveal some fun subordinate choices, including Pirate English and Upside Down English.

Running along the bottom of every Facebook page is a horizontal list of links called the *footer*. It's easy to overlook, but it has some useful resources.

- The **Language** link (next to the copyright statement) opens a dialog that lets you change which language you view Facebook in. (I use this to brush up on my French sometimes.)
- **About** takes you to the About Facebook page, which rounds up press information, hiring announcements, and other company-related info.
- **Advertising** links to information and tools for advertisers. (See the *Advertising and Promoting on Facebook* chapter.)
- **Developers** links to resources for creating Facebook applications.
- **Careers** provides info about professional opportunities at Facebook.
- **Privacy** gives you handy access to Facebook's privacy guide.
- **Terms** displays Facebook's Statement of Rights and Responsibilities.
- **Help** links to the Facebook Help Center, which also gives you access to Getting Started tips and Safety information.

The Profile Page

Your Profile page is the page about you on Facebook. It's the place your friends will visit to see what you've been up to lately, and it's one of the two pages you'll probably spend the most time on (along with your Home page).

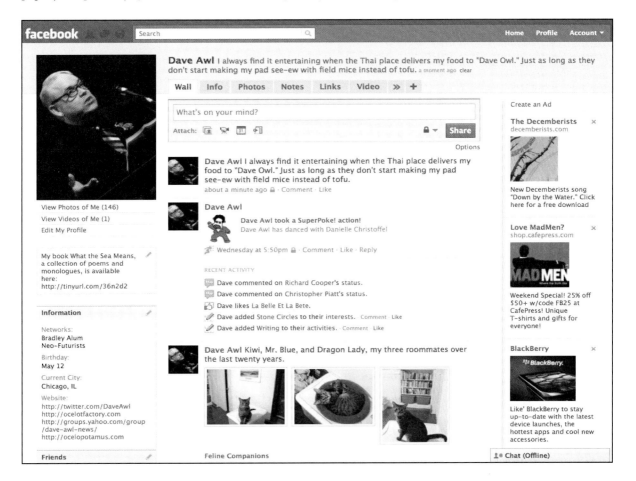

Your Status Update

Up at the top of your Profile page is your *status update*: a short (usually one- or two-sentence) answer to the question *What's on your mind?*

The status update at the top of the Profile page, and the tabs underneath it

TIP: Whatever you type for your status update will be visible on your friends' Home pages, and possibly other places around Facebook as well. You can think of it as sending out a little news release to your social circle.

TIP: In addition to the three default tabs on your Profile page, you can also add tabs for some of Facebook's other basic applications (such as Notes, Links, and Video), using the plus sign menu next to the tabs. See the *Applications and Other Add-Ons* chapter for details.

TIP: Who can see the information on your Profile page? By default, some parts of your profile can only be seen by your friends, some parts are also visible to people who are connected to your friends, and some of your information is visible to the general public. But you can control exactly who can access each part of your profile by taking charge of Facebook's privacy settings. See the *Privacy and Security* chapter for information on how to do that.

You can use your status update to tell your friends what you're working on, what you're planning on doing later today, what song is stuck in your head, something funny that happened to you on the way to work, or anything else you'd like to share with your friends.

The Three Main Tabs

By default, your profile page has three different tabs people can choose to see different kinds of information: the Wall, Info, and Photos. (Others can be added by choice—see the tip at left.)

Wall Tab

The Wall tab is the default view for your Wall. People can drop by your Wall to see what you've been up to on Facebook.

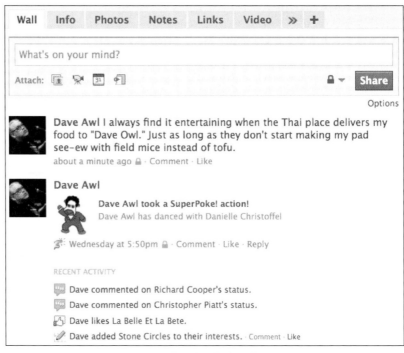

The Wall tab, with several News Feed stories displayed

Your Wall displays *News Feed stories*—short messages generated by Facebook to tell your friends what you've been up to lately: whom you've made friends with, what postings you've commented on, and so forth. (These are the same stories that appear in the News Feed area of the Home page, discussed later.) Think of Facebook's News Feed as your own personal PR bureau, keeping your legion of fans up to date on your doings. People can also write messages on your Wall (and you can return the favor on theirs).

 Dave Awl Hey there, Megan! I hope you're having such a terrific birthday that it makes the late news *and* they have to update the Wikipedia article on "Birthday" to address the resulting controversy.
October 3 at 9:15pm · Comment · Like

Info Tab

When people want to know a little more about who you are and what makes you tick, they click your Info tab. The Info tab rounds up basic data like your hometown, current city, and contact information, plus biographical information (your birthday, where you went to school, and where you've worked) and lists of your favorite music, books, movies, and TV shows.

Some of the information that can be displayed on the Info tab

TIP: By default, messages you write on someone's Wall are public, meaning that other people who visit that person's profile page will be able to read them—and they may show up in the News Feed as well. You can think of Wall posts as being kind of like tacking up a note on a neighbor's door, or dedicating a song to someone on the radio.

NOTE: The information on the Info tab is all optional. It's completely up to you what info you want to share, and how much detail you want to go into.

Photos Tab

Posting and sharing photos is one of the most popular pastimes on Facebook. Once you upload photos to Facebook, you can arrange them into albums and

NOTE: The Photos tab doesn't appear until it has content to display. So if you haven't posted any photos yet, and your friends haven't posted any photos tagged with your name, you won't see a Photos tab on your profile. But don't worry—the Photos tab will show up once it has a reason to be there.

invite your friends to come take a look at them—and maybe even scribble some trenchant remarks down in the comments area at the bottom of the page for each photo.

The Photos tab gives you and your friends quick access to any photos you've posted, as well as photos your friends have posted that include you.

The Home Page

You can always drop by your friends' individual Profile pages to find out what any specific pal of yours has been up to lately. But your Home page gives you one-stop shopping for news about your friends, including links and photos they've posted, their most recent status updates, and other good stuff.

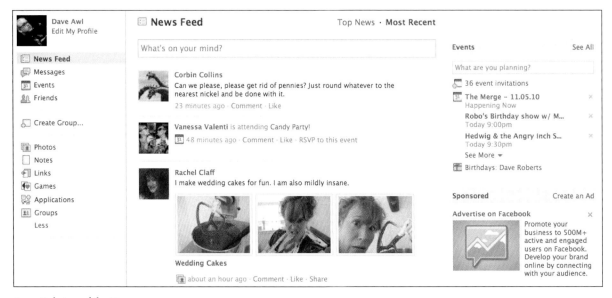

A partial view of the Home page

The News Feed

Right in the center of your Facebook Home page is the News Feed, which rounds up stories about your friends' activities on Facebook (like the ones described earlier in the "Wall" section).

The News Feed has two different views you can select: Top News, which shows you a selection of News Feed content Facebook thinks you'll be most interested in, and Most Recent, which shows you News Feed content in chronological order of when it was posted. You'll find all the details on the News Feed and how it works in the *Sharing Content on Facebook* chapter.

The Left-Hand Column

In the left-hand column of the Home page you'll find a list of bookmarks— quick links that either take you to various useful places on Facebook, or show you different kinds of content. Clicking the Messages bookmark, for example, opens your Facebook Inbox, where you can send and receive direct messages with other Facebook users. Clicking the Games bookmark takes you to the Games dashboard where you'll see invitations from your friends to play games with them on Facebook. Clicking the Photos, Notes, and Links bookmarks allows you to see just those specific kinds of content posted by your friends. All of these bookmarks are explained in detail in the chapters ahead.

The Right-Hand Column

There are some other goodies on your Facebook Home page, too, in the column on the right side of the page.

- **The Events area** lets you know about upcoming Events you've been invited to, as well as your friends' birthdays.
- **The Requests area** shows you a few of the most recent invitations you've received, and links to the main Requests page (discussed in the following section).
- **The Pokes area** displays any recent Pokes you've been sent. (Pokes are a special kind of "hello" message on Facebook; see the *Communicating on Facebook* chapter for details.)
- And down toward the bottom of the column is the **Get Connected area**, with some tools for finding people you know on Facebook and inviting other friends to join Facebook. (See the *Friends* chapter.)

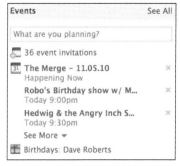

The Events area in the right-hand column on the Home page

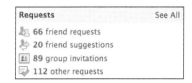

The Requests area. (Don't panic—the numbers you see won't be this high until you've been on Facebook a while and done a lot of procrastinating.)

The Pokes area

The Get Connected area

Other Kinds of Pages

In addition to your Profile page and Home page, there are a few other places you'll probably be visiting from time to time on Facebook.

The Requests Page

Clicking any of the links in the Requests area on the Home page takes you to the Requests page, where you can see various kinds of invitations you've received. When other Facebookers invite you to become their friend, the request shows up here. The Requests page also shows you invitations to attend Events, join Groups, play games, and interact with your friends using apps.

The Inbox

The Inbox is your Facebook message center—a place where you can send and receive direct, private messages to and from your friends on Facebook. See the *Communicating on Facebook* chapter for more about the Inbox.

The Notifications Page

When you click the Notifications icon in the blue bar, you'll see a handful of your most recent notifications. Click See All Notifications at the bottom to go to the Notifications page and see them all.

Notifications, as mentioned earlier, are little announcements that tell you something has happened that Facebook thinks you should know about. When someone writes on your Wall, comments on a photo you've posted, or accepts your friend request, you'll most likely find out about it through a notification.

All of your recent notifications are listed in chronological order on the Notifications page, which you can access by clicking the See All Notifications link at the bottom of the Notifications pop-up menu in the blue bar.

Groups

Groups are like little clubs on Facebook, where members can talk and post information related to something they have in common. You can create a Facebook Group dedicated to any subject under the sun, and invite people to join it—as long as it's not obscene, hateful, or otherwise in violation of Facebook's Terms of Use (as covered in the *Privacy and Security Chapter*). Groups currently come in two forms: new-style Groups and old-style Groups. See the *Group Dynamics* chapter for all the details on the distinction.

Events

Events are essentially home pages for calendar events. You can create Event pages for parties, performances, concerts, lectures, movie outings, rallies, or any other kind of gathering, and send out invites to friends you'd like to attend. Facebook allows the invitees to RSVP so you know whether or not they're planning on showing up, and gives you a page on which you and your guests can post information, photos, videos, and other content relevant to the Event in question. Events are covered in the chapter *The Facebook Calendar*.

Notes

Notes are short essays you write and post for your Facebook friends to read. You can think of them as blog entries, but instead of being posted to the whole World Wide Web, they're directed to the more intimate audience of your Facebook Friends list. You'll find all the info on Notes in the *Sharing Content on Facebook* chapter.

Official Pages

Individual Facebook members are represented by profiles. Public figures and entities like bands, theater companies, TV shows, books, and movies are represented by official Pages. An official Page on Facebook looks like a profile page, but instead of becoming friends with the entity the Page represents, you click a Like button to become a fan of the Page. See the *Pages* chapter for complete info on Facebook Pages.

Community Pages

Community Pages are pages that are automatically created by Facebook to round up information on various topics of interest to Facebook members. When you add activities and interests to your profile, they may appear as links to Community Pages dedicated to those topics—especially if no official Page for the topic exists.

Places Pages

Places Pages are pages that represent locations people check in to using Facebook's Places feature. Find out more about Facebook Places in the *Sharing Content on Facebook* chapter.

TIP: If you're familiar with Yahoo Groups or Google Groups, then you already have a pretty good idea how Facebook Groups work. And if you or your friends use Evite to send out party invitations, you'll find that Facebook Events work similarly.

Get By with a Little Help from the Help Center
Don't be shy about visiting Facebook's Help Center when you have questions or find something on Facebook you don't understand—especially new features that may have been launched after this book was published. You'll find basic instructions as well as useful tips which you can access by clicking in a directory of topics as well as by searching. You can visit the Help Center easily by clicking the word Help in Facebook's footer.

TIP: For keeping up with new features and changes to Facebook, I recommend following the official Page for Facebook itself, which you can find at facebook.com/facebook—click the Like button at the top of the page to get regular updates. It's also a good idea to check in from time to time on the official Facebook blog at blog.facebook.com.

Signing Up
and Setting Up
Your Profile

Life on Facebook begins with registering and setting up a personal profile. Your Profile page is where you get to express your personality, your style, your current interests, and your obsessions. It's the place your friends will drop by to see what's on your mind lately—as well as what's in your MP3 player, your video queue, and your book pile.

Your profile also serves as an introduction to new people you meet on Facebook—it's something like a business card, only with a playful streak, a listing of mutual connections, and dynamically updated contact info. (Not to mention the fact that you don't have to pay to have it printed up.)

If you're new to Facebook, this chapter will walk you through the process of creating an account and customizing your profile. And if you're already on Facebook, you can use this chapter as a reference on how to edit and update your profile, change your basic account info (including your password and your name), link your profile to set a username for your account, and customize the e-mail notifications you receive from Facebook.

Registering with Facebook

Before you join Facebook, there are a few things you might want to have at the ready—just so you don't wind up with an annoying case of *Facebookus interruptus*. Here's your checklist:

- First of all, you'll need a working e-mail address. Facebook will send a confirmation message to you that you'll need to respond to as part of the setup process. So make sure to use an address that you can actually check while you're signing up.

- You'll also need your date of birth, because you have to be older than 13 to join Facebook.

- You might also want to have a digital photo ready to use as your profile picture (although you can hold off on that till later if you want). Make sure the file size is less than 4MB.

Once you've got those prerequisites in order, the first step to joining Facebook is to point your browser to www.facebook.com, where you'll see the Facebook login page.

 No Need to Get Personal
Remember that on Facebook, profiles are used to represent individuals, and Pages are used to represent bands, businesses, and other collective entities. Pages are also the way to go for public figures, politicians, and celebrities who need to communicate with large groups of fans. So if you're looking to set up a presence for your company, or you're representing a public figure, you should set up a Page instead of a profile. (Of course you can still set up a personal profile for yourself.)

Also, if you're joining Facebook for work reasons—in order to set up a presence for your company, for example—and you don't want to set up a personal profile, you can create a business account instead. See the *Pages* chapter for full details on creating Pages and business accounts.

---

facebook

Email | Password |
Keep me logged in | Forgot your password? | Login

Facebook helps you connect and share with the people in your life.

Sign Up
It's free, and always will be.

First Name:
Last Name:
Your Email:
Re-enter Email:
New Password:
I am: Select Sex:
Birthday: Month: Day: Year:
Why do I need to provide this?

Sign Up

Create a Page for a celebrity, band or business.

English (US) Español Português (Brasil) Français (France) Deutsch Italiano العربية हिन्दी 中文(简体) 日本語 »

Facebook © 2010

Mobile · Find Friends · Badges · About · Advertising · Developers · Careers · Privacy · Terms · Help

Sign Up
It's free, and always will be.

First Name:
Last Name:
Your Email:
Re-enter Email:
New Password:
I am: Select Sex:
Birthday: Month: Day: Year:
Why do I need to provide this?
Sign Up

Signing up for Facebook begins with filling out this simple form.

NOTE: Although you do need to specify your year of birth to join Facebook (primarily so that Facebook knows you're old enough to use the service), you don't have to display it on your profile. You're allowed to hide your age from others on Facebook if you want to. See the "Editing Your Personal and Contact Info" section for details.

Fill out the form on the right side of the page as follows:

1. Type in your full name. It has to be your real name, not a pseudonym or alias. (See "The Importance of Being Earnest.")
2. Type in your e-mail address.
3. Choose and enter a secure password—one that contains both numbers and letters, and doesn't spell a word that can be found in a dictionary.
4. Choose Male or Female from the Select Sex menu. (You can choose not to display your gender on your profile, but at the present time Facebook does require you to specify Male or Female when you create a new account. See the "Gender Bending" sidebar for more about this.)
5. Enter your birth date.
6. Take a deep breath and click the Sign Up button.
7. Facebook may ask you to complete a security check, which consists of typing the words shown on the screen, to prove that you're a human being and not an automated program. If you can't read the words, Facebook gives you the option to change the words or try listening to an audio file.
8. Check your e-mail (the account you specified in step 2) for a confirmation message from Facebook. Inside the message you'll find a link to click to complete your sign-up process.

The Importance of Being Earnest (or Whatever Your Real Name Is)

As previously mentioned in the *Anatomy of Facebook* chapter, Facebook was founded on the concept of its members using their real identities, so you're required to sign up using your true legal name.

Pseudonyms and aliases are strictly a Bozo no-no. Creating what Facebook considers a "fake profile" is a violation of Facebook's Terms of Use, and grounds for deactivation.

Common nicknames like "Dave" for David or "Jenny" for Jennifer are generally fine, but signing up as Captain Creamhorn or Contessa Van Snorkel-Pudding is asking for trouble, smartypants.

Facebook takes this issue very seriously—it has a dedicated team that patrols the member rolls looking for fake profiles to deactivate. Facebook also has software that attempts to identify and block bogus names during the sign-up process.

Unfortunately, because truth is frequently more colorful than fiction, this has sometimes led to real people getting flagged for signing up with their honest-to-gosh given names. In the summer of 2008, Reuters reported on a Japanese author whose real name—Hiroko Yoda—was rejected by Facebook. Yoda is a relatively common surname in Japan, but Facebook thought she was trying to pose as Luke Skywalker's wizened Jedi master. Facebook eventually relented once Yoda proved her identity, but she's not alone: Genuine last names like Jelly, Beer, and Duck have also tripped Facebook's alarms.

If you sign up using your real name and Facebook mistakenly flags it as a fake name, your best bet is to contact Facebook directly to plead your case. Click the Help link in the footer on Facebook's Home page (it's visible even if you aren't logged in); then choose Sign Up and "My name was rejected during sign up" for a link to a contact form.

Getting Started

Once you've submitted the sign-up form, you'll arrive at Facebook's Getting Started page—or actually, page one of three.

The Step 1 page gives you the option to begin finding friends on Facebook by searching your e-mail account. Finding friends is covered at length in the next chapter, *Friends*, so for now we're going to click the "Skip this step" link at the bottom of the page and keep going.

The Step 2 page lets you fill out some basic profile information to get started with: where you went to school and where you currently work. Just as in Step 1, you can choose to skip this step if you want.

On the next page (which is still part of Step 2, if you're keeping score), Facebook will show you some names and faces of people it thinks you might know, based on whatever school or company info you provided. If you recognize anyone shown, you can click the Add as Friend link next to their name to send them a friend request.

❝ ❞ Gender Bending

Not everyone is comfortable identifying themselves as "male" or "female." For various reasons, some people prefer to avoid labels and gendered pronouns altogether.

Facebook used to simply use neutral pronouns for anyone it didn't know the gender of: "Dave Awl tagged themself in a photo." But rigid grammarians hated it, and Facebook's translators also complained about the difficulty of translating Facebook into other languages when no gender was specified.

So, in the summer of 2008, Facebook began requiring new members to select a gender, and gently badgering existing members who hadn't already specified one to do so. But Facebook also noted, in a posting on its official blog: "We've received pushback in the past from groups that find the male/female distinction too limiting. We have a lot of respect for these communities, which is why it will still be possible to remove gender entirely from your account."

That said, at the time of this writing I wasn't able to locate any control on Facebook that would allow you to "remove gender entirely from your account." The closest thing is an option to not display your gender on your profile. (Go to the Info tab on your Profile and click the Edit link next to About Me to edit your Basic info; then deselect the "Show my sex in my profile" checkbox.) Other than that, you can try contacting Facebook directly and asking them to allow you to go gender-neutral.

TIP: If you enter a high school or college in the Step 2 dialog, a pop-up menu will appear next to it that gives you the option to choose a class year.

Why Facebook Will Never Charge Admission

Bloggers have coined the term "zombie lie" to describe a certain category of pernicious untruth: No matter how many times you debunk it, it keeps on rising from the grave. One of the silliest zombie rumors about Facebook is the notion that sooner or later, Facebook is going to start charging its members a fee just to have an account. Facebook Groups with panicky names like We Will Not Pay to Use Facebook. We Are Gone If This Happens! continue to attract thousands of members, spreading the false alarm—even though it's been debunked numerous times by Facebook itself, as well as mainstream media outlets like CNN.

So why exactly is this particular rumor so unfounded? For one simple reason: The folks at Facebook aren't fools. They have a profitable business model, and that business model is based on advertising revenues—which depend on Facebook's membership continuing to grow. Requiring members to pay a monthly fee would restrict that growth, and maybe even cause Facebook's user base to shrink. A smaller audience would mean less advertising dollars for Facebook. In other words, charging people money would actually *cost* Facebook money.

So chill out, zombies! Facebook is free. Yes, Facebook may charge for certain premium features, or to buy credits that you can use to play games—but logging in and connecting with your friends is already paid for by the good old-fashioned magic of advertising.

Step 3 gives you the option to go ahead and add a profile picture, if you have one ready to go. (If you'd rather wait, you can skip this step—it's easy to add a picture later on.)

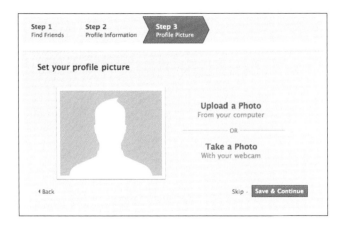

Choosing Upload a Photo opens a dialog that lets you browse to an existing picture on your computer.

If you have a camera connected to your computer, you can choose Take a Photo and snap a quick portrait of yourself.

When you click Take a Photo, the Take a Profile Picture dialog will open. It asks you to give Facebook permission to access your camera. Once you give it the green light, you're ready for your close-up.

Once you're done with all three steps, you'll arrive at your shiny new Facebook Home page.

At this point Facebook gives you a bunch of options for moving forward, including customizing your profile and searching for friends to add.

TIP: If you haven't responded yet to the confirmation message Facebook sent you when you signed up, you may see a reminder like the yellow bar along the top of the screen shot below.

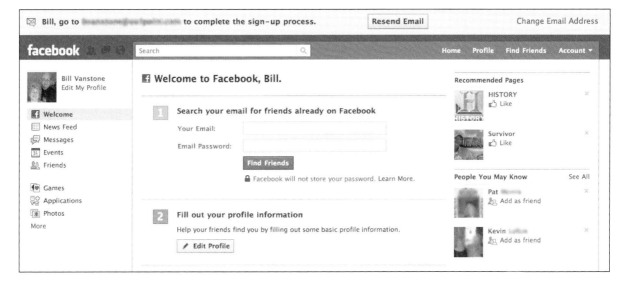

But before we invite any friends over to visit your new Facebook profile, let's spruce the place up a little by adding some information and making sure your basic account settings are in order.

Editing Your Profile

Whether you're setting up your profile for the first time or editing your existing information, Facebook's controls are basically the same.

If you've just completed the registration process, you'll find that Facebook gives you a handy Edit My Profile link on your new Home page so you can start filling in your profile info right away. (Clicking Profile in the blue bar and then the Info tab will get you pretty much the same results, but let's not look a gift link in the mouth.)

Once you've added some info, it's easy to add to it or change it.

TIP: Many of the Edit controls on Facebook are hidden by default, to keep the place looking tidy. So until you mouse over them, you'd never know they were there. If you're wondering how to change or edit something, it never hurts to run your pointer over it and see if a Pencil icon or some other helpful control magically appears.

Thumbnail and I

What's the Edit Thumbnail option in the Change Picture menu all about? Facebook uses your profile picture as an avatar to represent you in various places around the site, like the News Feed and within apps. This avatar version of you is usually square, and might crop your shot a little bit to fit the correct proportions. The Edit Thumbnail option lets you choose exactly how your shot will be cropped.

If you haven't added a profile picture yet, Facebook puts a couple of handy links right on the picture placeholder to make it easy.

Minding Your Own Birthday

Should you display your birthday on your profile? I think it's fine to show the month and date, so your Facebook friends can wish you happy birthday (an important Facebook ritual, as discussed in the *Facebook Calendar* chapter). But even if you don't mind your friends knowing your age, for security reasons, I recommend not displaying your year of birth—there's no real reason to disclose that, and your full date of birth could be useful information to identity thieves. In the About Me section, choose the "Show only month & day in my profile" option (shown below) from the pop-up menu next to the Birthday controls.

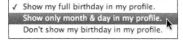

Changing Your Profile Picture

If you want to change your profile picture, go to your Profile page and move your pointer over your current picture. You'll see the Change Picture link appear. Click that, and you'll get a menu of options for choosing from your existing pictures or uploading a new one.

Left: The Change Picture control appears when you mouse over your profile picture. Right: The pop-up menu gives you a bunch of useful options for changing your picture.

Editing Your Personal and Contact Info

To edit (or add to) the information shown on your Info tab, click the Edit link next to the pencil icon for the section you want to edit.

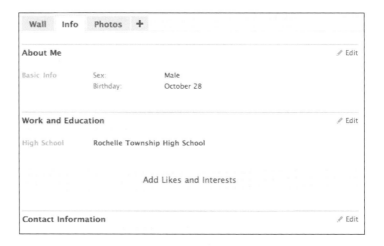

This will switch you to the editable view, which gives you various fields and menus for changing your info. Here's what the About Me section looks like after clicking the Edit link:

NOTE: The process I've just described works for the About Me, Work and Education, and Contact Information sections. Editing the Likes and Interests section of your Info tab works a little differently from the others, at least the first time you do it. But don't worry, I cover that in the "Adding Likes and Interests" section a little later in this chapter.

You can also edit the boxes that appear by default on your Wall and Info tabs, such as the Information box and the Friends box. Click the Pencil icon in the upper-right corner of any box for a pop-up menu with options related to that box.

Left: The Pencil icon in the Information box. Right: The menu options for the Information box let you pick and choose what info appears there.

Plain and Fancy

Facebook doesn't allow you to do much customization of your profile's visual design. Its philosophy is that keeping a neat, clean design that's consistent across the site helps people find what they're looking for more easily, and generally makes for a more pleasant browsing experience.

This makes neat freaks happy but is sometimes disorienting to people who come to Facebook from MySpace and expect to have the same control over colors, fonts, and layout—as well as their visitors' musical environment, with songs that start playing automatically.

But on Facebook, the idea is to express yourself with the content and information you post, rather than the design of your Profile page. You can jazz up the personality of your profile by adding fun applications, posting eye-catching photos and videos, and of course, engaging in colorful (not to say off-color) banter on your Wall.

One change you can make to the layout of your profile is that you're allowed to rearrange the locations of the boxes—some of them, anyway. The Information box and Friends box are fixed in place, but the boxes for apps such as Photos, Notes, Video, and Links can be moved. Just grab the blue title bar and drag the box until you see a dashed outline appear around a possible destination. Then release the mouse button to drop the box in its new location.

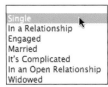

*The options in the Relationship
Status menu*

TIP: Keep in mind that
changing your relationship
status may trigger a News Feed story
that your friends will see. Changing
your status from *In a Relationship* to
Single, for example, can result in a
thread of 32 sympathy posts before
you've had time to exhale, and doing
it the other way around may generate
an equal number of congratulations
and requests for details.

Information

Relationship Status:
**Married to
Greg Kotis**

Children:
**India Kotis
Milo Kotis**

Birthday:
March 29

Current City:
Brooklyn, NY

Website:
http://www.ayunhalliday.com

*An example of an Information box
all decked out with a relationship
and family members*

TIP: Unlike relationships, with
family members Facebook does
allow you to enter the names of
people who aren't on Facebook. Their
names will simply appear as plain
text rather than links.

Setting Your Relationship Status

Facebook lets you indicate your current relationship status on your profile, so
others can see at a glance whether you're on or off the market. It's strictly optional, of course, but if you want to set a relationship status for yourself, click
the Edit link next to the About Me section of your Info tab and then click the
Relationships link in the left-hand menu. Then choose the appropriate option
from the Relationship Status menu.

Adding a Relationship

If you've got a significant other, the two of you can declare your relationship
on Facebook for all your friends to see.

NOTE: For the process below to work, your significant other needs to be on
Facebook and in your Friends list. If they aren't, you'll need to badger them to
sign up and friend you. Otherwise, although you can still change your relationship
status, it won't include the name of your significant other.

From the Relationship Status menu (discussed in the previous section),
choose any of the options that involve another person, such as In a
Relationship or Married. At that point, a With field will appear below
the Relationship Status menu.

Relationship Status:	In a Relationship ▾	with

You can type the name of your sweet baboo in the box and then press Enter.
Facebook will ask your baboo to confirm your relationship, and once they do,
a News Feed story will be generated announcing it to the world (or at least
the slice of it in your Friends list).

Adding Family Members

You can also add members of your immediate family to your Facebook profile. The process is pretty much the same for adding a relationship; type the
name of your relative and then choose the appropriate relationship from the
menu. Your family member will need to confirm the relationship before your
profiles are linked. Currently, the available options include only siblings, parents, and children. Facebook says extended-family relationships may become
available "in the future."

The "Write Something About Yourself" Box

Just under your picture on your Profile page is a little box that contains the words "Write something about yourself"—until you change that to something else. Click inside the box to type a short message.

This is your soapbox for whatever message you'd like to communicate, so be creative. It might be a biographical statement, a pithy quip, or a personal motto. You can also use this box to plug a current project or event, or draw attention to the link for your blog or website.

Edit My Profile

Write something about yourself.

The "Write something about yourself" box lives just underneath your profile picture.

Adding Likes and Interests

A big part of the satisfaction of setting up your Facebook profile is expressing yourself: creating a listing of your favorite bands, authors, TV shows, and movies, as well as your hobbies, activities, and other passions in life so that new friends can get a whiff of your scintillating personality, and old friends can check out what's on your mind these days.

TIP: If you've got an all-time favorite status update you've written, and it's not time-sensitive, you might want to recycle it for duty in the "Write something about yourself" box.

Plugging In to Pages
When I first joined Facebook, people displayed their interests on their profiles by typing short lists of their favorite things in life into various boxes. These days, Facebook makes the process a little more dynamic by using your connection to a Facebook Page as the primary way of expressing your interest in a subject. By connecting to an official or Community Page for, say, an author or a TV show—or even for an activity such as gardening or scooter riding—you're automatically linked to a gathering place for other Facebook users who share that interest, as well as a source of information about it.

If you haven't added any likes or interests to your profile yet, you can get started by clicking the Add Likes and Interests link on your Info tab. Start typing in any of the fields for the various categories in the form that opens, and Facebook will start searching for Pages that match.

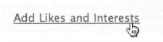

Add Likes and Interests

You can start adding your first likes and interests by clicking this handy link on your Info tab.

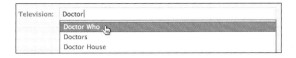

You can choose from the available matches, or, if nothing comes up, just keep typing what you want to say—Facebook will give you the option to add it to your profile anyway. If you accept, a brand-new Community Page will be generated to represent this hitherto-undocumented interest.

Once you've populated your profile with some Pages (note to self: add Alliteration to my interests), you can edit them any time you want by clicking the Edit link at the top of the section—add more interests, or delete the ones that are so very last week. You can delete an interest just by selecting it and then clicking Delete (or by going to the Page itself and clicking the Unlike link).

You can also rearrange their order (by dragging them around in the box after clicking the Edit link), so the stuff you're most passionate about is displayed first. In fact, whichever interest you award the first spot in a given category will be illustrated with a thumbnail image next to that category on your profile. (As in the shot below, where Russell Hoban gets the prestigious "favorite author" spot in my Books category.)

Books   Russell Hoban, Ursula K. Le Guin, Christopher Isherwood, James Joyce, Charles Dickens, Gore Vidal, Paul Monette, Kurt Vonnegut, Annie Dillard, Hermann Hesse, Jeanette Winterson, Rilke, Frank O'Hara, Allen Ginsberg, W. H. Auden and 2 more   Russell Hoban

Setting Your Status

Whenever you're ready to start sharing your deep thoughts, silly quips, or random cranial hiccups with your friends, you can set your first status update. You can do this easily on either your Profile page or the Home page by typing whatever you want in the Status Update field in the Publisher (which you'll find toward the top of both of those pages) and then clicking the Share button. Maybe something like, "I'm new to Facebook. Be gentle with me."

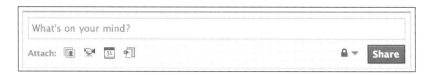

Editing Your Account Info

Your basic account info is always accessible on the Account Settings page. To get there, click on Account in the blue bar and then choose Account Settings. On the first tab, Settings, you can update your name if it changes (after a wedding, for example). You can also set the username for your account, change the e-mail address where you receive notifications, change your password, link to your accounts from other sites, add a security question, access your privacy and security settings, and deactivate your account if need be.

Setting a Username

Setting a username for your Facebook account accomplishes two things: First, it means you can log in to Facebook using your username in place of your e-mail address—which, depending on what you choose, may be easier to type. But it also gives you a handy, easy-to-remember URL for your Facebook profile that you can link to and share with others to help them find you. So, for example, if Herman Orff sets *HermanOrff* as his username, then Facebook.com/HermanOrff becomes his new URL. If he sets it to *afraidof-cabbage*, then Facebook.com/afraidofcabbage becomes the link.

You can set a username for your profile via the Account Settings page, or by navigating to Facebook.com/username.

NOTE: Usernames are not case sensitive, and periods are ignored. That means that *hermanorff*, *HermanOrff*, *Herman.Orff*, and *he.rm.an.or.ff* are all effectively the same username. So if you set *hermanorff* as your username, typing Facebook.com/Herman.Orff in your browser will still take you to Facebook.com/hermanorff.

TIP: Facebook only lets you change your username once, so think carefully about what you want it to be and make sure to proofread it cautiously before you click the button to set it. If you do need to change it, you can do so via the Account Settings page.

 Setting Up a Tab with the Payments Tab
As mentioned earlier, Facebook membership is free. So what's the Payments tab on the Account Settings page all about? At some point you may choose to buy Facebook Credits that can be used in various games and applications, or you might want to take advantage of Facebook's paid advertising options. You can specify a credit card and control the options for buying Credits and advertising via the Payments tab.

 The Changing Your Name Game
If you need to change the name you signed up for Facebook with, you can do so on the Account Settings page. The first time it's easy, and takes only about 24 hours. But after your first name change, for any subsequent switches you'll need to request permission by submitting a form to Facebook, and it could take up to a week to get a response. (So you might want to think twice about changing your name to Prunella McStoatwhistle for April Fool's Day. Like your mom used to say about making funny faces, you could get stuck that way.)

If your name changed when you got married, you might want to consider adding your maiden name as your middle name on your Facebook account. This will help old friends you've lost touch with recognize you more quickly on Facebook.

Facebook also allows you to display an "alternate name" on your account, to help people find you who know you by some other name. You can do this by clicking the Change link in the Name section of the Account Settings page, and then entering something in the Full Alternate Name field. If you select the checkbox to display your alternate name on your profile, it will appear in parentheses next to your primary name.

TIP: One more thought on usernames: If you're a performer, writer, politician, or other public figure, and you might be setting up an official Facebook Page at some point in the future—and if your real name is the name your fans know you by—you might want to consider reserving that for the username of your Page, and choosing something more nicknamey for the username of your personal profile.

TIP: Facebook's e-mail notifications can come in very handy if you're in an environment where you can read your e-mail but can't access the Facebook website—for example, if you're at a school or workplace location where Facebook is blocked. So if you post a question on someone's Wall before you leave for work in the morning, you'll still be able to read their response later that day, in the e-mail notification you get when they write on your Wall. And you can even keep the conversation going via e-mail: Facebook lets you respond to Wall postings, comments, and Inbox messages just by replying to the notification e-mail.

NOTE: Third-party applications you use on Facebook can contact you by e-mail, just like Facebook itself does. You can choose which applications are allowed to e-mail you on the Account > Application Settings page. See the *Applications and Other Add-Ons* chapter for more.

NOTE: Be sure to click the Save Changes button way down at the bottom of the Notifications tab when you're all done clicking buttons.

Changing Notification Settings

In addition to the Notification messages that appear within the Facebook site itself (as discussed in the previous chapter), Facebook sends you notifications as e-mail messages. When someone adds you as a friend, writes on your Wall, sends you an Inbox message, posts a photo that's tagged with your name, or does any of a variety of other things Facebook thinks you might want to know about, you'll get a heads-up when you check your e-mail.

If you don't want these notifications, you can choose to turn them off—and you can pick and choose what types of Notification e-mails you receive.

If you've activated a mobile device for use with Facebook, you can also control what notifications you receive on your phone. (See the *Going Mobile* chapter for more info on Facebooking by phone.)

To change your Notifications settings, go to Account > Account Settings and click the Notifications tab. You'll see a page full of checkboxes for the specific events Facebook can notify you about. Selecting a checkbox in the Email column means you'll get an e-mail when the event takes place; deselecting it means you won't. (The SMS column works the same way for notifications you can receive as text messages on your phone.)

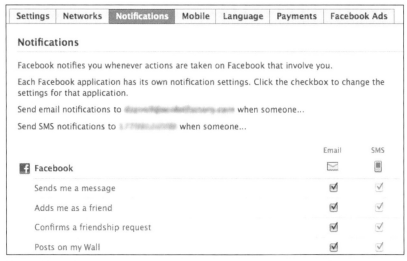

Some of the settings for e-mail notifications on the Account > Account Settings > Notifications page. There are also specific settings for actions related to photos, Groups, Pages, Events, Notes, Links, videos, and more.

Friends

In the previous chapters you've signed up with Facebook and learned how to set up and edit your profile. So far, so good. But if that's all there were to Facebook, there wouldn't be much point to it. It's friends, after all, who put the "social" in social networking.

So it's time to make some friends. Of course, chances are good that you signed up with Facebook because you got an invitation from a friend, and if you accepted it, then you've probably already got at least one friend displaying on your profile.

Then again, it's possible that you're starting with a clean slate—that you registered with Facebook because you keep reading news stories about it, or you stumbled across it in a web search, or maybe you have a friend or relative who keeps talking about it and you're curious what the appeal might be.

In either case, to get the most out of Facebook, you'll want to be connected to a number of friends with whom you can communicate, interact, share photos, play games, and more. How large or small that list of Facebook friends grows is entirely up to you.

Some of your friends are probably on Facebook already. Others may not be, but you can invite them to come join in the fun. And once

you've built up your Friends list a little, you can create special lists to keep track of them, you can introduce friends to other friends, and you can use existing friends to help you find your way to long-lost friends and make brand-new ones.

That's what this chapter is all about.

Connecting with Networks

Network, Schmetwork
These days, Facebook places a lot less emphasis on Networks than it used to. Up until early 2008, the blue bar included a Networks menu, and each Network had its own home page where members could post Events, write on the Wall, and browse for local Facebook friends. And Facebook used to offer Regional Networks for geographical areas, such as Chicago or Atlanta, in addition to its Networks for schools and workplaces.

Facebook says it removed the Network home pages because they weren't the most efficient way for users to connect, and the Network menu wasn't popular enough to deserve space on the blue bar. Facebook eventually eliminated its Regional Networks, too. But Networks for schools and workplaces still exist, and—at least for the time being— you can still join Networks and use them to help specify settings for who can see your profile and who can't.

Before you start connecting yourself to individual friends, it's a good idea to begin by connecting yourself to one or more communities that you already belong to in the 3D world: your high school, your college, or your workplace. Facebook calls these communities *Networks*.

Facebook gives you complete control over how public you want your profile to be. You can set it so that it's visible to everyone on the Internet; you can set it so that only very close friends can see it; or you can take advantage of a number of tools Facebook offers that allow you to choose a middle path— making it visible to various communities you belong to, without letting the whole world see in.

Networks allow you to open up your profile (or parts of it) to specific groups of people who are already part of your sphere. You might meet fellow students from your school in classes or at parties. And you might get to know anyone who works at your company in the normal course of doing your work, or sharing the elevator each morning. Joining a school or employer Network mirrors that social dynamic within Facebook itself. It makes it a little easier for people with whom you already have something in common to connect with you on Facebook.

If you entered the names of any schools or your employer when you signed up for Facebook, you may already belong to one or more Networks. But if not, you can choose to join them or leave at any time.

How to Join a Network

You can join Networks or leave Networks by visiting the Networks tab in your account settings. On the blue bar, choose Account > Account Settings, and then click the Networks tab.

Once you arrive at the Networks tab, your current Networks, if any, will be listed on the page.

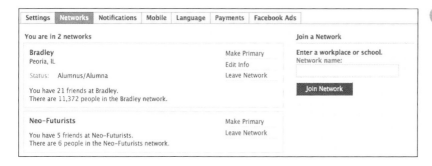

To join a new Network, type the name of a workplace, school, city, or region in the field on the right side of the page and click Join Network. (You may see Facebook suggest Networks for you to choose from if it begins to recognize what you're typing.)

From there, Facebook will advise you of any requirements to join and provide instructions for completing the process.

Networks and Privacy

Once you've joined a Network, you can use it as a way to control privacy settings for a variety of Facebook features, such who can find you by searching Facebook, or who can view photos or specific applications installed on your profile. You might create an album of photos from your college debate team, for example, and specify that it can be viewed by anyone who belongs to your school's Network as well as your friends. (See the *Privacy and Security* chapter for the full scoop on how to control specific privacy settings.)

TIP: If Facebook doesn't recognize the name you type, you'll get an error message saying "No matches found." Which means that a Network doesn't currently exist for the school or workplace you're trying to join. If that's the case, and you feel that the community in question deserves its own Network, you can contact Facebook and request that one be created.

What Networks Can You Join?

- **Workplace Networks** require you to have an actual working e-mail address from the company in order to join. So, for example, if you work for Spacely Sprockets, you'll need to be able to confirm your relationship to the company using an address such as *george@spacelysprockets.com*.

- **High School Networks** require you to be enrolled at the school before you can join them. (In order to provide maximum protection to high school–age Facebookers, it's strictly students only—even alumni and teachers aren't allowed to join high school Networks.) Of course, even if you can't join your high school's Network, you can still list your school's name in the Education area of your profile.

  College Networks are similar to Workplace Networks: You'll need a working address from your current school or alma mater. If you're an alumnus and you don't already have a school-issued e-mail address like *rincewind@unseenuniversity.edu*, you'll need to set one up. (Most colleges make e-mail addresses available to alumni these days, so you can still join your alma mater's Network even if, like me, you went to college in the days of typewriters and kerosene lanterns.)

Stranger Danger
Before you approve any friend request, especially from someone you don't know very well, you should do a little scouting and vetting. Take a look at whatever info is visible on their profile to make sure there isn't anything that causes you concern. Check to see if you already have any mutual friends—and if you do, you might consider sending those friends a message asking them if they can vouch for the new person or supply any useful info. If you feel any doubt or discomfort at all, then you shouldn't feel any urgency about accepting the request. Take a few days to think about it, if you need to—the request will still be there, waiting for you to accept or reject once you've made up your mind.

Click the friend requests link in the Requests area of the Home page to go to the page where you can view and respond to requests. (And yes, this is what it looks like when you let your requests pile up a little bit.)

A friend request notification in the blue bar.

Adding Friends

When someone else on Facebook wants to be your friend, you'll receive a friend request, which you'll have to approve before Facebook officially pronounces you to be pals and you show up in each other's Friends lists.

You may have received some invitations from friends before you ever joined Facebook, in which case it's possible that you may have one or more friend requests already waiting for you to respond to. But if not, you'll have plenty of friend requests to look forward to in the future.

Friend requests are flagged out on your Home page, in the Requests area in the right-hand column. (New friend requests also appear as notifications in the blue bar.) You'll also receive an e-mail notification, unless you've tweaked your settings so as not to allow such e-mails. (You can change that setting on the Account > Account Settings > Notifications page.)

Approving or Rejecting Friend Requests

When you receive a friend request, click the friend requests link on your Home page (or the link in the e-mail notification you received). You'll be taken to the page where friend requests you've received but haven't responded to are displayed.

Each friend request displays the person's name and profile picture (if they have one). If they've included a personal message, that will also be visible.

If you and the person who sent the request have any mutual friends on Facebook, the request will say something like "2 mutual friends" (or however many there are). The phrase "2 mutual friends" is a link—click it to see a listing of friends you have in common. This can be a real lifesaver if your brain is having trouble making a connection to the person's name or picture, because mutual friends can clue you in to how you know the sender.

Notice that the name of the person who sent the request is in blue, which means you can click it to go take a look at the person's profile. (Facebook grants you temporary access to the profile of anyone who sends you a friend request, even if you wouldn't normally be allowed to see it.)

It's a good idea to always check out the profile before you approve a request. If you're having trouble figuring out whether you know the person or not, it may contain clues that tip you off, like the fact that you went to the same grade school or summer camp. You might also spot red flags that suggest the person isn't someone you'd get along with, or may not be who they say they are. (See the sidebar "Stranger Danger" for more.)

Once you've made up your mind, you have two choices: Confirm, which will add the person to your Friends list and give them access to your profile, or Not Now, which will hide the request without approving it.

If you choose to confirm the person, you have the chance to add them to one or more Friend Lists, which help you keep your friends organized in convenient categories. (See the "Friend Lists" section, later in this chapter.) Click the Add to List button that appears after you accept the request, choose the list you want to add your new friend to, and then click Confirm.

Once you've confirmed the person, Facebook displays a message that invites you to visit your new friend's profile and may also suggest mutual friends.

If you click the Not Now button, Facebook moves the request into your Hidden Requests area. You can view it again by clicking the See Hidden Requests link at the bottom of your list of friend requests on the Requests page. When you display your hidden requests, you have the option to confirm them or click Delete Request to remove a request permanently.

TIP: If you choose to delete a friend request, or leave it hidden indefinitely, keep in mind that Facebook isn't in the business of sending out rejection slips. So when you hide or delete someone's request, they won't get any kind of official message notifying them of that fact, and you don't have to feel like you've dumped a bucket of cold water over their head. It's true that if they're paying attention to their Friends list, eventually they may notice that you're not there. Or they may visit your profile and see that the Add as Friend button has reappeared (and the "Awaiting friend confirmation" message has disappeared), from which they can infer that you've chosen not to accept their request. But all in all, it's a fairly quiet and subtle form of rejection.

A friend request as it appears in the blue bar's pop-up notifications menu. One downside to responding via these buttons: If the person who sent you the request included a message, it won't be visible here. For that reason I always click through to the Requests page using the See All Friend Requests link.

Clicking on the number of friends you have in common opens the Mutual Friends dialog.

Click the name of the person who sent the request to check out their profile.

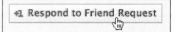

If you make up your mind while you're checking out the profile of the person who sent the request, you don't have to go back to the Requests page—just click the handy button at the top of the profile.

Clicking the Add to List button that appears after you accept a friend request reveals a pop-up menu that lets you add the person to any of the Friend Lists you've created.

You can add the same person to more than one list, so if they belong in more than one category, just keep clicking till you've selected all the lists you want. Check marks indicate the lists you've already selected.

" " Serious Sleuthing
If basic and advanced search aren't enough to turn up your friends, never fear. Facebook offers a slew of other advanced tools for searching up your friends on the "Find Your Friends on Facebook" page. See the "How to Pump Up Your Friends List" section, later in this chapter, for full details.

TIP: If you get multiple results with the same name as the person you're searching for, see the sidebar "Finding a Needle in a Friendstack" for tips on figuring out which one is your actual pal.

There's one other action you can take if you're not sure how to respond to a friend request. The "Send [Name] a Message" link on the person's profile lets you send them a note, which you can use to request more info as to why they'd like to be your friend (or to diplomatically explain why you're keeping your friend list on the small and private side if you think you'll be declining).

Sending a Friend Request

Now that you've taken care of the friend requests you've received, it's time to send some out yourself. Odds are good that you know plenty of Facebook members who aren't yet aware you've arrived—so all you have to do is find them. Fortunately, Facebook makes that easy with the handy search field that lives in the blue bar.

Start by thinking up names of one or more close, trusted friends. (Feel free to jot a short list on a sticky note or a napkin or something.) Type the first person's name into the search field and hit Return/Enter. You may get a list of several people who have the same name, or one person if your friend has a very distinctive monicker. If Facebook doesn't find any exact matches for the name you typed, it'll suggest some names it found that seem similar, in case one of those is the friend you were looking for.

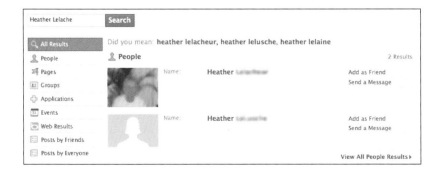

If you click the People filter in the left-hand column (or the View All People Results link at the bottom), you'll narrow the results to personal profiles (filtering out Groups, Pages, Events, and other named entities on Facebook that might have similar names).

Clicking the People filter also presents you with the option to refine your search by entering a location, school, or workplace—or if you know the person's current e-mail address, you can search by that as well.

Once you do identify someone you know and want to bond with, all you have to do is click the Add as Friend link next to their entry in the results. The Add Friend dialog will appear.

The Add Friend dialog

TIP: Notice that you have the option to type a short message to the recipient by clicking the "Add a personal message" link. I *highly* recommend doing that if there's any chance they might not recognize or remember you by name. If it's someone you know only slightly, or an old school chum you lost track of two decades ago, you'll earn good karma (and possibly a faster approval of your request) by erring on the side of providing their brain with a little context—which will give them the opportunity to respond with something graceful like, "How could I possibly forget you?" even as they're silently thanking you for not making them scrape their gray matter to figure out why your name rings a bell.

Your 5,000 Closest Friends

How many friends can one human being have? On Facebook, the answer is easy: 5,000. As celebrities as diverse as Stephen Fry and Yoko Ono have discovered, Facebook places a firm limit of 5,000 on the number of friends you can add to your profile. Even Santa Claus has been stymied by that limit—according to an item on *Wired* magazine's blog, a man whose legal name is Santa Claus, and who runs an advocacy group for children called the Santa Claus Foundation, reached the 5,000 friend limit within a month of joining Facebook. And not all of his elves and reindeer working together could persuade Facebook to raise the ceiling. (The item noted that Facebook did cut him a break by allowing him to sign up as "Santa Claus" in the first place, once he proved that it was his legal name.)

Facebook's position is that your profile's Friends list should emphasize personal relationships with people you actually know. But if you're a public figure or politician whose fans and supporters number in the thousands, don't despair: Facebook has a solution for you. You can set up a Facebook Page. Facebook Pages are free, and they look like profiles, but they give you more powerful tools for communicating with and keeping track of your enormous fan base—with no limit on the number of fans your Page can have. And you won't have to spend all your time approving endless friend requests, either: When someone chooses to become a fan of your Facebook Page by clicking the Like button, the connection is automatic. (After all, if you're a rock star, you don't get to choose who wears your band's T-shirt.) See the *Pages* chapter for full info on how to set up and manage Facebook Pages.

TIP: When someone you've added accepts your friend request, you'll get a notification from Facebook letting you know that the friendship has been confirmed.

TIP: If you send a friend request and then change your mind, you can cancel it. Just go to the person's profile and click the X next to "Awaiting friend confirmation" at the top of their profile.

Clicking on the words "Add a personal message" in the Add Friend dialog opens up a field where you can type a personal note—so your friend request seems a little less out of the blue.

Once you've submitted your request, you can search for other friends and lather/rinse/repeat to your heart's content. Then sit back and wait for the love to roll in.

Finding a Needle in a Friendstack

So you typed "Joe Smith" or "Amy Johnson" into the Facebook search field and surprise, surprise, you got a huge list of people to choose from. How do you know which if any of the results is your own personal Joe or Amy?

If they've posted an accurate picture, it shouldn't be too hard to pick them out of the lineup. But if they're camera shy, they may have chosen to hide behind a picture of a family pet or a favorite cartoon character—or they may have no picture at all—in which case you'll need to do a little sleuthing.

Facebook tries to help you by sorting the most likely results to the top of the list—so people you have things in common with will be listed first. That means that if your friend went to your high school or college, works at your company, lives in your town, or has a number of friends in common with you, odds are good they're higher on the page rather than lower.

Your first step is to see if you can click through to any of the profiles listed. If the likely candidates have set their privacy settings to make their profiles public, or even open to mutual friends, then you may be able to see some or all of their profile information (see the *Privacy and Security* chapter for details).

If you can't click through, the best clue left to you at this point is mutual friends. Take a look under each person's name. If you have any friends in common you'll see a link there telling you how many (subject to the person's privacy settings). Clicking that link will show you the list. If you can spot your friend's significant other, sibling, roommate, sidekick, or anyone else you both know, you've got a bull's-eye.

If all else fails, you may still have the option of sending a polite inquiry to whomever seems most likely to be the person you're looking for (assuming they haven't disabled this option). Click the Send a Message link and compose a bashful missive along the lines of, "Forgive me if I've got the wrong person, but are you the Amy Johnson I used to steal Tater Tots from during 'C' lunch period in 1985? If so, I think I owe you a bag or two of Idaho's finest . . . "

WARNING: Although you are allowed to make new friends on Facebook, and occasionally send friend requests to people you don't already know in the non-Facebook world, Facebook also wants to protect its members from spammers and con artists who want to friend large numbers of users for not-so-honorable purposes.

In order to prevent this, Facebook flags certain friend requests as "suspicious." When you send a friend request, Facebook looks at whether you have any mutual friends with the recipient, and also whether anybody has marked you as someone they don't know after ignoring a friend request in the past. If you don't have many friends in common with the other person and you have a history of getting marked, then Facebook may consider your request suspicious—in which case you'll get a dialog telling you it can't be sent (and allowing you to contact Facebook if you feel there's been a mistake).

This is one more reason why it's always a good idea to include a message with your friend request if you think there's any chance the recipient might not recognize your name—doing so will reduce the chances of your friend request getting marked as inappropriate.

Inviting Friends Who Aren't on Facebook

It's possible that some of your favorite people aren't on Facebook yet. If that's the case, maybe it's your destiny to recruit them. You can easily invite anyone you want to join Facebook, as long as you know their e-mail address and they're over 13 years of age.

Navigate to your Facebook Home page and scroll down to the link that says "Who's not on Facebook? Invite them now" toward the bottom of the right-hand column. Click that link and you'll be taken to a page with an easy form to fill out.

Click the "Invite them now" link on the Home page to invite friends who aren't on Facebook yet.

In the top field, type the e-mail addresses of the people you want to invite, separated by commas. In the bottom field, type an optional message to the recipients. If desired, you can change the language in which the invite will be sent by clicking the "[change]" link next to "Invites will be sent in English (US)." Click Invite to finish, or Cancel if you're having second thoughts, and you're done.

There are two other options you'll notice on the Invite Your Friends page. Import E-mail Addresses lets you invite a batch of friends from various

If a friend you're inviting would be more comfortable viewing Facebook in a different language, use the pop-up menu to choose the best language for the invitation. (Only a few of the available options are shown here.)

Personalize It
When you're inviting someone to join Facebook, you'll almost always get better results if you take advantage of the optional message field. Type a short personal greeting that demonstrates to the person (or persons) you're inviting that it's really you, and not a spammer, that's sending the invitation. Addressing them by name and working in a reference to how you know them, a mutual friend, or an in-joke are good ways to boost the credibility of the invite.

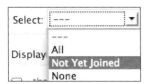

The links at the top of the Invite History page

The options in the Select menu on the Invite History page

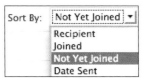

The options in the Sort By menu on the Invite History page

online address books you might use. See the "How to Pump Up Your Friends List" section later in this chapter for more info.

The View All Invites link in the lower-right corner of the form takes you to the Invite History page, which lets you see all the people you've invited to Facebook in the past, including who has accepted your invitation and who hasn't—yet. (Don't be surprised if people who don't accept your invitation right away eventually pop up on Facebook many months later.)

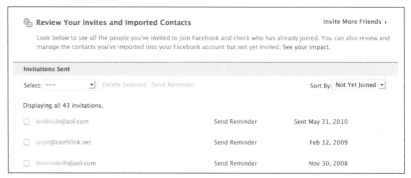

The Invite History page shows you all the Facebook invitations you've sent at a glance, and lets you send reminders if you want to follow up on the ones that haven't been accepted.

The Invite History page comes with various management tools. You can select the checkboxes next to the names of anyone you want to remove from the list, and then click Delete Selected at the top of the list. You can send reminders to those who haven't responded by clicking the Send Reminder link next to their name, or selecting their checkbox and clicking Send Reminder at the top of the list.

The Select menu lets you automatically select the checkboxes for everyone, no one, or just those who haven't yet joined Facebook. The Sort By menu lets you choose the order in which your invitees are displayed: by name, by date of invitation, or by whether or not they've accepted your invite.

But the fun's not over yet: If you click the "See your impact" link at the top of the page, you'll be taken to the Impact page, where you'll see the total number of people you've invited to join Facebook, a sampling of the people who've joined because of you, and a leaderboard of your friends that shows you exactly where you rank in terms of how many innocent souls you've drawn into Facebook's web. Looks like your friend Robbie has successfully invited more people than you? Better step up your game!

Suggesting Friends

If you have two Facebook friends who know each other in the real world but haven't found their way into each other's Friends lists yet, Facebook gives you a handy way to point them out to each other.

You can also use this feature to play Facebook Cupid, and introduce two people who don't know each other yet, but who you're pretty sure will be likely to hit it off. If you go that route, however, you should exercise a little discretion—and by all means send an introductory message, as discussed in the "Suggestion Box" etiquette note on the following page.

To suggest friends, go to the profile of the person you'd like to suggest as a friend for someone else. If the person has recently joined Facebook, you'll see a "Suggest Friends for [name]" link underneath their profile photo. If they're a Facebook veteran, it won't be quite so prominent, but you can still find it toward the bottom of their profile (make sure you're on the Wall or Info tab).

Click the link and you'll be presented with a dialog that allows you to choose the people you'd like to send friend suggestions to.

The Suggest Friends link

Suggest Friends for Tracey

Both Tracey and the friends you choose will receive a friend suggestion from you.

Find Friends: Start Typing a Name

Filter Friends ▼   All   Selected (0)

✕ You are viewing 40 friends from Facebook Me!   Select All

Herman Cabeje	Ian Belknap	Jason Rothstein Ill. Chi...
Jennifer Senft	Jill Bernard	Jocelyn Prince The Publ...
Karen Christop...	Karen Heiney Brown	Kevin Spengel Friends
Kristin Shout Amondsen Sassi	Laura Pexton Ross Pearson ...	Lori Dana

Send Suggestions   Cancel

🗨 Suggestion Box

If you suggest that two people become friends on Facebook, unless you're 100 percent sure that they already know and will recognize each other, as a matter of courtesy you should send them a friendly little note telling them exactly why you think they might want to befriend each other. Otherwise they'll be stuck scratching their heads and wondering whether they've met before.

You might reasonably expect Facebook to include an option to do this in the Friend Suggestion dialog itself—but as of this writing it still isn't there, so you'll need to send a separate Inbox message.

For this reason I often skip the automatic friend suggestion feature altogether, and simply send an Inbox message to the two friends I'd like to introduce to each other. That way I can give them a little background on each other and let them know why I think they'll be simpatico. I only use the automatic suggestions for people I know are already friends. (See the *Communicating on Facebook* chapter for the skinny on sending messages to your Facebook friends.)

You can click the Filter Friends menu to choose recipients from a Friend List you've created (see the section on Friend Lists later in this chapter) or any Network that at least one of your friends belongs to. (You can reverse the filtering process by clicking the little X next to the words "You are viewing [number] friends from [name of Friend List or Network]." Clicking the X takes you back to the All Friends view.)

Once you've chosen the people you want to send the suggestion to, click Send Suggestions, and you're done.

> **NOTE:** Friend suggestions used to be one-way: You had to pick which friend would get the suggestion to add the other, which could be confusing. But these days, friend suggestions travel in both directions simultaneously—so no matter which person's profile you visit to click the link, both prospective friends will get a notification that you've suggested them as friends for each other.

Removing a Friend

If you decide that you need to *defriend* someone—removing them from your list of friends altogether—Facebook gives you a number of ways to break up. (I'm not sure if there are 50 ways or not—you'd have to ask Paul Simon.) Here are two of the simplest: You can go directly to the person's profile and click the Remove from Friends link toward the bottom of the page, or you can find their entry on your Friends page (Account > Edit Friends) and click the "X" button over on the right-hand side.

Either way, you'll get a dialog asking you to confirm that you really want to give this person the heave-ho. (This step can't be undone—at least not without crawling to your brand new ex-friend and begging them to refriend you—so make sure you really want to do it before you click Confirm.)

Suggest Friends for Paul
Report/Block this Person
Remove from Friends
🔊 Share

The dreaded Remove from Friends link—Facebook's equivalent of the pink slip

The Remove Friends dialog asks you if you're sure you really want to do that.

Alternatives to Defriending

Time and experience have shown that people take defriending on Facebook very, very seriously. As author and Boing Boing blogger Cory Doctorow put it in an *InformationWeek* essay: "Removing someone from your Friends list is practically a declaration of war."

Case in point: One of my friends made the mistake of defriending a couple of old college pals with whom he'd been having political disagreements. He thought he was taking the gentle approach—removing the opportunity for conflict and allowing time for everyone to cool off. Instead, the defriended parties quickly noticed that they'd been given the boot, took mortal offense, and seized the opportunity to paint him as a friendship-betraying scoundrel on the Walls of all their mutual friends.

A cautionary tale, indeed. And here's the thing: Some people take the drastic step of removing other people from their Friends list simply because they aren't familiar enough with Facebook's controls to know that there are less socially suicidal ways to deal with the small annoyances of life on Facebook.

The good news is that you almost never need to defriend anyone on Facebook—unless you actively dislike them and you really do want to sever your social connection with them. For almost all other cases, Facebook provides tools that will allow you to eliminate the source of friction without breaking the bonds of Facebook friendship and thereby creating bad blood.

- First of all, if someone is posting content that annoys you—littering your Home page with obnoxious status updates, uninteresting links, or endless games and quizzes you couldn't care less about—all you have to do is hide their postings from your News Feed, or filter it so they're not included in the people whose postings you see. (I cover how to do all that in the *Sharing Content on Facebook* chapter.)

- Coming from the other direction, you can also hide your own postings from any friends you don't want reading or commenting on them. If you have co-workers whom you don't really want to know about what you get up to on the weekends, or a hot-tempered friend who tends to start flame wars when certain sensitive topics arise, you can choose to make all of your postings—or specific postings on a case-by-case basis—invisible to the people you don't want to see them. (See the *Privacy and Security* chapter as well as the *Sharing Content on Facebook* chapter.)

> **Defriend vs. Unfriend**
> The terms *defriend* and *unfriend* have both been in circulation for a while as synonyms for the act of removing someone from your Friends list. *Unfriend* got a boost in 2009 when the New Oxford Dictionary picked *unfriend* as its word of the year. But I personally prefer *defriend*, and am sticking with it for this book, because I find *unfriend* clunky and it's been my experience that *defriend* is the choice of people who've been on Facebook longer and use it more heavily. Facebook co-founder Chris Hughes agrees with me: *The Post-Standard* reported that prior to a lecture he gave in 2009 he expressed surprise that the dictionary went with *unfriend*, noting that *defriend* is the term he and his friends use.

> **NOTE:** If you do defriend someone, they won't receive any kind of official notification message, so the only way they'll find out about it—assuming you don't tell them—is if they go looking for you in their Friends list and discover you've gone missing, or visit your profile and see that the Add as Friend button has reappeared.

- If someone is pestering you with endless Event invitations you're not interested in, before you give them the heave-ho, try sending them an Inbox message and diplomatically asking them to take you off their invitations list. (If they persist after a polite request, then they probably do deserve to be defriended—but at least you gave them a fair shake.)

Ultimately, of course, there are plenty of legitimate reasons for defriending people on Facebook. Abuse and harrassment shouldn't be tolerated—and if a friendship has run its course, or you need distance from an ex, so be it. For smaller matters, though, it's good to know how to avoid accidentally declaring war when you were only trying to keep the peace.

In Memoriam: When Facebook Friends Pass Away

Being defriended on Facebook can be painful — but of course it's nothing compared to the pain of having someone close to you pass away.

Interestingly, though, Facebook has proven that it can be a source of comfort to those who are grieving for a friend or family member they've lost. The Facebook profiles of people who have recently died become online gathering places where friends and relatives of the departed can come together to express their feelings of loss and grief, provide solace, and share memories of their loved one with each other—a kind of 24-hour virtual wake.

On the other hand, there have been some awkward situations, too. Facebook's automatic suggestions have sometimes recommended that people become friends or "reconnect" with people they know who have died—which can give survivors the unsettling feeling of encountering a ghost in the machine.

Facebook has responded by allowing profiles for deceased members to be "memorialized"—an option that converts profiles into tribute pages. People who were already Facebook friends with the user can still view the profile, but no new friends can be added. The account can no longer be logged into, and Facebook removes information it considers "sensitive," such as status updates and contact information, from the profile.

Memorializing an account should also prevent it from showing up in friend suggestions, or in reconnect messages on the Home page. However, the profile's Wall remains active so that friends and family can post their remembrances.

Facebook also honors requests from immediate family members to deactivate a deceased user's account completely, so that no one can view it.

To memorialize a profile, a friend or family member can fill out a form that Facebook provides (which can be found at http://www.facebook.com/help/contact. php?show_form=deceased). The person making the request must also provide proof of the death, by including a link to an obituary or news story that can be reviewed by Facebook's staff.

There is some potential for mischief here. The *New York Times* has reported on cases where a living person has found their page memorialized as a prank, by a friend who submitted an obituary for someone with the same name. A software engineer from Germany named Simon Thulbourn was locked out of his own Facebook profile for a while after this happened to him—though he was eventually able to get his account back by proving to Facebook that reports of his death had been somewhat exaggerated.

Viewing Your Friends

By the time you've got more than a couple dozen Facebook friends—which often happens in the first day or so—you may need a little help keeping track of them all. Fortunately, Facebook gives you a number of tools for doing that.

The Friends Box

By default, Facebook displays a little sampler of six randomly chosen friends in the Friends box that appears on the Wall and Info tabs of your profile. A different selection displays every time the page is loaded, unless you change that (see below).

You can set some additional options for the Friends box by clicking the Edit (pencil) icon in the upper-right corner:

- Use the Show menu to choose the number of friends who are displayed (the choices are 6, 9, or 12).
- The "Always show these friends" option lets you type the names of a few of your bestest pals that you want to always show in the box.
- The "Include friends from" checkboxes let you choose to include or exclude specific Networks when Facebook chooses random friends to display. So if you want to hide all co-workers from your office or all class-mates from a certain school, you can deselect those boxes. (But note that this will only work if the people in question have joined the relevant Net-works. So if you have a classmate from Riverdale High who never joined the Riverdale Network, they might still show up even if you deselect the Riverdale box.)

> **TIP:** If you don't want the Friends box to be visible on your profile at all, you can hide it—or you can restrict it so that it's only visible to certain friends. Clicking the Change Visibility Options link in the Friends box's options will take you to your privacy settings, where you can control that. (More info in the *Privacy and Security* chapter.)

The Friends Dialog and the Friends Page

To see all of your friends at once, you can click the See All link in the upper-right corner of the Friends box, which opens the Friends dialog. However, if you have a lot of friends, the small Friends dialog isn't really the most comfortable way to view them. Visiting the main Friends page gives you the same controls along with your full browser window to scroll around in. To go there, choose Account > Edit Friends in the blue bar.

The Friends box as it appears by default

Setting options in the Edit dialog for the Friends box

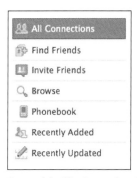

Some of the filtering options in the left-hand column of the Friends page

The Pop-Up Friend Preview

As you're merrily clicking your way around Facebook, reading various postings and comments, you may occasionally see names that you'd like to know a little more about, without necessarily taking the time to click through to the profile. That's when Facebook's pop-up friend preview is just the ticket.

To activate it, just move your cursor over the name of someone you'd like info about. (Depending on your connection speed, you may need to wait a few seconds before the preview appears.) You'll see a slightly larger version of the person's profile picture, any Networks they belong to, and a listing of mutual friends. There's also a link you can use to send them an Inbox message—and if you aren't friends with them yet, a link to send them a friend request if you'd like to.

If you click the Browse link at the top of the Friends dialog—or the Browse button in the left-hand column of the Friends page— you'll see a pop-up menu that lets you browse your friends by several categories, including school and workplace Networks, as well as location.

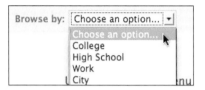

On the main Friends page, there are even more options for filtering your list of friends. The Recently Added button shows you the newest friends you've added on Facebook, and the Recently Updated button shows you friends who've made changes to their profiles. But for my money, the most useful option here is ...

Facebook Phonebook

This is a tool that can be a real lifesaver if you're traveling, at work, or otherwise separated from your usual address book, primary computer, or scribbled-on pile of coffee-stained sticky notes. If you need to find the phone number for one of your Facebook friends, try clicking the Phonebook button on the Friends page. You'll get an alphabetized listing of all of your friends who've posted their numbers on Facebook, and have set their privacy options to allow you to view them.

> **NOTE:** Facebook gives you very specific control over who can see any phone numbers you choose to include in your profile information. You can limit the visibility of your numbers to specific friends using Friend Lists, or you can opt out of Phonebook entirely by simply choosing not to display your numbers to anyone on Facebook. See the *Privacy and Security* chapter for details.

The Politics of Friending

How many Facebook friends should you have? And should you friend people you don't know very well, or limit your Friends list to proven pals?

As with so many questions in life, there's no absolute right or wrong answer to that question—it all depends on what you personally are comfortable with.

Some people take a "more the merrier" approach, approving every friend request automatically, and sending invitations to anyone and everyone who seems remotely interesting.

At the other end of the scale are the people who prefer to keep a small, carefully pruned Friends list consisting of only their nearest and dearest—the people they feel they could be happy living on a small wooden raft with. No strangers or casual acquaintances need apply.

And then there are the rest of us, who fall somewhere along the spectrum between those two extremes.

When I first joined Facebook, I had the idea that my Friends list would be limited to only people I knew fairly well. The first time a complete stranger sent me a friend request, I wasn't sure what to do. Fortunately, I was able to deduce by looking at our mutual friends that the person in question was a fan of my old theater company, and after approving his request I was glad I got to know him.

From that early experience, I learned that Facebook can be a great place to make new friends in addition to reconnecting with old ones. I realized that as a writer and performer it made sense for me to broaden my social network, and I began to think of my Facebook profile as somewhere in between public and private.

Your mileage may vary, of course. Ultimately, only you can decide exactly where you fall on the scale between "the more the merrier" and "less is more." But thinking about the following questions can help you make up your mind about how social you want to be.

1. **How introverted or extroverted are you?**

If you've ever taken the Myers-Briggs Type Indicator test, then you may already have a good sense of whether you generally chart as an extrovert or an introvert. But even if you're muttering, "The Myers what now?" at the moment (Google is your friend), you should have some sense of whether you're the outgoing sort who likes to surround yourself with tons of friends, or the quiet type who feels more comfortable with a smaller social set.

Of course, just because you're shy in the real world doesn't mean you're that way online. Some people find that the Internet liberates them to be more outgoing, and feel more confident expressing themselves in writing than speaking. If you're the sort who blossoms socially when you go online, then your Facebook Friends list may quickly outgrow your offline address book.

2. **How open to making new friends are you at this stage of your life?**

Even if you're generally a people person, you might find yourself at an age where you're already surrounded with dear old friends you never have enough time for, so you don't feel the urge to make a lot of new ones.

On the other hand, if you've just moved to a new community or are feeling like your social scene could use some new energy, then making new friends might be moving up your list of priorities fast.

3. **How conservative do your employers or your profession require you to be?**

The news has been rife with stories of people who've gotten in trouble for posting something they probably shouldn't have to their Facebook profile, MySpace page, or personal blog. Some companies do keep tabs on their employees' Internet presence—especially if they access their profiles on company time or use them in the course of their work.

If your co-workers or your boss are on Facebook, that provides some added incentive to make sure your profile hews to a professional image. And even if you're still in school, or not currently working for a large company, it pays to think ahead a little. Everyone should know by now that employers sometimes check out the Facebook and MySpace profiles of job candidates, looking for red flags before they make final hiring decisions.

Obviously there are some professions that require you to keep more of a clean-cut, button-down image than others. If you're a musician, massage therapist, or interior decorator, you may have a little more freedom of self-expression than if you're the local pastor or a lawyer hoping to become district attorney one day. (See the *Facebook at Work* chapter for more on this topic.)

Of course, even if the above considerations apply to you, keeping your Friends list on the small side isn't the only way to avoid getting into trouble. Facebook gives you a variety of specific tools and settings to control who can view certain photos, applications, or information on your profile. (See the *Privacy and Security* chapter for the full details on those controls.) And there's no substitute for exercising some basic caution about what you post in the first place.

4. **Does your livelihood depend on exposure and keeping yourself on other people's radar?**

Some careers thrive by staying in view of other people. If you're a musician, actor, comedian, or writer, for example, then you want to build a following of fans, and remind the various colleagues, agents, producers, directors, and editors who can hook you up with work that you exist. Facebook can be an excellent way to keep yourself in other people's line of sight.

By the same token, if you're an independent professional, freelancer, or entrepreneur of any kind, Facebook can help you keep in touch with your clients, co-workers, and other members of your professional network, so that you're top of mind when they're looking to hire someone.

On the other hand, if you're a public figure with a very large following of fans, or running a business that needs professional promotion, then you might want to consider setting up a Facebook Page for your fans and customers, and reserving your profile for personal friends only. See the *Pages* chapter for complete info on how to set them up, and how to take advantage of their sophisticated tools for communicating with fans, supporters, and customers.

Either way, it behooves you to do a little thinking at the outset about how your Facebook presence can work for you, and how public versus private you want it to be.

5. **Do you have anything you want to promote on Facebook, and is that a significant part of your reason for being on Facebook?**

This is closely related to the previous question—but if you've got a book or a film to sell, a blog or podcast to promote, a dog-walking business you're launching, a proposed local ordinance you're campaigning to defeat, or anything else you'd like to maximize word of mouth about, a larger Friends list will increase the audience for your status updates, Facebook Notes, viral videos, and other posted items.

6. **Are there people from your past (or present) you don't want to find you?**

Sometimes people have very legitimate reasons for not wanting to be found. Maybe you've got a problematic ex (or six). Maybe you're feeling antisocial these days and not in the mood to relive your high school years just now. Maybe you're in the Witness Protection Program. Maybe you're Peter Parker and you don't want Harry Osborn to track you down until he's cooled off about the dad thing a little.

Depending on the seriousness of your reasons, you may want to give a little extra thought to whether you should be on Facebook at all, and you'll want to make sure you pay a visit to the *Privacy and Security* chapter so that you can take full advantage of Facebook's privacy settings.

But it's also important to understand that as your Friends list grows, so does the set of people who are friends with your Facebook friends, increasing the likelihood that old acquaintances will spot you on a mutual friend's profile. So keeping your list small may (I stress the word *may*) help to limit your exposure somewhat.

7. **How much do you enjoy interacting with people online?**

Some people were born to chat, e-mail, and text—others prefer face-to-face interaction or using the phone. The larger your Friends list, the more likely you are to get Pokes, messages, Wall posts, application requests, and other virtual forms of communication.

I personally enjoy the semiotics of Facebook—if I didn't, I wouldn't be writing this book. I love waking up to Wall posts from college friends, SuperPokes from former co-workers, and Inbox messages from friends I met while traveling the UK a few summers back.

But I've had one or two friends decide to leave Facebook simply because they didn't like responding to all the messages piling up in their Inbox, or didn't like feeling obligated to return the various pokes and Wall posts and Farm-Ville invitations they received from their friends. (If you found that last sentence puzzling, don't worry—it's all explained in upcoming chapters.)

So if you're someone who hates typing when you could be talking, keeping your Friends list small might be a way of reining in the total volume of messages you receive.

On the other hand, this is another case where friend control isn't your only option for keeping things within manageable bounds. Take a deep breath and remember:

- You're not obligated to respond to requests from anyone just because they're in your list of friends. (If your friendship doesn't survive an unreturned SuperPoke, it was probably on thin ice already.)
- There's no law saying you have to reply to a message using the same medium. If you'd rather respond to a friend's Wall post by texting or picking up the phone and giving them a jingle, that's your prerogative, and they'll probably appreciate it just as much.
- You can uninstall any application that brings you more annoyance than pleasure.

8. **How are your time-management skills?**

There's a popular button in the Pieces of Flair application that reads, "Facebook—you didn't want to go outside anyway."

Hey, this is the 21st century. Even Zen monks feel rushed, overbooked, and short of time. Facebook can absolutely be part of a healthy balanced diet, and with a little self-control and moderation you can tend your virtual Farm on Facebook and still make it outside to smell the nonvirtual petunias well before the sun sinks in the west.

But there's no denying that Facebook can be seriously addictive, and if you know you have a hard time saying no to playing games when you should be working, and you have the kind of obsessive personality that lets the dirty dishes and the bills pile up while you engage in Wall banter with your A-list amigos, then limiting the number of people who are empowered to distract you online might be a sensible approach.

This is the small People You May Know box that sometimes appears on the Home page. Click the See All link to go check out the much larger sampling on the "Find Your Friends on Facebook" page.

The "Find your friends" link on the Home page takes you to the "Find Your Friends on Facebook" page.

People You Don't Know
If you're certain you don't know a specific person, you can click the little X next to their entry to make them go away. (Don't worry—they'll never know you did it, and it won't sour your chances of becoming friends in the future if you meet them at a party or something. However, it *will* prevent you from being recommended to the person you X'ed out by their own People You May Know listing.)

How to Pump Up Your Friends List

If you're in a social mood, and you'd like to connect with as many of your real-world friends as possible on Facebook, you're in luck—Facebook gives you lots of great ways to find them.

People You May Know

One of Facebook's best tools for finding your friends is the People You May Know tool. It lives on the "Find Your Friends on Facebook" page, but may sometimes put in a cameo appearance on the Home page as well.

Here's how it works: When you have a certain number of friends in common with another Facebook member, the system figures it's likely the two of you know each other. So Facebook serves up a regular sampler of folks who meet certain criteria (which may include such things as school and work info, in addition to mutual friends).

To take a look at the people Facebook thinks you might know right now, click the "Find your friends" link in the right-hand column of the Home page. That will take you to the "Find Your Friends on Facebook" page, and now you're cooking with gas. In the middle of the page you'll see a selection of possible friends (and you can click the More link to see a super-sized helping). If you recognize someone you know, click the "Add as friend" link to send a friend request.

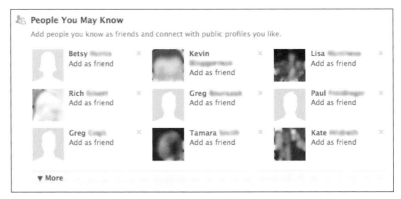

The full-size People You May Know section on the "Find Your Friends on Facebook" page gives you a much larger selection of possible friends to choose from.

If you're not sure whether you know the person or not, you can click their name or picture to check out their profile (or however much of it the person's privacy settings allow you to see).

You may find that the People You May Know tool shows you a slightly different selection of people every time you visit if there are plenty of good candidates out there. So if you're looking to build your Friends list, you might want to get into a habit of visiting the "Find Your Friends on Facebook" page on a regular basis to see who Facebook is suggesting to you.

The Friend Finder

The Friend Finder—Facebook's contact importer—also lives on the "Find Your Friends on Facebook" page, under the Find People You Email heading. You can access it easily from the Home page by clicking the "Find your friends" link in the right-hand column's Get Connected section.

If you use a web-based e-mail account, this handy tool can search your address book to find friends who are already on Facebook, identifying them by their e-mail address. It works with webmail accounts from "almost any" common provider, including Yahoo, Hotmail, AOL, Gmail, Comcast, and more.

The catch is that you'll need to type in your e-mail address and the password for your webmail account—giving Facebook temporary access to your account. Facebook promises not to store your password, and provides a "Learn More" link to its current policies on how your contacts' e-mail addresses may be used to help you connect with friends. If you decide you're not comfortable entering this info, then you'll want to take a pass on using this tool.

Find People You Email   Upload Contact File

Searching your email account is the fastest way to find your friends on Facebook.

Your Email: [   ]

Email Password: [   ]

[**Find Friends**]

🔒 Facebook will not store your password. Learn More.

You can also get around the password-sharing issue by clicking the Upload Contact File link, which lets you provide Facebook with a listing of your address book contacts generated by a program such as Outlook, Thunderbird, Mac OS X Address Book, and more. You may see instructions specific to whatever platform Facebook detects you using, as well as other options below that. (Clicking the "How to create a contact file" link will give you

NOTE: The People You May Know tool can be helpful, but it's not a sure-fire thing. One friend of mine refers to it as "People You've Been Trying to Avoid," because of its uncanny ability to serve up the people in your social circle you're not so fond of.

Friends of Friends
Although Facebook's automatically generated People You May Know tool is pretty sharp, it doesn't catch everyone. So the manual approach works pretty well, too. If you're looking for old pals, one of the best places to find them is lurking in the Friends lists of people you're already friends with, who know some of the same people. Spend a little time clicking on your friends' Friends lists and scanning them for familiar faces. It's a small world, and you may be surprised to discover some of the friends you have in common.

access to instructions for the full range of e-mail applications that are compatible with this process.)

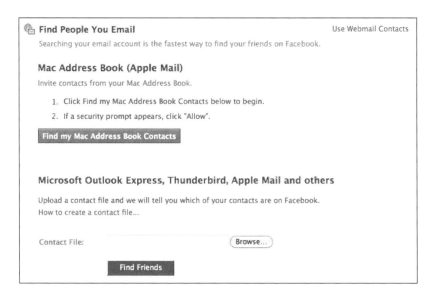

Similarly, if you use instant message programs, you can let Facebook comb through your AIM Buddy List or Windows Live Messenger Contacts list (among other options) to find people you know who've listed their IM handles on Facebook. Scroll down to the Find People You IM section at the bottom of the page, and click the appropriate link.

Class Consciousness
The high school and college advanced searches focus on your year of graduation by default. But if you had lots of friends older or younger than you, fear not. You can use the pop-up menu at the top of the results page to change the year and search for the seniors you worshipped or the freshmen you terrorized.

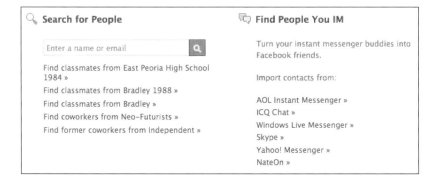

Advanced Search

You may have already searched for friends using the basic search field that lives in the blue menu bar. But there are some advanced search tools on the "Find Your Friends on Facebook" page, under the "Search for People" heading. Here you can search for classmates from your high school or college, or co-workers from your workplace Networks.

Invitations

As discussed earlier in this chapter, you can use the "Invite Your Friends" form to send invitations to join Facebook to anyone who isn't already registered and for whom you have a current e-mail address. You might even want to jot down a short list of your favorite pals, search for them one at a time, and if they aren't on Facebook, send them invitations.

TIP: Clicking the More Search Options link on the Results page will take you to a page where you can search for people by any school or any company—not just the ones you attended or worked for yourself.

Invitation Swarming: The Magic of Piling On

If you have a good friend you really, really want to join Facebook, and you have several mutual friends already on Facebook, there's a sneaky trick that almost always works: the coordinated attack. After all, getting one invitation from an old friend is compelling, but getting three or four on the same day feels like the stars are aligning.

I know from firsthand experience, because that's how I wound up joining Facebook myself, after getting several invitations from old friends on the same day.

So suppose at a previous job you were part of a tight-knit group of co-workers with your pals Buddy, Sally, and Rob. Buddy and Sally are already on Facebook, but for some reason Rob hasn't shown up yet. You can drop Buddy and Sally a message letting them know you're about to send Rob an invite, and suggest that they might want to send him one at around the same time. There's no guarantee that Rob will take the bait, but the odds have definitely improved.

Creating and Using Friend Lists

It's time to talk about one of the most important and underutilized features on Facebook: Friend Lists. A significant share of the problems people regularly ask me for help with on Facebook can be solved by setting up Friend Lists and learning how to use them.

Whether you realize it consciously or not, you probably already sort your friends and acquaintances into categories. You may have one set of old friends from high school, a group of co-workers you enjoy hanging out with, and another group of friends from your church, your bowling league, or your favorite dance club.

Friend Lists you've created are displayed in the left-hand column of the Friends page.

These groupings come in handy when you're organizing social events. If you're planning a dinner party, for example, and you invite six of your old high school pals along with your friend Phil from the office, Phil might feel a little overwhelmed, especially when you're off in the kitchen carving radishes into little rosebuds and putting spray-cheese on Triscuits. So if you're a good host, you think to yourself, hmm, maybe I should invite a few more people from the office so Phil has someone to talk to while the ice is getting broken.

Just as you do in the 3D world, Facebook's Friend Lists can help you keep track of the various categories your friends fall into—which ones already know each other, which ones would need to be introduced, and which ones are most likely to attend, say, a night at the theater, a golf outing, or a Sunday morning brunch.

In upcoming chapters, I'll show you how to use Friend Lists in all sorts of useful ways—not only to home in on the people you want to invite to a particular Facebook Event or Group you're creating, but to help you keep track of the people who matter most to you on Facebook.

> **TIP:** In fact, Friend Lists are key to one of the most useful features on Facebook: the ability to control who can see specific status updates, photos, posted links, or other kinds of content that you may want to share with some friends but not others. (For more info on this, see the *Sharing Content on Facebook* chapter.)

For now, here's how to create a new Friend List. First, click Account on the blue bar and then choose the Edit Friends link. You'll be taken to your main Friends page, with the Recents list (friends you've interacted with recently) showing by default.

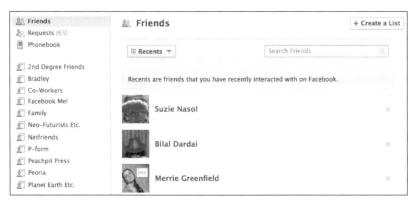

The Friends page allows you to create and manage your Friend Lists.

The column along the left is where your created Friend Lists will be displayed, if and when you have any. Click the "Create a List" button at the top of the page to add one. The Create a New List dialog will open up.

Click the Create a List button on your Friends page to set up a new Friend List.

TIP: You can put the same friend on more than one list, so if Phil is in your scuba club as well as working at your office, you can add him to your "Diving Buddies" list right after you add him to "Co-workers."

NOTE: You can add only people you're already friends with to a Friend List. If you type the name of someone you haven't already bonded with on Facebook, they won't show up in the dialog.

The first step is to type a name for your list in the Enter a Name field. Keep it short or Facebook will truncate it to fit the left-hand column width, and make sure the name is something clear that won't leave you scratching your head trying to figure out what it means later.

Step two is to add some friends to your newly named list. You can either click on friends' pictures to select them in the Friend Selector area, or start typing a name in the cleverly named Start Typing a Name field to narrow the visible choices. When you've selected everyone you want for this particular list, click the Create List button to finish up.

You can create up to 100 different Friend Lists, and each list can contain as many as 1000 friends.

If a list has fewer than 20 people, you can use it to conveniently send an Inbox message to all the members at once. Just type the name of the list in the To field when you're addressing your message. (See the *Communicating on Facebook* chapter for more on sending Inbox messages.) If the list has more than 20 members, you'll get an error message telling you it's too big. You might want to consider breaking it up into several smaller lists for messaging purposes—and since redundancy is okay on Friend Lists, there's no need to delete the original big list before you create the smaller ones.

By the way, your friends have no way of knowing what lists you do or don't add them to, so if you decide to create a list called "PWDLM" (People Who Dance Like Monkeys) or something, the people you add to it will be none the wiser. (Of course, your karma might take a hit.)

Editing a List
You can edit any of your Friend Lists by selecting it in the left-hand column on the Friends page.

Deleting a List
You can delete a Friend List at any time by selecting it and then clicking the Delete List link at the bottom of the list. But be careful— deleting a list is irreversible.

To Friend or Not to Friend—When You're on the Fence

Facebook brings with it some tricky and unexpected dilemmas. You'll get plenty of no-brainer friend requests from your best chums, and some wonderfully out-of-the-blue invitations from long-lost friends you've been missing for years.

But you'll also get some that make you scratch your head a little. Should you be Facebook friends with your boss? Your in-laws? Your old college roommate's mom? The kid from your grade school who made you eat a live centipede and apparently now wants to make amends?

And then there are the friendly strangers who show up on your Requests page. They may turn out to be wonderful people you're glad you've met, but they may also turn out to be creepy stalkers with no sense of boundaries. What to do?

As for your boss, see the *Facebook at Work* chapter for some perspective on that. For the strangers, see the "Stranger Danger" tip earlier in this chapter. And for the other head-scratchers, the advice is largely the same as for strangers:

1. Take your time to think it over.
2. Check out the relevant profiles.
3. Get input from mutual friends.

Once you've done all that, run the available data through that amazing biological computer known as your "gut," and see what answer you get.

Keep in mind that there may be less social cost to ignoring a friend request than to friending someone and then removing them later. As discussed earlier in this chapter, defriending someone is usually seen as a serious rejection and may cause lasting animosity—whereas simply ignoring a friend request can be passed off as mere negligence.

In the real world, skin comes in all degrees of thickness. One person may never notice that you ignored their friend request, while some other melodramatic soul takes it as a denial of their human worth.

You can't control other people's feelings, of course, or what molehills they mistake for mountains, and you have to do what's right for your own comfort and sanity. But it's also worth taking a moment to evaluate what you know of the person you're considering, how easily their feelings get hurt, and how much you care about keeping their good will.

One good rule of thumb for Facebook is that the less you know someone, the less you owe them. But it's also true that sometimes our best friends—and most valuable business contacts—are the ones we're just about to meet.

Privacy and Security

If you keep even half an eye on the news, you're aware that privacy and security are critically important issues online—and that's especially true in the social networking world. On sites like Facebook and MySpace, you can expose yourself to identity theft or fraud, just as with online shopping or banking sites. But on social networking sites, you also risk embarrassment or even censure if you wind up revealing the wrong details to the wrong people. Because you're on Facebook to make connections and share information, it can be easy to cross the line into revealing too much information. Sometimes it's hard to figure out where the line even is.

But don't panic. As long as you exercise a little caution, there's no reason the time you spend on Facebook should be any more perilous than a night on the town with friends. In both cases, it's important to keep your wits about you, know the lay of the land, and think before you share too much info with people you don't know very well.

In this chapter I'll give you tips on how to balance self-expression with discretion, and I'll explain the settings that Facebook provides to help you protect your privacy. But before we discuss Facebook's privacy and security tools, let's start by talking about the one you bring to the party yourself: your common sense.

An Ounce of Discretion Is Worth a Ton of Privacy Settings

Most people have many different sides—and they often choose to share those sides with different sets of people. You might talk music with one set of friends who tend to share your taste, and sports with another set of friends. You might avoid talking politics or religion with certain friends because you know you don't see eye-to-eye with them.

But on Facebook, your friends will all see the same persona, consisting of whichever parts of your personality you use Facebook to express. Unless you use Facebook's privacy settings to carefully separate your social groups, as we'll discuss later in this chapter, friends with whom you don't normally discuss politics will see your political comments. Friends who have different taste in music from you might discover your passionate love of Barry Manilow or Night Ranger.

Family and friends mix together on Facebook, too. You may have friends with whom you tend to engage in salty repartee that you'd never want your mom to overhear, but if she's one of your Facebook friends, she very well might.

There can also be academic and professional repercussions to how you express yourself on Facebook. Colleges have revoked admissions for students because of inappropriate postings on Facebook and MySpace, and employers increasingly check out the profiles of job candidates before making hiring decisions. Chatting about conditions at your current office can be a pitfall, too: If your boss is friends with anyone in the conversation, he or she could overhear the whole thing.

You shouldn't necessarily let those considerations stifle your self-expression on Facebook, but when you post, it might help to imagine that you're speaking to a large and diverse group at a party, rather than to a few intimate friends at your kitchen table.

It's true that using Facebook's privacy settings can provide some control over who sees what. But don't let those settings lull you into a false sense of security. Words and images posted on the Internet have a way of reaching a wider audience than originally intended, and once they do, trying to recall or erase them is like trying to put the proverbial toothpaste back in the tube. Or maybe more like trying to put Silly String back in the can.

The fact is, there's only one way to absolutely guarantee that a photo, video, or snatch of ribald banter won't be seen by more people than you want it to: Don't post it online in the first place.

Facebook's official privacy policy puts it this way: "Although we allow you to set privacy options that limit access to your information, please be aware that no security measures are perfect or impenetrable. We cannot control the actions of other users with whom you share your information. We cannot guarantee that only authorized persons will view your information. We cannot ensure that information you share on Facebook will not become publicly available. We are not responsible for third party circumvention of any privacy settings or security measures on Facebook."

In other words, Facebook's privacy and security tools can greatly *reduce* the chance that your information will be seen by the wrong eyes, but they can't rule it out entirely. You may be a Yoda-like master of Facebook's privacy settings (clicked all the pop-up menus, you have!), but your info can still get away from you. For example, a trusted friend could easily fail to realize that a photo you posted was intended to be seen by only a very select audience, and might repost it somewhere else or e-mail it to a group of mutual friends—or people you don't even know.

Remember also that law enforcement officials can get a court order to view Facebook profile information—and these days, they sometimes set up "plain-clothes" Facebook profiles to investigate and track illegal activity online. I've also heard one anecdotal account of a job seeker being asked by her prospective employers to log into Facebook and then leave the room while they reviewed her profile. If your potential bosses get to look at your profile the way you see it, privacy controls become irrelevant.

The bottom line is if you're truly worried that a bleary-eyed photo of you holding a plastic cup at a party could get you in trouble if it were seen by a prospective employer, an admissions board, or certain very conservative relatives, the safest approach is to simply not post it at all.

That doesn't mean you should censor yourself excessively or squelch every playful impulse. But you should consider the risks and benefits, and find a reasonable middle ground for self-expression that's within your personal comfort zone.

The Facebook Privacy Wars
In the time since I wrote the first edition of this book in 2008, there have been a number of high-profile controversies about privacy on Facebook. Facebook has sometimes pushed its members in the direction of sharing more info publicly than many users are comfortable with (for example, by setting the default for sharing content to Everyone rather than Friends Only). Many individuals and advocacy organizations (such as the ACLU and the Electronic Frontier Foundation) have at times questioned whether Facebook's privacy tools were truly effective, and some have questioned whether Facebook's commitment to protecting users' privacy is sincere. In response, Facebook has revised its privacy controls, attempted to make them easier to understand, and reiterated its commitment to protecting user privacy.

Trying to cover the Byzantine history of these controversies, and Facebook's various missteps and corrections, would require far more time and space than the scope of this book allows me. But when all is said and done, I think the best response is to reiterate the advice I've given from the beginning: Remember that the Internet is the Internet, and anytime you post content or information online (whether it's on Facebook, a personal blog, or anywhere else), you surrender some control over its privacy.

Your first, best, and strongest privacy control is your own prior restraint. If you're truly worried about keeping your home address or your phone number private, then by all means err on the side of caution and don't post it online. All in all, the safest approach you can take to privacy on Facebook is to simply think of your profile as a public website—just like a blog or a personal home page—and then restrict what you decide to post there accordingly.

Friend Management: The Key to Choosing Your Audience

Unless you keep your Friends list small and exclusive, you'll find yourself friending and being befriended by more than just the dear old friends you'd trust with your house keys and your unlocked diary.

There will also be co-workers, casual acquaintances, friends of friends you met at a party, and old schoolmates you lost track of years ago, as well as all sorts of other gray-area cases. You may even be using Facebook to make friends with interesting new people you don't know very much about at all, just yet.

Fortunately, Facebook's Friend List feature (as explained in the *Friends* chapter) is a great tool for sorting and grouping your friends. And by organizing your friends according to your degree of intimacy with them, you can use your Friend Lists to filter how much and what you reveal to whom.

The Three-Level System

One simple system you can use is to sort your growing Facebook circle into three basic lists.

Start by creating one list that's just for your nearest and dearest: the inner-circle friends who already know all your business, and whom you trust enough to grant total security clearance to your Facebook profile. Call this list something like Trusted Friends.

Next, create a second list for all the people in the middle. The people you don't know well enough to let them see you with your hair in curlers, or share your home address with, but also don't have any reason to feel wary of. Call this list something like Casual Friends or Acquaintances. This will probably be the biggest list and the one you add people to by default.

Finally, create a third list for people you don't know very well, aren't entirely sure how much you trust, or just want to keep an eye on until you have a better sense of what makes them tick. You can call this list something like Restricted Access or Watch List. (I call mine PIDRK, which stands for "People I Don't Really Know," but you might not find unwieldy acronyms as entertaining as I do.)

Once you've got those lists set up, it's time to perform a simple triage operation. Go through your All Friends list (choose Account > Edit Friends in the blue bar and then choose All Friends from the menu at the top of the page), and assign everyone to one of those three lists.

Adding a friend to the Trusted Friends list.

Going forward, each time you add a new friend, you should automatically assign them to the appropriate list.

Here's another refinement: If you have family members whom you love and trust but still don't want seeing certain photos or comments you post, you might create a fourth list for them, called Family Members.

Once you get the hang of them, you can use Facebook's custom Friend Lists to sort your friends into as many different levels of security clearance as you want (up to Facebook's maximum of 100 lists), and as you'll see, there are lots of ways to put your custom lists to work.

Privacy Settings: Controlling Who Sees What

Facebook gives you some very specific settings for controlling what parts of your Facebook life are visible and who gets to see them.

Your home base for most of the settings you'll want to change is the Privacy Settings page. To find it, choose Privacy Settings from the Account menu in the blue bar.

The current incarnation of the Privacy Settings page was launched after a number of high-profile controversies about privacy on Facebook, and in response to a widespread feeling that many users didn't understand exactly how much of their profile info they were sharing by default on Facebook, or how to control that.

In creating this version of the page, Facebook had a difficult balancing act to pull off: serving the needs of two very different types of users. On the one hand, Facebook has a history of providing very specific, customizable controls for users who want to be able to choose the exact audience for each kind of content on their profiles. So Facebook wanted to keep those granular privacy controls available for those who've come to depend on them.

 Friend Lists vs. Groups
One of the reasons Facebook launched its revamped Groups feature in the fall of 2010 was to provide another solution to the privacy and audience issue that I address in this section. Facebook's new Groups give you another way to post content where only certain groups of your friends can see it. However, I still think Friend Lists are the superior tool for controlling who sees what you post. For one thing, anyone who joins a new-style Group can add other members to it—so you never have complete control over who makes up your posting audience in a Group. Whereas with Friend Lists, you (and only you) are 100% in charge of who gets put on each list.

Part of the reason Facebook launched the new Groups is because they found most users didn't really understand Friend Lists and never bothered to create any. But the fact that you're reading this book sets you apart from the herd—it means you're willing to make the effort to learn about Facebook and how to get more out of it. If you're also willing to take the time to set up Friend Lists and learn how to use them, it'll pay off for you in convenience and control.

Choose Privacy Settings from the Account menu in the blue bar.

On the other hand, Facebook also needed to provide a solution for users who found those granular controls confusing and complicated.

Facebook's solution to this problem is to provide two levels of privacy controls for content you share:

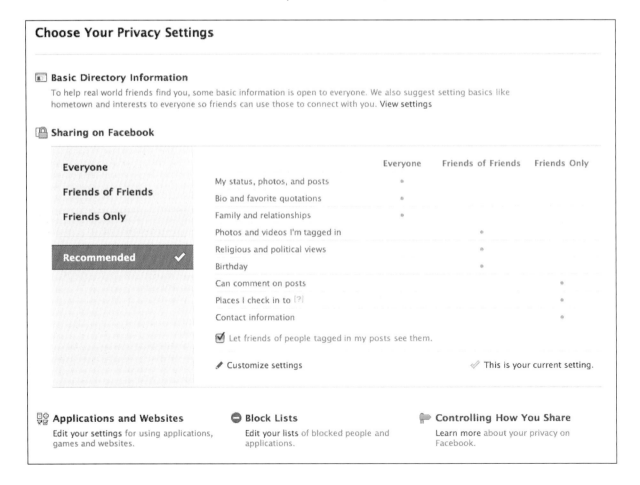

- **Simplified settings:** Four easy options to choose from, setting Privacy for your entire account with one click
- **Customized settings:** The advanced controls that let you pick and choose privacy levels for each part of your account

TIP: Don't panic! The Simplified and Customized settings mentioned here will be explained in detail in the upcoming "How to Control Who Sees Content You Share" section, a few pages hence.

Additionally, Facebook provides a separate set of controls for what it calls your Basic Directory Information—which consists of information that can help friends find you on Facebook, such as your location, work or school, friends, and interests. I'll cover all of those settings in the pages ahead.

To get us started, here's what Facebook's Privacy Settings page looks like by default when you first arrive at it, with a brand-new account:

Choose Your Privacy Settings

Basic Directory Information
To help real world friends find you, some basic information is open to everyone. We also suggest setting basics like hometown and interests to everyone so friends can use those to connect with you. **View settings**

Sharing on Facebook

		Everyone	Friends of Friends	Friends Only
Everyone	My status, photos, and posts	•		
	Bio and favorite quotations	•		
Friends of Friends	Family and relationships	•		
	Photos and videos I'm tagged in		•	
Friends Only	Religious and political views		•	
	Birthday		•	
	Can comment on posts			•
Recommended ✓	Places I check in to [?]			•
	Contact information			•

☑ Let friends of people tagged in my posts see them.

✏ Customize settings   ✓ This is your current setting.

⊞ Applications and Websites
Edit your **settings** for using applications, games and websites.

⊖ Block Lists
Edit your **lists** of blocked people and applications.

⚑ Controlling How You Share
Learn more about your privacy on Facebook.

How to Customize Your Basic Directory Information

The very first item at the top of the Privacy Settings page, Basic Directory Information, consists of a bunch of information and settings that Facebook assumes you'll want to make public—primarily because doing so helps your various friends and acquaintances track you down and connect with you on Facebook, so your network can keep growing.

By default, then, these settings are all set to "Everyone"—meaning that anyone on the Internet can see the basic information here, and contact you via Inbox messages or friend requests. And if you're fine with that, you don't have to do anything with these controls.

But of course, not everyone on Facebook wants to be found by people they're not already Facebook friends with. So by clicking the View Settings link in this area, you can set a specific level of privacy for each of these controls.

Here's an example: Scroll down to the control labeled See My Education and Work.

TIP: You can control who can see your list of friends on Facebook using the "See my friend list" setting on the Basic Directory Info page. Keep in mind that the ability to look at your Friends list or send you an Inbox message may help a long-lost friend identify whether you're the person they used to know—or just someone with a similar name.

🗂 See my education and work	This helps classmates and coworkers find you.	🔒 Everyone ▾

By default, its pop-up menu is set to Everyone, which means that your Education and/or Work information is visible to the general public. If you want to restrict it, click the pop-up menu and you'll see four choices: Everyone, Friends of Friends, Friends Only, and Customize.

The next step down in visibility from Everyone is the Friends of Friends option: This information will be open to all of your Facebook friends, *plus* any friend of one of your Facebook friends. It's more restrictive than Everyone because a person has to share at least one mutual friend with you before this info is visible to them.

The next setting, Friends Only, is fairly self-explanatory: Only people you've added as a friend on Facebook will be able to view your information.

The fourth setting, Customize, opens the Custom Privacy dialog. The settings here are a little more complex but very useful, giving you more options for controlling who can see your information. If you want to slice up your profile information and serve different segments to different audiences, this is the place to do it.

The options in the pop-up menu for each privacy control. (But note that the top three controls, which control how people can contact you, don't include the Customize option.)

NOTE: For info on the three controls at the top of the Basic Directory Settings page, see the upcoming section "How to Control Who Can Contact You on Facebook."

Friends of Friends

The theory behind the Friends of Friends option is that someone who shares a friend with you is part of your larger social circle, and someone you have a good chance of meeting socially. And at least one person you know made the decision to add this person as a friend, for whatever that's worth. Keep in mind, though, that sharing a mutual friend with you is not a guarantee that someone is trustworthy, because lots of people on Facebook make friends with people they don't know very well. Here's a little thought experiment: think of someone you know who you don't really trust, and wouldn't want to share your info with on Facebook. Then see if you can think of anyone you're friends with who is also friends with that person. If the answer is yes, you might want to avoid the Friends of Friends setting.

The top part of the Custom Privacy dialog controls who your information is visible to: You can choose Friends of Friends, Friends Only, Only Me, or Specific People, which will open a field where you can type the names of specific friends or any Friend Lists you've created. Your info will then be visible only to those people.

The bottom part of the dialog allows you to exclude specific people—which effectively hides the info in question from those people. Just type the names of the people or Friend Lists you want to hide your info from. When you're all done, click the Save Setting button to exit the dialog.

How to Control Whether You Show Up in Search Results—on Facebook and on Search Engines

The first setting on the Basic Directory Info Page controls who can find you by searching on Facebook.

 **Search for me on Facebook**   This lets friends find you on Facebook. If you're visible to fewer people, it may prevent you from connecting with your real world friends.

The default setting is Everyone, which means anyone who searches Facebook can find you. (This doesn't mean they can see your profile—just the search result itself.) You can restrict your search visibility with the other choices in this menu, which work the same way as the privacy controls already discussed. (But note that there's no Customize option for this one—the three choices in the menu are Everyone, Friends of Friends, and Friends Only.)

You can also control whether your Facebook profile shows up on search engines like Google or Bing. By default, Facebook creates a Public Search

Listing for all personal profiles belonging to users who are over the age of 18. By default this listing doesn't display your entire profile—just a preview showing some of your basic directory information. The privacy settings you choose for the various parts of your profile determine what can be accessed by search engines—only those parts of your profile for which you choose the Everyone setting can turn up in public search engine results.

But if you don't want your profile to be found on search engines at all, you can make it completely off-limits to them by turning off your public search listing. To do this, go to the main Privacy Settings page (Account > Privacy Settings) and look for the "Applications and Websites" area.

 NOTE: If you're a minor (meaning your age is listed on Facebook as under 18), no public search listing will be created for you, regardless of whether you enable the public search listing checkbox.

⯐ Applications and Websites
Edit your settings for using applications, games and websites.

Click the "Edit your settings" link to go to the Applications, Games, and Websites page and scroll down to the Public Search area.

Public search	Show a preview of your Facebook profile when people look for you using a search engine.	**Edit Settings**

Click the "Edit Settings" button to go to the Public Search page.

Public search	Public search controls whether people who enter your name in a search engine will see a preview of your Facebook profile. Because some search engines cache information, some of your profile information may be available for a period of time after you turn public search off. See preview
	☑ Enable public search

On the Public Search page, deselect the "Enable public search" checkbox shown above, and your public search listing will be removed.

If you'd like to see what your public search listing looks like, you can take a look at it by clicking the "See preview" link. (It's semi-hidden at the end of the paragraph of text just above the checkbox in the shot above.)

How to Control Who Can Contact You on Facebook

There are two settings toward the top of the Basic Directory Info page that control how (and whether) people can contact you if you aren't already friends with them on Facebook—by sending you friend requests or Inbox messages. Like the search control, there's no Customize option for these controls—your choices are Everyone, Friends of Friends, and (for Inbox messages) Friends Only.

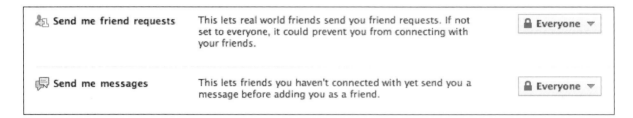

As you can see, Facebook does a pretty good job of explaining right on the page why it's helpful to leave these controls set to Everyone. You might be tempted to restrict the ability of people you're not friends with to send you Inbox messages in order to prevent spam, but that isn't really a problem— Facebook is pretty aggressive about preventing users from sending Inbox messages to large numbers of people.

How to Control Who Sees Content You Share

Now that you've got your Basic Directory Info locked down, it's time to look at the main part of the Privacy Settings page: the Sharing on Facebook area. This is where the two levels of privacy controls (Simplified versus Customized) I talked about earlier come into play.

 Setting Privacy for Specific Posts
In addition to the global privacy settings discussed here, Facebook also gives you the opportunity to choose the audience for each and every post you make, by applying a custom privacy setting in the Publisher. For all the details on how to do that, see the *Sharing Content on Facebook* chapter.

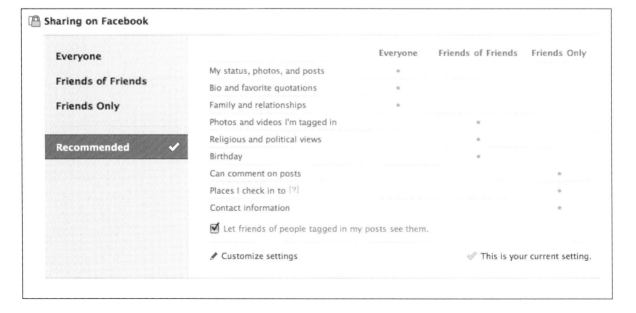

In the shaded column on the left, you can see the four Simplified settings: Everyone, Friends of Friends, Friends Only, and Recommended. Over on the right, you can see a table listing the various elements of your profile that are controlled by these settings: everything from content you post on your Wall (the "My status, photos, and posts" item) to your birthday and contact info.

The Recommended option shown here is chosen by default, and it applies the settings Facebook thinks most people will want. The bullets in the three columns of the table (Everyone, Friends of Friends, and Friends Only) show you who can see which parts of your profile using this option:

- **Everyone** can see your status, photos, and other Wall posts; your bio and favorite quotations; and your family and relationships
- **Friends of Friends** can see photos and videos you're tagged in, your religious and political views, and your birthday
- **Friends Only** are allowed to comment on your posts, can see places you check into using Facebook's Places feature, and can see your contact info.

Clicking any of the other Simplified settings on the left-hand side will move the bullets around in the three columns to reflect your new setting. For example, if you choose Friends Only, then all of these profile elements will be visible to only your friends (and you'll see all of the bullets appear under the Friends Only column heading). Choosing Everyone moves all the bullets into the Everyone column. But note that the Friends of Friends setting behaves somewhat unexpectedly here: Some of the bullets move into the Friends of Friends column, but a few of the most sensitive pieces of data, such as your birthday and contact info, remain in the Friends Only column.

That covers the four Simplified settings. But what if you want precise control over each one of these profile elements? What if you'd like to choose exactly which column each bullet goes into? That's where the Customized controls come in.

To tailor your settings exactly the way you want, click the "Customize settings" link at the bottom of the table. You'll arrive at the Customize Settings page, where you'll see a separate Privacy control for each of the items in the table, with a pop-up menu just like the ones on the Basic Directory Info page. From there you can assign the exact level of privacy you want to each kind of information.

Notice that there are even separate controls for each part of your contact information—your mobile phone number, your e-mail address, and your home address, for example—so that if you choose to share those things you can choose exactly who gets to see them.

TIP: The checkbox labeled "Let friends of people tagged in my posts see them" means that if you tag your friend Peggy in a status update, Peggy's friend Joyce will be able to see the posting in her News Feed and on Peggy's Wall—even if Joyce isn't one of your own Facebook friends. Leaving this setting enabled is logical because one of the primary reasons for tagging someone else is to allow the posting to appear on their Wall.

Public vs. Private Channels: Know the Difference

One of the biggest mistakes newcomers to Facebook make is not knowing the difference between which means of communication on Facebook are private, and which are public. I can't tell you how many news stories I've seen where someone got in serious trouble—in some cases losing their job or jeopardizing a court case—because they posted something in a public area of Facebook that should have been confined to a private message. Even rock stars have fallen into this trap: Courtney Love made headlines in March of 2010 when she accidentally shared her mobile phone number with the world by posting it on the Wall of an entertainment mogul—clearly misunderstanding the nature of a Facebook Wall. So in case you need a cheat sheet, here's the breakdown:

- **Private**: Inbox messages (except for messages addressed to groups of people) and Chat sessions between individuals.
- **Public** (subject to privacy settings): Wall posts and any content you post using the Publisher, such as status updates, Notes, Links, photos, and videos.

NOTE: Although Facebook automatically generates News Feed stories about many actions that you take on Facebook, such as making a new friend or Liking a Page, there are certain kinds of actions that Facebook never announces in the News Feed. Among them: sending Inbox messages (which are private, as opposed to Wall posts); viewing profiles, photos, and Notes (Facebook doesn't report on your reading and browsing habits); and removing people as friends.

Social Plugins and Instant Personalization

If you're logged into Facebook when you visit other websites, you may see various widgets and boxes called Social Plugins that display Facebook activity. For example, the site for a newspaper might display which friends of yours have Liked certain articles. Social Plugins don't share any info about you with the sites that host them, but if you don't want to see them, you can simply log out of Facebook.

When you visit certain sites with whom Facebook has partnered, such as Bing, Yelp, and Pandora, you might also see a feature called Instant Personalization, which draws on information you've made publicly available via the Everyone setting (if any) to customize what you see. If you want to opt out of Instant Personalization completely, you can do so by going to the Privacy Settings Page, clicking "Edit your settings" under Applications and Websites, and then clicking the Edit Settings button for Instant Personalization.

Social Plugins and Instant Personalization are discussed in more detail in the *Sharing Content on Facebook* chapter.

How to Use Friend Lists to Fine-Tune Your Control

Privacy settings are one of the places where organizing your friends into Friend Lists (as I encouraged you to do at the beginning of this chapter) really pays off. As we've seen, many of the controls in both the Basic Directory Info and the Sharing on Facebook areas include the Customize command, which opens the Custom Privacy dialog. And by plugging your Friend Lists into the Custom Privacy dialog, you can make specific content visible or invisible to entire categories of people you're friends with on Facebook. You could choose to set your work e-mail so that it's only visible to co-workers, for instance, or choose to hide the photos you're tagged in from certain family members.

Here's an example: Say you want to set your mobile phone number so that it's only visible to your Trusted Friends list. Go to the Privacy Settings page, click Customize Settings, and scroll down to the Mobile Phone setting in the Contact Information area. From the pop-up menu, choose Customize to open the Custom Privacy dialog.

Then, in the top part of the dialog, under "Make this visible to," choose Specific People from the pop-up menu.

A field will open that lets you enter the specific people you want to be able to see your mobile phone number. You could type a bunch of friends' names, of course, but it's easier to type the name of the Trusted Friends list you've created for this very purpose.

The "Hide this from" field in the bottom of the dialog works the same way, only it subtracts people from the audience instead of adding them. This is where you get to put up the velvet rope that blocks access to specific parties. Anyone you enter there will be excluded from viewing the info in question, *regardless* of whether they belong to any of the categories or Friend Lists you granted access to in the top of the dialog. So if you already have a Friend List called Restricted Access, for example, here's where you can put it to good use.

How to Preview What Your Profile Looks Like to Other People

Once you've got your privacy settings all set up the way you want them, Facebook gives you the ability to view your profile as any specific person you're friends with will see it—so you can make sure you're getting the results you intend. So, for example, if you've set your controls so that Uncle Leonard can't see photos you're tagged in, you can take a look at your profile through Uncle Leonard's bifocals and make sure he's seeing what you expect him to.

Here's how: Go to the Privacy Settings page and click Customize Settings. At the top of the page, click the Preview My Profile button.

On the Preview My Profile page, type Uncle Leonard's name in the field.

Privacy Settings for Photos and Videos
You can edit privacy settings for photo albums or videos on the Edit Info page for the album or video in question. As with applications and the various information on your profile, you can use Networks and Friend Lists to specify exactly who you do and don't want to see what you've posted. See the *Photos and Videos* chapter for full details on creating and editing photo albums and videos.

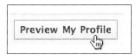

The Preview My Profile button

This is how your profile looks to most people on Facebook

Preview how your profile appears to a specific person: | Start typing a name

‹ Back to Privacy Settings

Presto! The profile preview shown in the lower part of the page will magically change to reflect the privacy settings that apply to Uncle Leonard.

How to Block People

If you don't want any contact with someone else who's on Facebook, you can block them on the Privacy Settings page. (This is an especially important step to perform if someone has harassed or threatened you in any way—right before you report that person to Facebook. See the upcoming section "Reporting Abuse" for how to do that.) Blocking someone on Facebook not only prevents them from using Facebook to contact or communicate with you on Facebook, it makes you virtually invisible to them—like Harry Potter's magic cloak.

To block someone, go to the Privacy Settings page and find the Block Lists area at the bottom. Click the "Edit your lists" link to go to the Block List page.

Privacy Settings for Applications
Looking for info on how to set the privacy options for applications? That's all covered in the *Applications and Other Add-Ons* chapter.

Block Lists
Edit your lists of blocked people and applications.

Block users	Once you block someone, that person can no longer be your friend on Facebook or interact with you (except within applications and games you both use).

Name: [   ] **Block This User**

Email: [   ] **Block This User**

You haven't added anyone to your block list.

TIP: If you need to reverse the blocking process in the future, you can do so by coming back to this page and clicking Unblock next to the person's name.

In the "Block users" area, type the name or e-mail address of the person you want to block in the box and click Block This User. Facebook will show you a results page listing people who match what you typed, so that you can pick the precise person whom you want to block. Click Block Person next to the appropriate listing, and presto! You're done.

What's the Deal With Social Ads?

From time to time, you may see ads in the sidebar that mention the fact that one or more of your friends have (for example) Liked a certain Page on Facebook or have clicked to confirm that they'll be attending a certain Event. And by the same token, your friends may see ads that mention your own actions. Facebook calls this form of advertising Social Ads.

It's important to note that only people who are already your confirmed friends on Facebook will be able to see you appear in Social Ads.

From a privacy standpoint, this isn't much different from the stories that show up in the News Feed mentioning that you've Liked a Page or will be attending an Event. The only differences are that Social Ads appear in the sidebar, and somebody somewhere has paid for them.

An example of a Social Ad, which mentions that two of my Facebook friends are fans of the artist in question

Facebook Security 101

Here are some basic tips for a safer and more secure Facebook experience. These are mostly common sense, but even if you're a veteran Facebooker, it doesn't hurt to be reminded of them.

- Choose a secure password for your Facebook account (one that uses both numbers and letters, isn't a word that can be found in a dictionary, and isn't something anyone else could guess). Change your password regularly and *never* share it with anyone else.

- Be careful about whom you friend. See the "Stranger Danger" and "To Friend or Not to Friend" sidebars in the *Friends* chapter for some perspective on this. And remember that online, people aren't always who they seem to be.

■ Be suspicious of links to external sites, and don't enter your passwords or other sensitive info unless you're certain the site you're on is legitimate.

■ If someone uses Facebook to threaten or harass you, report them to Facebook immediately. (See the following section for how to do that.)

Reporting Abuse

If you see hateful, abusive, or otherwise objectionable content that violates Facebook's terms, you can report it anonymously to Facebook. You can also anonymously report individuals who post offensive content, or who harass or threaten you or any other Facebook users. Facebook will investigate, and if the complaint is legitimate, Facebook will take the appropriate steps to warn or remove the parties responsible.

Clicking the X (Hide or Remove) link next to any Wall posting opens a pop-up menu that includes a Report as Abuse link, which allows you to send a report to Facebook. (You may need to mouse over to the right side of the posting to see the X.) If you spot a profile with objectionable content, you can click the Report This Person link toward the bottom of the profile. Groups have a similar link (Report Group) on their pages that you can use to report objectionable Groups, and so do Pages, photos and Notes.

Phishing Lessons

The term *phishing* refers to a kind of online fraud in which criminals try to trick people into revealing their passwords, credit card numbers, and other sensitive data. You may already be familiar with phishing e-mails, which are spam messages disguised to look like e-mail from your bank or other sites you do business with, such as PayPal and eBay. Clicking a link in a phishing e-mail takes you to a fake site that's mocked up to look like the real thing, where the phishers hope you'll trustingly enter your information.

You can often identify phishing e-mails because they don't address you by your real name the way your bank would, or because they're littered with typos and bad grammar. (For some reason that escapes me, highly literate people rarely seem to choose phishing as a career path.) Threats are another giveaway—phishing e-mails often claim that dire consequences will occur if you don't do what's requested. It's all just an attempt to intimidate you into clicking that bogus link.

WARNING: If you use a shared computer or access Facebook from a public space, make sure to deselect the "Keep me logged in" checkbox when you log in to Facebook. And don't forget to log out when you finish your Facebook session. Otherwise you may wind up giving the next person to use the computer complete access to your Facebook account.

What's "Objectionable"?
Obviously, deciding what's objectionable can be subjective, but Facebook's terms expressly prohibit nudity, pornography, harassment, and unwelcome contact. Objectionable content, according to Facebook, includes "content that *we deem* to be harmful, threatening, unlawful, defamatory, infringing, abusive, inflammatory, harassing, vulgar, obscene, fraudulent, invasive of privacy or publicity rights, hateful, or racially, ethnically or otherwise objectionable." In other words, the definition of *objectionable* is ultimately up to Facebook's judgment.

An example of the Report as Abuse link in the pop-up menu for the X (Remove) link next to a Wall posting

Become a Fan of Facebook Security

The Facebook Security Page is a good central resource for information about phishing, viruses, and other security topics. You can find it easily by typing *Facebook Security* into Facebook's search box.

By clicking the Like button at the top of the page, you'll be signed up for updates from Facebook related to security and safety topics. (And your News Feed will most likely mention that you've become a fan of Facebook Security, helping to spread the word about this resource to your friends. One good deed for the day done!)

I've also found the official Facebook Page for the computer security firm Sophos to be a useful resource for news and info on Facebook security issues. You can find it by searching for *Sophos* in the blue bar.

On Facebook, phishing commonly takes the form of a message or Wall posting that *appears* to come from someone on your Friend List—but in reality, your friend's account has been compromised, and the message has been sent by scamsters using the login information they stole from your friend. The phishers are hoping you'll trust the message because you trust your friend, and click the link and enter your information before you have time to realize that the message is, well, phishy. If you take the bait, and the phishers gain access to your own user name and password, very shortly your other friends will start to get phishing messages that appear to come from you.

What Phishing Looks Like

If you see a posting like this appear on your Wall, you'll know the friend who supposedly posted it got phished.

Note the telltale signs of a dodgy post: the all caps, the bad punctuation and spelling. And of course, the most important clue of all—the whole point of the post is to get you to visit a spammy web site, which is no doubt crawling with viruses, malware, and other nastiness.

Phighting Back: Tips for Not Getting Phished

Phishing is common enough on Facebook that sooner or later you'll come across it, if you haven't already.

Education is your best weapon against phishers—once you know how phishing works, you're less likely to take the bait. So here's a bucketful of tips to help you keep from getting phished:

- Make sure your browser is up to date and secure. Current browsers are getting better at identifying and warning you about suspicious sites. Make sure you've got the most up-to-date version of whatever browser you're using.
- Don't click any links, especially links to external web sites, if you're not sure where they go. And pay attention to the URL in your browser. Mouse

over the link before you click it, and look at the URL that appears in the status bar of your browser. If it doesn't match the address the link is supposed to take you to, that's a reason to be suspicious.

- Be suspicious of any Wall posts or messages that don't sound like the friend who supposedly wrote them. If the grammar, spelling, or syntax isn't what you'd expect from the person you know, that's a red flag.
- Set up a security question for your Facebook account. If phishers do manage to take control of it, Facebook's User Operations team can help you restore your access by having you provide the answer to your security question. (You can set your security question on the Account > Account Settings page.)
- Remember that Facebook will never ask you to provide your password in an e-mail or Inbox message.
- Help police Facebook by watching your friends' backs—if it looks like a friend of yours has been phished, let them know immediately.

What to Do If You Get Phished

If you discover that your Facebook account has been accessed by phishers, there are three steps to take immediately.

1. **Reset your password** on the Account > Account Settings page. (As mentioned earlier, if your login information no longer works, you may need to provide Facebook with the answer to your security question so they can restore access to your account.)
2. **Report abuse to Facebook.** Click the Help link in the footer on any Facebook page. Then type the words *report phishing* in the search box for a link to the form where you can submit a phishing report to Facebook.
3. **Run antivirus software** to check your computer for any malware you may have picked up.

TIP: One caveat regarding security questions: Make sure the answer to your question isn't something that anyone else could guess or discover from publicly available information. If someone can find out the name of your pet by Googling your name, for example, then don't use the name of your pet.

Beware of Links Bearing Trojans

Phishing isn't the only reason to be careful where you click on Facebook. Facebook has also had problems with viruses. One notorious example was called Koobface—technically a worm delivered by means of a Trojan horse—which spread via Inbox message spam on Facebook.

If you got one of those messages—which could appear to come from a friend whose computer had been infected—you saw a link to an online video player. Once you arrived at the video page, a message informed you that you wouldn't be able to play the video without downloading an upgrade to your video software. But if you clicked the link, you'd wind up downloading the Trojan and potentially infecting your own computer.

I've seen this one in action myself. One morning I woke up and logged onto Facebook to find a message in my Inbox from an old college friend. It was just a one-sentence message, of the "Hey, look at this" variety, with a link included. I was still half asleep and not thinking suspiciously, so I clicked the link. (Only later, when I was little more awake, did it occur to me that the friend in question almost never sent me messages littered with misspellings, smileys, and LOLs.)

After clicking, here's what I saw:

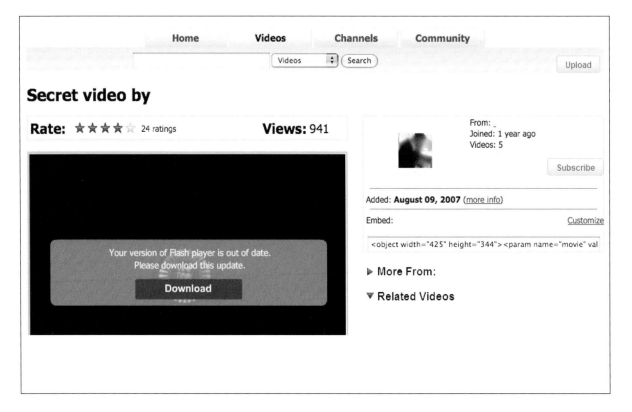

Fortunately, I'd read about this particular Trojan, so I knew enough not to download the bogus video software. And now you do, too.

Clickjacking 101

One kind of spam-generating scam that's spread rapidly on Facebook in recent months is *clickjacking*. Clickjacking is a way of tricking you into clicking on something you didn't really mean to click on, by using malicious code to create an invisible button or link that's hidden underneath other content. Simply put, you think you're clicking on something innocuous, but instead you wind up clicking on the hidden link or button, which then triggers an action you didn't mean to take.

On Facebook, the form this takes has been dubbed *Likejacking*, because the object of the scam is to get you to click a hidden Like button, sending out a News Feed story saying that you Liked a Page or a link that you haven't, in fact, Liked. When your friends see the story in their News Feed, they click on it too, and the whole thing perpetuates itself virally.

Here's an example of how it works: You click on a posting on someone's Wall, and it takes you to a website where you're encouraged to click on a button to play a video clip (usually something sensational like "OMG LADY FINDS BABY ALLIGATOR IN HER HAPPY MEAL BOX!!! CLICK TO WATCH VIDEO!!!!") But when you click what appears to be the Play button, instead of playing the video, your click is actually recorded as Liking a bogus Page.

The best precautions you can take to fight the clickjackers are the obvious ones:

- Keep a close eye on your Wall and immediately delete any postings that don't belong there.
- Be careful about clicking on links to external websites, and clicking on links you find on sites you're not familiar with.
- Distrust any messages that contain excessive capital letters and multiple exclamation marks (this is a good rule for life in general).

For those who want a stronger level of protection, there's one other step you can take. If you use Firefox as your web browser, you can add a free extension called NoScript that prevents any scripts from being executed without your consent. Because clickjacking depends on the use of scripts, this effectively protects you from getting clickjacked—unless you relax your guard and enable the wrong site. (The downside, of course, is that you'll spend a lot of time tediously approving the sites you visit that aren't malicious, but security always comes at a cost.) You can find NoScript at www.noscript.net.

 Can a Status Update Get You Burglarized?

Security experts have long warned that announcing online when you're away from home might serve as an invitation to thieves. And indeed, in recent months there have been news reports of Facebook users being burglarized by people in their Friends lists after posting status updates mentioning that they were on vacation or just out for the evening. In September of 2010, it was reported that New Hampshire police had busted a burglary ring that was responsible for more than 50 break-ins, and specialized in targeting people based on their Facebook postings.

So a little caution would seem to be in order. If you want to be on the safe side, avoid announcing in advance where you're going and when. Instead, wait till you get back home, and then post your concert or vacation pictures and tell everyone what a great time you had. And if you use Facebook's Places feature, which allows you to broadcast your whereabouts by checking into locations using your mobile phone, you might want to restrict its visibility to only your Trusted Friends list on the Privacy Settings page.

If You're Under 18

💬 **If You're a Parent**
If you have children of Facebook-using age, the first thing you should do is visit Facebook's Safety Center at www.facebook.com/safety, and read through the materials there. You can also become a fan of the Facebook Safety Page (facebook.com/fbsafety) to see regular updates on safety-related topics.

Make sure to talk with your children about the potential dangers that can arise online. Have them familiarize themselves with the basic safety and security tips in this chapter, as well as on Facebook's Safety page. And stress that they should report inappropriate messages and behavior to you as well as to Facebook.

Facebook doesn't allow children under 13 to access Facebook—and suggests that parents consider carefully whether children over 13 should be supervised when they use Facebook.

Just as you need to look out for your own privacy rather than depending on Facebook's settings, you can't assume (and Facebook doesn't guarantee) that the site is "entirely free of illegal, offensive, pornographic or otherwise inappropriate material, or that its members will not encounter inappropriate or illegal conduct from other members." Members are encouraged to report any such material, and full instructions on how to do so are given on the Safety page.

Finally, if you have children on Facebook who are minors, be sure to read the "If You're Under 18" section, and have your kids read it, too.

If you're legally a minor—or if you have family members who are minors using Facebook—you need to pay extra attention, and give extra weight, to the security warnings and safety tips in this chapter.

The sobering reality is that people online are not always who they pretend to be, and predators do use the Internet to stalk and "groom" underage victims. Online bullying is also a sad reality, and people have been known to assume false identities for this purpose.

Facebook does its best to identify fake profiles and shut them down—and in fact has sometimes taken criticism for being too aggressive in its approach. But Facebook's security team isn't omniscient, and despite its efforts, fake profiles do get created and do get used for some dishonorable purposes.

In addition to the general security and safety tips shared elsewhere in this chapter, minors on Facebook should take these precautions:

- Don't post your address or phone number online, anywhere. Don't trust Facebook's privacy settings to limit access to them. Let e-mail be your first point of contact for anyone who doesn't already have your number.

- Don't friend anyone you don't already know and trust.

- Make sure you familiarize yourself with Facebook's privacy settings, and set them carefully. Check them every so often to make sure you're still comfortable with the level of privacy you've chosen.

- Don't arrange to meet anyone offline for the first time without other people you know and trust being present and knowing in advance about the meeting.

- Don't feel obligated to post an actual photo of yourself as your main profile pic. Your profile picture can show up in all sorts of places on Facebook other than your profile itself (including search listings, Groups, third-party apps, and more), so it may be seen by people you aren't friends with. Lots of people on Facebook use an avatar other than their own photo—such as an image of a pet, a favorite possession, or even an illustration—that says something about them but doesn't compromise their privacy.

- Block anyone who sends you inappropriate communications (see the info on how to block people earlier in this chapter) and report them to Facebook (see "Reporting Abuse"). And as Facebook says on its Safety page, "We strongly encourage users under the age of 18 to talk to their parents or a responsible adult immediately if someone online says or does something to make them feel uncomfortable or threatened in any way."

Keeping a Low Profile

Lurking is a time-honored tradition on the Internet. Some people are shy. Others need to fly under the radar for reasons related to their careers or personal lives.

If you're one of those people, you may wonder whether it's possible to lurk quietly on Facebook at all, given that Facebook's default approach is to announce what people do.

But it is possible to keep a low profile on Facebook, by setting your privacy controls to the maximum and declining to post any personal info on your profile.

Once you've followed the steps below, nobody you haven't explicitly chosen to be friends with on Facebook will be able to tell you're on Facebook at all. And even your friends won't see much information about you, if any. You can lurk to your heart's content.

Of course, you'll be missing out on most of the fun of Facebook, which is about interaction, after all—but fortunately, all of the steps are reversible if and when you decide to come out of your shell.

So here's your step-by-step guide to Facebooking on the down-low:

1. Set all of your Basic Directory Information and Sharing controls to the narrowest possible setting (in most cases Friends Only) on the Privacy Settings page.

2. Be sure to set your Search Visibility to Friends Only (the narrowest possible setting) on the Basic Directory Info page, and turn off your public search listing if it was enabled.

3. You may also want to delete personal info from your profile, using the Edit links on your Info tab, if you've entered any. The only info you can't erase from your profile is your name. Everything else—your location, your birthday, your bio—is optional. (Note that although you may not be able to remove your gender, you can hide it so it isn't displayed.)

4. On the Applications You Use page, deauthorize all applications. (See the *Applications and Other Add-Ons* chapter for how to do this.)

5. Leave any networks you've joined. You can do this by visiting the Account > Account Settings > Networks page.

 There's No One Watching the Watchers

For the record, there's no way you can see who's visited your profile on Facebook, or for anyone else to know that you've been looking at their profile (unless you deliberately leave behind some evidence, like a comment or a Wall post). This has been a perennial kind of scam on Facebook: Over time there have been an abundance of bogus applications, Pages, and Groups on Facebook claiming that they can show you who's been looking at your profile— and making that claim is a solid-gold clue that whoever made it is untrustworthy. Facebook acts to remove these scams as soon as it becomes aware of them.

WARNING: One thing I *don't* recommend you do is use a pseudonym on Facebook, or create multiple profiles—that's a violation of Facebook's terms and can get your profile(s) shut down, without warning, and you may even find yourself permanently banned. (See the *Signing Up and Setting Up Your Profile* chapter.)

Quitting Facebook

Some people resist joining Facebook precisely because of the popular misconception that once you set up a Facebook profile, you can never remove your information. I have one friend who starts singing the lyrics from "Hotel California" (*you can check out any time you like/but you can never leave*) anytime the word Facebook is mentioned.

So in case you're afraid of being assigned a permanent residence at the Hotel Facebook (and having an Eagles song stuck in your head for all eternity), I'm going to tell you exactly how to pack up and leave Facebook if you ever decide you need to.

There are two ways to leave Facebook:

1. **Deactivating temporarily.** If you choose this option, you'll vanish from Facebook for the time being, but the door will be open if you want to come back at some point in the future.

   To temporarily deactivate your Facebook account: Go to Account > Account Settings and click the Deactivate link. Fill out the form letting Facebook know why you're deactivating, and then click the Deactivate button to confirm.

    NOTE: If you choose temporary deactivation, you can reactivate your account at any time by logging in to Facebook with your e-mail and password.

   TIP: While you're deactivated, your friends will no longer see you in their Friends lists. You might want to let them know you're deactivating, so that they don't think you've defriended them.

2. **Permanently deleting your account.** If you choose this option, you'll be submitting a request to Facebook to permanently remove your profile from Facebook. This step is not reversible (that's why it's called "permanent").

   To erase your Facebook account forever, click Help in the footer and then type *Delete* in the Help Center's search field. Click "How do I permanently delete my account?" on the results page, read the instructions, and click the link to the Delete Account form.

Are you sure you want to deactivate your account?

Deactivating your account will disable your profile and remove your name and picture from anything you've shared on Facebook.

Reason for leaving
(Required):

- ◯ I have another Facebook account.
- ◯ I don't feel safe on Facebook.
- ◯ I have a privacy concern.
- ◯ I don't find Facebook useful.
- ◯ This is temporary. I'll be back.
- ◯ I get too many emails, invitations, and requests from Facebook.
- ◯ I don't understand how to use Facebook.
- ◯ I spend too much time using Facebook.
- ◯ Other

Please explain further:

The options on the Account Deactivation form let you tell Facebook why you're leaving.

Delete My Account

If you do not think you will use Facebook again and would like your account deleted, we can take care of this for you. Keep in mind that you will not be able to reactivate your account or retrieve any of the content or information you have added. If you would like your account deleted, then click "Submit."

[Submit]   Cancel

The dialog for deleting your account warns you that this step is permanent.

Sharing Content on Facebook

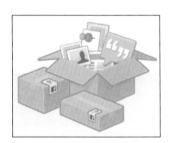

Here's where the fun of Facebook truly begins. Spiffing up your profile and collecting friends is all well and good, but the secret ingredient to Facebook's success is the way it keeps you connected to your friends—making it easy to share news, links, photos, and videos.

Before Facebook came along, you might have dug up old friends on the Internet whom you hadn't seen in years and swapped an excited e-mail or two in an attempt to catch up. But unless you really *worked* at keeping in contact, all too often you'd find that within six months or a year you'd fallen out of touch again.

Fortunately, Facebook takes the heavy lifting out of staying connected. Facebook's profiles give you an easy way to check in on any specific friends to see what they've been up to lately, while the News Feed that appears on your Home page gives you a big-picture briefing on what's going on with your social circle from day to day and week to week.

But Facebook's sharing tools are more than just a form of social glue. They're the reason why Facebook is so effective at spreading the word about all kinds of things, and why it's become one of the primary ways people find out what's going on in the world—and discuss it with each other. In this chapter, we'll explore how all of that works.

The Facebook Publisher: One-Stop Posting and Sharing

Up at the top of the Wall tab on your profile lives a special area, which (although it isn't labeled as such) is called the Facebook Publisher. The Publisher makes it easy to post all sorts of content to your profile: messages, links, photos, videos, and more. You can also use the Publisher on your friends' profiles to post content to their Walls.

You'll find the Publisher on the Home page, too, as well as the pages for Groups, Events, and official Pages. And depending on where you find it, the Publisher's appearance can vary somewhat. In fact, at the time of this writing there are no less than *three* different versions of the Publisher on Facebook: the one that appears on personal profiles and official Pages, the one that appears on Facebook's new-style Groups, and the one that appears at the top of the Home page. But they all function basically the same way: To post something, click the button for the type of content you want to share. This causes the appropriate fields and controls to appear. (If you don't choose any button at all, you'll be posting a status update or text-only message.)

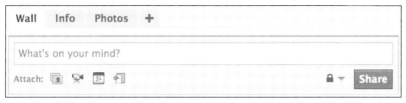

The Publisher as it appears on a personal profile. Underneath the "What's on your mind?" field are buttons for posting (from left to right) photos, videos, Events, and Links.

News Feed

Top News · Most Recent 300+

What's on your mind?

The Publisher as it appears on the Home page. You have to click in the "What's on your mind?" field before the buttons for posting content appear.

Share: Post Link Photo Video Event Doc

The newer version of the Publisher as it appears on a Group page. This incarnation—which Facebook also refers to as the Share Menu—is probably the wave of the future, and by the time you read this, it may be the version you see on the Home page and personal profiles, too. Just click the button for the type of content you want to post.

Feeding the News Feed

So, what does it mean to post something to your profile? As a matter of fact, there are two things happening at once.

First of all, when you post something to your profile, you're posting it on your Wall—a story about the item will appear among the other stories on your Wall, and friends who drop by your profile to check out what you've been up to will see it there.

But you're also engaging in a kind of targeted broadcasting. Facebook will generate a News Feed story about the item you've just posted, which your friends may see the next time they look at the News Feed area on their Home pages. So when you post an item to your profile, you're also sharing it with your friends—saying, in effect, "Hey, everyone—look at this!"

NOTE: We'll look at the specifics of posting Wall messages, status updates, Links, Notes, and Places in the course of this chapter. (Photos and videos are discussed in the *Photos and Videos* chapter, and Events are discussed in the *Facebook Calendar* chapter.)

💬 **Taking It Private**

Wall posts, by design, are public conversations—like talking to a friend at a party where the other people gathered around can hear. But if you want to talk privately with a friend on Facebook, you can do that, too, by sending them an Inbox message or by using Facebook's Chat application. Both are discussed in detail in the following chapter, *Communicating on Facebook*.

NOTE: In some cases, you may not see the Publisher when you visit a friend's Wall—which means the friend in question has chosen not to allow Wall posts by friends. (See the upcoming section "How to Control Who Can Post on Your Wall and See What's Posted There" for how that works.) In that case, you'll have to send your friend an Inbox message instead of writing on their Wall (or, in some cases, you may still be able to comment on existing stories on your friend's Wall).

💬 **Whose Wall Is This, Anyway?**

One common mistake Facebook newbies make (and even more experienced Facebookers, sometimes) is getting confused about exactly whose Wall they're writing on. You'll sometimes see people posting messages as their own status updates that were clearly intended to be a greeting on someone else's Wall— and from the other direction, you might see someone accidentally post their own status update on the Wall of a friend.

So here's how to keep it straight: If you're using the Publisher at the top of your own profile or the Home page, then you'll be posting the content to your own Wall. But if you're using the Publisher on someone else's Wall, then the content you post will appear on their Wall as a message from you.

Wall Basics

The Wall tab on personal profiles is where a big chunk of the direct, person-to-person social interaction on Facebook takes place. It's where you and your friends can leave each other social messages that other friends are allowed to see, and the place you drop by to see what's going on in the brain of any particular friend you'd like to catch up with.

How to Write on Someone Else's Wall

Writing on someone's Wall is easy. Just go to their profile and type your message in the Publisher at the top of their Wall—just like you'd do if you were posting a status update on your own Wall, only in this case the text will show up as a message on your friend's Wall. (If you see the newer kind of Publisher shown on the previous page, you might need to click the Post button before the field where you type your message is displayed.) Click the Share button when your message is ready to post.

In addition to writing messages, you can use the Publisher to post links, photos, or videos on your friends' Walls—all the same kinds of items you can post to your own profile. Just choose the appropriate button on the Publisher.

Care and Feeding of Your Wall

Facebook gives you a fairly generous amount of control over what appears on your Wall—it's your place, after all.

How to Control Who Can Post on Your Wall and See What's Posted There

Having friends write friendly messages on your Wall can be one of the most satisfying parts of life on Facebook—especially when your birthday rolls around. But not everyone is comfortable with the public nature of Wall postings by friends—or trusts completely in their friends' sense of discretion. So Facebook lets you choose whether or not your friends are allowed to post to your Wall. It also lets you specify exactly who can view what your friends post. To do this, start by clicking the Options link at the top of your Wall, over to the right just underneath the Publisher.

Clicking the Options link reveals the controls that let you change the view for your Wall (discussed in the following section), and also displays the Settings link over to the right. Click the Settings link.

Facebook will display the Wall settings area, where you'll see the Stories Posted by Friends controls. Use the "Who can see posts made by friends" pop-up menu to restrict the level of access. If you want, you can use the Customize command to limit visibility to people on a Friend List you've created, such as your Trusted Friends.

Stories Posted by Friends

Posting Ability:	☑ Friends may post to my Wall
Who can see posts made by friends?	🔒 Friends Only ▾
Combine Posts:	☑ Show posts from friends in the default view

How to Change the View for the Wall

Along the top of your Wall you'll find a set of links that let you change what's displayed on your Wall. As shown in the previous section, you'll need to first click the Options link to reveal these controls. The default setting is [Your Name] + Friends, which means postings by your friends are visible alongside your own postings. But if you click Posts by [Your Name], the view will change to show you only what you've posted to your profile yourself. Clicking Just Friends shows you only what your friends have posted to your Wall.

Note that when you click these links, you're not actually removing anything from your Wall, and you're not changing what other visitors to your Wall see—you're just temporarily changing what's displayed to you personally.

The same view options are available when you're reading your friends' Walls, or the Walls for official Pages, too. So if you're visiting Tracey's Wall, for example, you can click the Filters link underneath the Publisher, and then click Just Tracey to see only what Tracey herself has posted, or Just Friends to see what Tracey's friends have contributed to her Wall.

TIP: You can also control which (if any) applications are allowed to post stories to your Wall, using the settings on the Applications You Use page. See the *Privacy and Security* chapter for details.

TIP: If you deselect the checkbox for "Show posts from friends in the default view" in the Stories Posted by Friends area, your friends will see only your own posts by default when they first arrive at your Wall. They'll need to change the view for the Wall using the view controls in order to see postings by your friends.

TIP: Changing the view for a Wall can be useful in a variety of circumstances. You might be looking at the Wall for an official Page and want to screen out postings by the Page's fans in order to see just the content posted by the Page itself. Or you might be trying to find a link you posted on your own Wall a few months ago—in which case, filtering out postings by your friends will narrow the field.

How to Delete Wall Stories

You have the option to remove any story that appears on your Wall if you don't want it to be there. To delete a story, move your pointer over the right side of it until the X (Remove Post) button appears. Click that and then choose Remove Post from the menu that appears. (You can also use this menu to flag spam or report abusive posts if any appear on your Wall.)

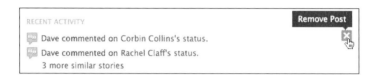

The Social Section
Imagine that you're reading the morning news on a web portal where your news is arranged into sections. You click on the World tab for your international stories, the Tech tab for computer-related news, the Entertainment tab for movie and music news, and the Sports tab to keep track of your teams.

Now imagine that there's a tab there called Friends, and when you click on it, you get updates about what's going on in your personal social sphere. You might find out that two of your friends have gotten engaged and that several others are going to a concert this weekend. You might also read a political rant by your friend Kevin and some philosophical musings by Maria, and then see some freshly taken photos of Kurt's trip to Germany.

That's basically how the News Feed on Facebook's Home page works. If you make a habit of visiting the Home page on a regular basis, Facebook will gradually catch you up on the developments—big and small—that your friends choose to share on Facebook.

Feeding Frenzy: Using Feeds to Keep Track of Your Friends

I've said earlier that Facebook makes it easy to stay on top of what's going on with your friends, and the News Feed area on Facebook's Home page is where that happens. (See the "Social Section" sidebar at left for an explanation of what it's all about.)

Facebook gives you some useful options for changing what kinds of stories you see in the News Feed, and homing in on stories featuring the friends you're most interested in.

How to Change the Display for the News Feed on Your Home Page

At the top of the News Feed on the Home page are two links: Top News and Most Recent. Clicking these switches you back and forth its two main views.

- **Top News** is the default view—think of it as a kind of "Facebook Digest." Facebook automatically analyzes a number of factors and then chooses a handful of stories it thinks you'll be interested in. (See the sidebar, "Some Posts Are Edgier Than Others" for more on this.)

■ **Most Recent (also known as the Live Feed)** is the much less filtered experience—most of the News Feed stories about your friends appear here in chronological order. If you have a lot of friends, you probably won't be able to read through it all, but clicking on it occasionally gives you a level of detail—and some interesting surprises, sometimes—that you won't get from the Top News view.

Facebook's Ever-Changing Home Page

Like just about every other part of its site, Facebook redesigns the Home page fairly often—it's been overhauled at least three or four times since I first started planning this book in early 2008. In fact, even as I'm writing this, I'm expecting Facebook to launch another version of the Home page sometime soon.

This ongoing process of change can be fairly frustrating to regular Facebook users, who find it disorienting to discover controls they've spent time learning how to use suddenly renamed and rearranged. Logging on to Facebook after a Home page update can feel a little like waking up and tripping over the ottoman because someone rearranged the furniture in the middle of the night. (And imagine how you'd feel if it was your job to write a book explaining how to use Facebook, knowing full well that many of the screen shots and instructions you're laboriously assembling will no longer match the

site sometime soon—maybe even before the printing presses are done churning it out. Okay, I'll stop before my violinist asks for a raise.)

Ultimately, it's all part of life online, and experienced Facebookers (and Facebook authors) learn how to roll with the changes. So if the Home page looks different from what you see here, remember that its basic function tends to stay the same. It's there to help you keep track of what your friends are posting, and its various controls are designed to help you slice and dice that stream of postings in various ways, so you can see different categories of information when you want to. As I mentioned back at the beginning of the book, once you understand the principles behind the way Facebook works, you can usually figure out how to do what you're trying to do—with a little patience and a willingness to experiment with new controls.

How to Filter the News Feed on Your Home Page

Lots of people filter their water these days, to improve its flavor and quality—in fact, plenty of people I know wouldn't dream of drinking it straight out of the tap. Some people even filter the air in their home to remove allergens and odors. Well, you can apply the same approach to your News Feed to improve the flavor and quality of your Facebook experience.

Because here's the thing: When you have less than 100 friends on Facebook, you'll probably find it easy to keep up with everything your friends are posting. But by the time you have several hundred friends, there aren't enough hours in the day to read everything they're all sharing—and updates from people you barely know are crowding out postings by the people you care

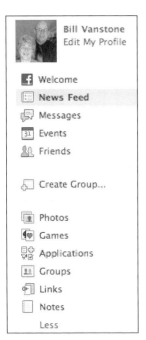

The bookmarks that appear in the left-hand column of the Home page by default. You may need to click the More link at the bottom of the column to display them all. And if you've been using any apps, you'll see bookmarks for recently used apps, too.

When you click the Friends bookmark, a submenu appears with a Status Updates bookmark along with bookmarks for any Friend Lists you've created.

about most. At that point, you have a choice: You can resign yourself to reading a random sampling of Facebook potluck every day, or you can attempt to filter out some of the noise to focus in on the people who really matter to you. So here are some of the ways Facebook lets you sift through the content on your Home page to home in on what you're interested in.

USING THE DEFAULT FILTERS

If you're interested in seeing just one particular type of content—say, only status updates, or only photos—you can do that. Among the bookmarks in the left-hand column of the Home page are several that can be used to filter News Feed content. Clicking the Links, Photos, or Notes bookmarks, for example, will show you all the recent postings by your friends that fit into those categories. And clicking the Friends bookmark will reveal a submenu with a Status Updates bookmark, which allows you to see only status updates.

THE BEST WAY TO FILTER YOUR HOME PAGE: USING A FRIEND LIST

Here's the option I recommend—the way I read my own News Feed every day. If you've created any Friend Lists, they'll be displayed in the submenu that appears when you click the Friends bookmark in the left-hand column (the same submenu that contains the Status Updates bookmark mentioned in the preceding section). Clicking the bookmark for any of those Friend Lists will give you a version of the News Feed that contains only postings from the friends who belong to that list. Presto! You can filter the News Feed by any category of friends you want to create.

I recommend creating a Friend List called something like Favorites that's just for reading the News Feed. Add to that list anyone whose postings you want to make sure you don't to miss—the people you're closest to, and the people who tend to post the most interesting content. Then you can start the day by reading your Favorites first. Once you've caught up with your inner circle, you might check other lists, like your Co-Workers list or your Family list or the people from your book club. Or you might head to the Most Recent view of the News Feed to sample some less-filtered postings from your full list of friends.

HIDING SPECIFIC PEOPLE, PAGES, AND APPS FROM YOUR NEWS FEED

As you're reading the News Feed, if you see postings from specific friends, Pages, or apps that you'd rather not be seeing, you can hide those postings—or even choose to hide all postings from that source from appearing in your News Feed in the future.

The Hide button, which looks like a little X, is hidden itself (how ironic!) by default, but it'll show itself if you move your mouse over to the right side of any posting in the News Feed.

Phil Ridarelli That didn't take long.

The Hide button at the right side of a posting. (Phil, if you're reading this, don't worry—I didn't really hide you.)

When you click the Hide button, a menu appears that lets you choose to hide just this specific post or all future posts by the friend, Page, or app in question.

Hide this post
Hide all by Phil

Mark as spam

How to Edit the Options for the News Feed

Way down at the bottom of the News Feed area on the Home page is a link that's easy to overlook: Edit Options.

Older Posts ▾   Edit Options

Clicking it opens the Edit Options dialog, which contains some additional settings for controlling who and what appears in your News Feed.

There are two versions of the Edit Options dialog—depending on which view you're in when you click the Edit Options link at the bottom. The one for the Top News view simply allows you to unhide any friends, Pages, and apps you've chosen to Hide in the past.

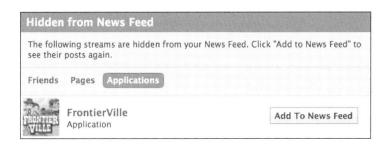

Hidden from News Feed

The following streams are hidden from your News Feed. Click "Add to News Feed" to see their posts again.

Friends   Pages   **Applications**

FrontierVille
Application   Add To News Feed

Some Posts Are Edgier Than Others

It's something everyone wonders about from time to time: How exactly does Facebook decide which postings appear in the Top News view of your News Feed? There are no human editors involved, of course. Instead, Facebook uses a system of algorithms called EdgeRank to decide which postings rise to the top of the heap.

EdgeRank takes its name from the fact that it evaluates postings for newsfeedworthiness based on whether they have certain distinguishing factors called edges—including feedback such as Likes, comments, and tags. The more edges a posting has, the higher it ranks.

But not all edges are created equal. EdgeRank also weights the edges themselves based on three factors:

1. Affinity score. Facebook analyzes how often you interact with each of your friends on Facebook, by (for example) viewing each other's profiles or exchanging messages. People you interact with more get a higher affinity score. So a posting will rank higher in your News Feed if the friend who posted it, or the people who've Liked and commented on it, have higher affinity scores because they're people you tend to pay attention to.

2. Type of edge. Some edges carry more weight than others. Comments may affect the posting's rank more than Likes, for example.

3. Time decay. Edges lose their edginess as time goes by, so the older the posting and its edges are, the less likely they are to rank highly enough to appear in your News Feed.

To sum it all up: Fresher items that have gotten a lot of response from friends you care about are probably most likely to get promoted by EdgeRank.

Are You Being Heard?

Remember that just because people connect to you on Facebook, or follow you on Twitter, doesn't mean they're actually listening to you. Some of your friends and fans on Facebook may be paying close attention to what you post; others may have chosen to hide you from their News Feed, or may be filtering their Home page using a "Favorites" Friend List that doesn't include you.

Much of the time this is perfectly natural. By the time they've been on Facebook for a few months, most people have too many friends to follow everyone in their News Feed, so they have to do some filtering. (And Facebook does some of its own filtering, too, automatically.) So you can't assume that just because you post something to your profile, everyone in your friends list will see it in their News Feeds—and you shouldn't necessarily take that personally.

On the other hand, no one likes the feeling of posting into a void. If you aren't getting the response you expect to your postings, it might not hurt to do a little bit of audience analysis: Pay attention to which postings of yours *do* tend to get responses, and think about how you can make what you post more appealing, engaging, and relevant to your friends' interests.

The Edit Options dialog for the Most Recent view, however, has some additional controls.

News Feed Settings

Live Feed automatically determines which friends to include based on who Facebook thinks you want to hear from most. You can manually adjust this list below.

Show More   **Hide**

Type a friend's name   Type a friend's name

The top part of the dialog lets you type the names of friends you'd like to see more content from on the left, and friends you'd like to hide from your News Feed on the right. (Once you've added people to either of these lists, you can remove them from the list by clicking the X next to their name.)

Number of Friends

Control how many friends you want shown in Live Feed. A higher number means you will see new posts more frequently.

250   Maximum number of friends shown in Live Feed

View Recommended Friends

Save   Cancel

The bottom part of the dialog contains the Number of Friends control. By default, Facebook limits the number of friends who can appear in the Most Recent view (aka Live Feed) to the 250 people it thinks you'll be most interested in. If you'd like to open up your News Feed to your full list, you can set this number to 5000 (the maximum number of friends Facebook allows you to have). Or pick a number anywhere in between.

The Tao of Status Updates

Once your Friends list grows to a significant size—by the time your friends number in the several dozens, say—reading status updates becomes not only a form of entertainment, but a surprisingly useful way to learn things. Clicking on the Status Updates tab on the Home page can feel like you're accessing the collective psyche of your social sphere, the *zeitgeist* of your Friends list—only instead of the spirit of an age you're tapping into, it's the spirit of a particular morning, afternoon, or evening.

If you're new to Facebook, I highly recommend getting in the habit of checking your friends' status updates on a regular basis. You may be surprised at some of the things you learn. For one thing, status updates can alert you to interesting trends among the people you know. You might discover that an alarming number of your friends are coming down with colds or sniffles (giving you an opportunity to stock up on zinc lozenges), or that a bunch of them are excited about the new season of *Mad Men*, or that several are heading to a nearby state to volunteer for flood relief work.

I'm amazed at how often I first hear about breaking news events on Facebook. Barack Obama's victory in the 2008 Iowa caucuses, the deaths of Heath Ledger and George Carlin, earthquakes in California and Illinois—these are all news events I learned about from reading my friends' status updates before clicking over to Google News for the full details. And the day I found out that several of my friends had been laid off from different employers in the same afternoon served as a local, human counterpoint to reading about unemployment figures in the news.

How to Post a Status Update

Posting a status update is easy—it's the default setting for the current version of the Publisher, so all you have to do is start typing in the "What's on your mind?" field. (If the Publisher has changed by the time you read this, you might need to click a button that says Status or something similar before the field where you type your message is displayed.)

Note that Facebook currently limits status updates to 420 characters—much more generous than Twitter's 140, but not enough to let you post a chapter of your novel or anything. (Hey, that's what Notes are for.) If you go over the magic number, you'll see a little knuckle-rapping dialog box that tells you to edit your post a little and try again.

Status updates have one special property that separates them from other kinds of things you can post on your Wall—they also appear at the top of your profile, so they're one of the first things that catch the eye of any visitors.

> **Dave Awl** startled a raccoon the size of a chubby 5th grader on Berwyn Avenue last night. It unsuccessfully attempted to hide behind a tree. about a minute ago clear
>
> Wall   Info   Photos   Notes   Links   Books   »   +

How to Tag Someone or Something in a Status Update

If you're typing out a status update and you find yourself mentioning someone or something with a profile or page of any kind on Facebook (including personal profiles, Pages, Groups, and Events), you can tag that person or thing in your posting.

Reading Facebook Content Using RSS

If you use an RSS reader such as Google Reader, you can use it to access your Facebook notifications. Go to the Notifications page (click the Notifications icon in the blue bar, then the See All Notifications link). You'll find a Subscribe via RSS link at the top of the page. This gives you an alternate way to keep up with Facebook content without visiting Facebook itself—and might come in handy if you're in a situation where Facebook's website is blocked.

TIP: You can also update your Facebook status from your mobile phone. (See the *Going Mobile* chapter for more info.)

NOTE: Status updates are meant to be timely in nature. So if you don't change your status for a full week, Facebook will automatically clear it for you at the seven-day mark to keep your status update area from getting moldy. (It's kind of like the rules for the refrigerator at work.) Note that the posting doesn't disappear from your Wall itself when this happens—just the area at the top of your profile.

TIP: This method of tagging works in Link posts as well as status updates.

Status Updates Versus Links
Occasionally I hear from a frustrated friend who's been trying to post a status update, but can't get their posting to appear up at the top of their profile where status updates live. What's the deal, Neil?

The deal is, Liz, that you've been trying to include a URL of some kind in your status update, and so Facebook is automatically treating it as a Link post. By definition, a status update on Facebook is a posting that contains only plain text (or tags). As soon as you include a web link of any kind, it leaps into the category of Link postings, at which point Facebook helpfully attempts to generate a preview image and text to illustrate it. And of course, that preview area doesn't fit in the status update area at the top of your profile.

If it helps, you can think of the link preview area as being like ballast that makes your posting too heavy to float to the top of your profile the way status updates do ... or maybe not, it's up to you. I just throw these things out there. At any rate, if you want to use your status update to draw attention to a link, you can always say something like, "Hey, check out the link I posted a little lower down on my Wall ..."

TIP: If you're the admin for an official Page on Facebook, you can connect your Facebook Page to a Twitter account by visiting www.facebook.com/twitter.

To activate the tagging function, just type the @ symbol and then start typing the name of the entity you'd like to tag. After a moment, Facebook will load the tagging menu with a list of possible choices.

Click the one you want, and Facebook will turn the name into a tag. The tagged text will appear in blue text in your finished post.

Tagging someone or something in a post accomplishes two things: It turns the name of the tagged party into a link (aha, so that's why it's blue), which people can click to visit the profile or page you've tagged—and it may also cause your post to appear on the Wall for that profile or page. (Note that because Pages on Facebook are public, your tagged posting won't appear on the Wall for a Page unless your privacy settings allow it to be seen by everyone. See the section "Choosing the Audience for Each Post," later in this chapter.)

Syncing Your Facebook Status with Twitter

If you're a Twitter user, it's possible to connect your Facebook and Twitter accounts so that your status updates do double-duty as tweets on Twitter.

The easiest way to accomplish this for a personal profile is to install the Twitter application for Facebook, which lets you post to both Twitter and Facebook at once. You can find it by searching the word Twitter in the blue bar (or the Application Directory). See the *Applications and Other Add-Ons* chapter for all the skinny on how to add applications and manage them.

That said, although you can save a few seconds here and there by posting to Facebook and Twitter at the same time, I don't actually recommend it. Why not? Well, for one thing, your most loyal friends—your "true fans"—are likely to follow you in more than one place. They'll appreciate it if you add some fresh, unique content to each stream so they aren't seeing the exact same series of posts multiple times.

But the even more important consideration is that context and style matter. Each medium has its own conventions and formats. For example, Twitter's hash tags and @replies don't work on Facebook. So if you post a Twitter tweet, complete with hashtags and @ symbols, on Facebook, you look a little like someone who shows up at a Christmas party dressed for Halloween—like you're not really paying attention to your context. (I have one friend who says he hides anyone from his News Feed whose postings contain "Twitter litter.")

And then there's the character count issue: Facebook gives you a generous 420 characters, whereas Twitter limits you to 140. You can use those extra characters to express yourself more fully on Facebook if you post separately (and maybe get rid of some of the unlovely abbreviations Twitter can force you into). And instead of using the shortened URLs that Twitter demands, you can take advantage of Facebook's ability to illustrate your links with eye-catching preview images and text.

So for best impact, I recommend posting each update manually, and adapting it to the forum where you're posting it. It takes a little longer, but you'll reap the benefits in audience appreciation.

Ways to Use Your Status Updates

Status updates are an interesting medium, because despite their brevity, you can use them to say so many different types of things.

Status updates can serve as a personal journal, in which you record the little details and experiences of your day; a standup comic's microphone, where you crack jokes and serve up wry observations; or an activist's mega-phone that lets you disseminate information and share your perspective on current issues and events. Most likely, your status updates will be a mix of all of those different modes, and more.

You can also use your status updates as a promotional space if you want: to draw attention to an upcoming performance, a new product launch, or anything else you're proud of and want your friends to know about. (Just be careful not to overdo it—if your status updates start to feel like a steady stream of spam, people may start to tune them out or even defriend you.)

Here are a few very practical ways you can put your status updates to work:

- Access your brain trust by asking questions. My friend Amy, who's just learning Photoshop, used her status to ask for help changing the resolution of a graphic and got responses back in a matter of minutes. I've also seen people request recommendations for doctors, dentists, and other service providers.

- Let people know when you're traveling, so friends in the area you'll be visiting can give a yell if they want to get together with you.

- Remind people about upcoming Events. ("Don't forget to reserve your booth for the big craft show, people!")

- Let people know you're all right in the event of some-thing worrisome going on in your corner of the world (earthquake, tornado, campus lockdown) that your friends might hear about.

- Get moral support. Ask for sympathy, positive vibes, or prayers when you're in the hospital, under the weather, or just having a lousy week.

Word of Face: Reaching Your Audience on Facebook

Facebook's News Feeds are a big part of what makes the site so entertaining and addictive. But thanks to a nifty phenomenon called *passive endorsement*, they can also make Facebook a powerful tool for spreading the word about—well, almost anything.

I know, I know. Passive endorsement sounds like a corporate buzz phrase. Something your boss might make you watch a bad training video about. But bear with me—because if you've got a creative project, a business, or a cause to promote on Facebook, passive endorsement can add extra oomph to your efforts.

Here's how it works. Suppose you see an ad for a movie on TV. That's *active endorsement*—the advertisers are deliberately promoting the film to you, with the explicit goal of persuading you to see it. For your part, you know you're being advertised to, so you take whatever claims are made about the movie with a grain of salt. ("One of the year's best, huh? We'll see about *that!*")

On the other hand, suppose you overhear several of your co-workers chatting about seeing the movie—saying how hilarious and moving and thought-provoking it was. Assuming they're people whose opinions you respect, your ears perk up a little and you think, *Hmm, maybe I need to check that out.*

That's the impact of passive endorsement. Your co-workers didn't collar you and order you to go see the movie—which might have been counterproductive. They simply expressed their sincere appreciation for it.

On Facebook, this effect can manifest itself in a wide variety of ways. If you keep an eye on the News Feed, you'll see stories when friends of yours join a Group, become a fan of a Page, or plan to attend an Event. Third-party apps can generate stories, too: If your friends buy tickets for a concert using iLike, add a book to their Visual Bookshelf, or decide to support an organization using Causes, Facebook's News Feed may tell you about it.

How can you make use of this? Here's an example: Suppose you're planning a big benefit for a local organization you're on the board of. You've arranged for superb food and lined up top-notch entertainment. You know your guests will be getting their money's worth; all you have to do is get the word out.

When it's time to promote the event, you can send invitations to the organization's mailing list. You might pass the invite along to your personal friends, too. And you might even ask everyone who gets the invitation to pass it along to all of *their* friends—which would exponentially increase your audience. But will they really do that? Odds are that some of your most loyal friends will pass the invitation along, but most will feel they've done their part just by buying their own tickets.

Now suppose that you post the same event on Facebook and send invites to everyone in your Friends list who might be interested. Each time one of them clicks Yes to accept, Facebook generates a News Feed story saying, "Virgil Brown is attending the 4th Annual Disco Lasagna Bowl Benefit" (subject to their chosen privacy settings, of course). Which allows each person who accepts the invite to passively endorse it, thus helping to spread the word about it to all of *their* Facebook friends. And suddenly your benefit is going viral, reaching a whole new level of exposure.

Obviously, it's possible to substitute all kinds of events in the above scenario: a nightclub party, a poetry slam, a performance by your band, an exhibition of your artwork, or the grand opening of a new business you're launching.

It works the same for any Pages you may create to promote a band or a comedy group or a coffeehouse or a freelance photography studio, for example. As you'll see in upcoming chapters, Pages give you great tools for communicating with fans and customers; but they also allow those fans and customers to announce their loyalty to you via News Feed when they decide to become a fan of your official Page by clicking its Like button.

That's a kind of advertising you can't buy—but if your fans and customers love what you do, on Facebook they can choose to give it to you for free.

Admittedly, tapping into the power of passive endorsement can be a little like trying to bottle lightning. It's not enough just to create a Page or an Event on Facebook—passive endorsement only works if your content is compelling enough to engage people's interest and strike a collective nerve.

But then again, if you're looking to promote something on Facebook, hopefully you've already done the prerequisite work of analyzing what your audience is interested in and creating something that will appeal to them. In that case, you've got nothing to lose by putting it out there where Facebook users can choose to embrace it—and much to gain if you do manage to tap into a massive wave of passive endorsement.

Notes: Blogging on Facebook

TIP: On the Notes application's Home page, you'll see a roundup of all the Notes recently posted by your friends. So even when you don't have a Note to write yourself, dropping in here can be a good way to catch up on what your friends are writing. In the submenu that appears underneath the Notes bookmark when you click it, you can click the My Notes bookmark to see all the Notes you've written in the past, and the Notes About Me link to see any Notes in which you've been tagged by your friends.

Notes
My Drafts
Notes About Me
My Notes

When you click the Notes bookmark, a submenu appears beneath it with additional bookmarks.

Tag, You're It

What does it mean to tag someone? Anyone whose name you enter in the "Tag people" field will get a Notification telling them that you've tagged them—so it's essentially a way of saying, "Hey, come look at this." You should think of tagging as the Facebook equivalent of tapping someone on the shoulder—which can be annoying if you don't have a good reason for doing it. So it's best to use the tagging feature sparingly and tag people only if they're actually mentioned in the Note or there's some other reason they'd want to know right away that you posted it. If you repeatedly tag people in your Notes for no good reason, they may start ignoring your tags altogether.

If you've got a message you'd like to share with your friends that's too long for a status update, Facebook's Notes application has you covered. Writing a Note is Facebook's answer to blogging. You can use Notes to share deep thoughts or goofy non sequiturs, political rants, personal journal entries, poems of the day, or anything else you might post on a blog.

Notes are also famous for spreading memes like "25 Random Things About Me" and various lists of favorite books, movies, albums, and so forth. People write their own lists and then tag several friends in the Note, encouraging them to write their own version and keep the chain going. (How you feel about being tagged in a Note like that probably depends on how much time you have for writing Notes and how you feel about task-oriented Internet memes in general.)

When you post your Note, it will appear on your Wall and also in the News Feeds of your friends.

How to Post a Note

There are a couple of different ways to post a Note on Facebook. For the most full-featured Note-writing experience, you can go into the Notes application itself—accessible by clicking the Notes bookmark on the Home page. (Notes is one of the basic Facebook applications that comes with your account by default, so you don't have to worry about installing it.) To start writing your Note, click the Write a Note button at the top of the page.

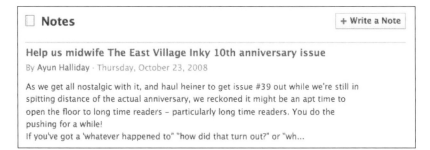

On the next page you'll find an easy form with fields for the title and body of the Note. Down at the bottom there's a Photo control that lets you upload a picture from your computer to illustrate the Note. And there's also a field that lets you tag any of your friends who are mentioned in the Note.

If you'd like to take your Note beyond the realm of plain text, you can spruce it up with boldface, italics, and other styles using the buttons along the top, (or by using basic HTML tags if you're familiar with those). A privacy control at the bottom of the form lets you specify who can view the Note.

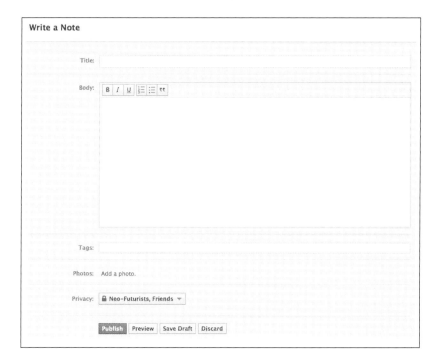

The Write a Note page in the Notes app gives you all the controls for writing, formatting, tagging, and setting the privacy of your Note.

Importing Stories from an Outside Blog as Notes

If you've got an existing blog out on the web somewhere, you can import your blog posts as individual Notes on Facebook. To do this, go to the Import a Blog page, which currently lives at www.facebook.com/editnotes.php?import. (You can also get there via the Edit Import Settings link that appears on certain pages within the Notes app.)

On the Import a Blog page, you'll be asked to enter your blog's public URL or RSS/Atom feed address. Facebook will then import your previous blog posts as individual Notes.

Once you enable importing, Facebook will continue to import activity every time you update the account or blog that you've enabled. If you want to stop importing at any point in the future, you can disable it by reversing the operation: Click the Stop Importing button on the Import a Blog page.

TIP: If you have trouble importing your blog, consult Facebook's Help center (via the Help link in the footer) for some tips and troubleshooting advice.

NOTE: Whether Facebook imports some or all of your previous activity on an external site or blog depends on what it's able to access from the feed.

Posted Items: Sharing Links on Facebook

If you're like me, several times a week (maybe even several times a day) you find yourself reading a fascinating news story, or a witty or insightful blog post, or watching a hilarious video on YouTube, and thinking: "This is brilliant—other people need to see this!"

So how do you share the link with your friends? You could forward it to them via e-mail—but if you do that too often, you run the risk of annoying your friends by cluttering up their already overstuffed inboxes. (And if e-mail has proven anything, it's that one person's brilliant "joke of the day" is another person's spam to be deleted unread.)

Fortunately, Facebook gives you a much less intrusive and more convenient way to share links with your friends: the Links application. (Like the Notes application, Links is one of Facebook's basic apps and is installed to your account from the get-go.) When you post a link on Facebook, it appears on your Wall and also goes out to your friends' News Feeds. So your friends will see it the next time they check their Home page, without feeling like you've spammed them.

In a sense, the links that appear in the News Feed are like a kind of collaborative group blog that you and your friends create together, each and every day. Links even get their own bookmark in the left-hand column of the Home page, so you and your friends can easily keep track of each other's recommended links for reading and browsing.

How to Post a Link

There are a number of different ways to post links on Facebook, but the most obvious route is to go to the Publisher at the top of your profile and click the Link button, which reveals the field where you can enter the URL for the Link you want to post.

Enter the URL and click the Attach button to see how your Link post will appear on your Wall and in the News Feed.

TIP: When you post a YouTube video to Facebook, you don't need the full embed code like you would if you were posting it on your blog or on MySpace. (In fact, if you try to use the embed code it will show up as gibberish when you post it.) All you need is the regular URL for the video. Enter that in the Link field, and Facebook will magically turn it into the embedded video player.

TIP: You can tag profiles and other Pages in Link posts the same way you do in status updates, as described earlier in this chapter.

The Link button on the Publisher

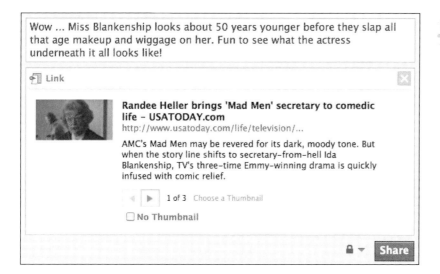

How to Edit the Preview for a Link

You can edit the preview text for a Link by clicking in the text area, which will turn it into an editable field. Choose a photo to illustrate the Posted Item by clicking the arrow buttons to cycle through the available choices, or click the No Thumbnail checkbox if you don't find any of the photos appropriate.

You can also type a comment of your own in the field up above the preview area. Whatever you type here will appear just above your link, so you can tell you friends what you think is interesting or entertaining about the link, or just editorialize a little. When you're happy with how it looks, click the Share button to send it out over the News Feed.

Using the Share Button

You don't necessarily have to head back to your Wall to post an item on Facebook. If the link you'd like to post is on Facebook itself—such as a Group, an Event, a Page, a Note, a photo or video, or even someone's profile—you can just look for the handy Share button that Facebook thoughtfully provides on most pages of the site.

When you click the Share button, you'll get a Share dialog with two choices:

You can find the Share button lurking somewhere on most of the pages on Facebook.

- **Post to Profile** shares the item on your Wall and in the News Feed—just like using the Publisher.
- **Send as a Message** lets you share the link privately, with one or more specific people, by sending them a direct Inbox message with the link attached.

Using the Share Button on the Facebook Toolbar

If you use Firefox or Internet Explorer as your web browser, there's a free Facebook toolbar you can download and install. Among other useful controls, the Facebook toolbar gives you a handy Share button that you can use to share whatever page you're currently visiting on the web, without going back to Facebook. For more information on the Facebook toolbar, see the *Applications and Other Add-Ons* chapter.

Facebook Places: Location, Location, Location

Facebook's new Places feature is its built-in answer to services like Foursquare, which allow you to keep your friends notified of where exactly you are in the world, by "checking in" to the places you visit using your mobile phone. So, for example, you might use Places to let your friends know when you pop into a restaurant for lunch, or are hanging out at your favorite watering hole, in case there's anyone in the vicinity who wants to come join you. Checking in to a location using Places generates a News Feed story that appears on your Wall, and that your friends can see on their Home pages, just like any other kind of content you share on Facebook.

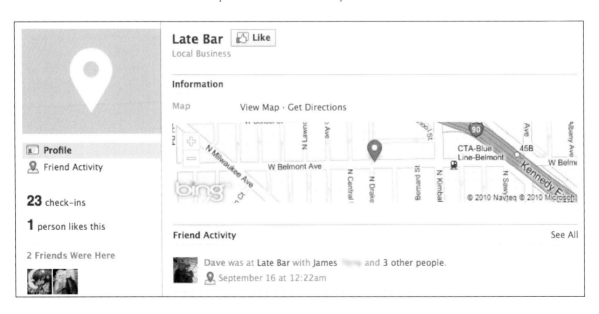

The first time someone checks into a location, Facebook creates a Places page for that address. Places pages show a map, as well as any recent check-ins at that location by friends whose privacy settings allow you to see their Places activity.

People can also be checked into places by other Facebook friends, if the privacy settings of the person who's being checked in allow it. The idea here is that if (for example) you're the only one at the party with a mobile phone, some of your Facebook friends who are there can ask you to go ahead and check them in at the same time you're checking in yourself.

Note that if someone else checks you into a location, Facebook will notify you and give you the opportunity to remove the check-in from your profile. And if you want to prevent this altogether, you can disable friends' ability to check you into Places in your privacy settings (see the warning on this page for more).

At the time of this writing, Places is only available to users in select countries who either have access to the Facebook for iPhone app, or use a touchscreen device that can access the touch.facebook.com site.

To check in somewhere using the Facebook application for iPhone, select the Places application on the home screen and tap OK when you're prompted to share your current location. To check in somewhere using another web-enabled mobile device, go to touch.facebook.com and tap the Places tab, and then tap Share Location when prompted.

If you need to edit or delete a Places page you've recently created by checking in, you can do it as long as you act quickly. Navigate to the Places page for the location in question using your web browser and click "Edit Page" in the top right corner. From there, you'll be able to edit the Place's name and description or delete the Place, as long as too much time hasn't passed. (How much time is "too much"? Your guess is as good as mine.)

> **WARNING:** Obviously, there are important privacy and security concerns that come with announcing your whereabouts online. See the *Privacy and Security* chapter—particularly the sidebar "Can a Status Update Get You Burglarized?"—for more on this subject. If you do decide to use the Places feature, I strongly recommend using a Friend List to restrict the visibility of your check-ins to *only* the friends you trust with that information. You can control who can see your Places activity on the Account > Privacy Settings > "Customize settings" page. In particular, be sure to take a look at the "Friends can check me in to Places" control in the "Things others share" area and disable it if you're not comfortable with that happening.

> **TIP:** For more on using Facebook with your mobile phone, see the *Going Mobile* chapter.

Choosing the Audience for Each Post

The *Privacy and Security* chapter explains how to configure your privacy settings to decide who can see various parts of your profile, including content you share using the Publisher. But Facebook also gives you a privacy control in the Publisher itself that lets you decide who can see each and every posting you make, on a post-by-post basis. This works for every type of posting, including status updates, Links, Notes, photos, and videos.

To access the privacy control for the Publisher, click the padlock icon next to the Share button.

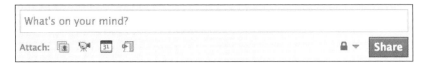

The options in the privacy menu for the Publisher

Clicking the padlock opens the Publisher's privacy menu, from which you can choose the level of access for the content you're about to post. If you choose Customize, the Custom Privacy dialog will open. As previously covered in the *Privacy and Security* chapter, the Custom Privacy dialog lets you make the post visible or invisible to specific people. You can even restrict its visibility so that it can only be viewed by the people on a specific Friend List, such as your Trusted Friends or Family.

Commenting on Facebook Stories

Facebook's feed stories aren't just one-way telegrams transmitted to your friends—they can also be conversation starters. Certain kinds of feed stories, including status updates and Links, have Comment links that appear underneath each story when it shows up on someone's Wall or in the News Feed on the Home page.

WARNING: If you post a comment and then have second thoughts about it, you can delete it from Facebook by clicking the little X at the upper-right side of your comment. But remember that Facebook's default setting is to send you an e-mail notification whenever someone comments on a story about you. So the friend whose story you've just commented on may very well see your comment in e-mail form *regardless of whether you delete it or not.* Moral: Think before you click!

TIP: In addition to deleting comments you make on other people's stories, you're allowed to delete any comments your friends make on stories about you that appear on your Wall or in the News Feed.

Clicking the Comment link opens up a field where people can type a short response to the story, creating a discussion thread about it.

And of course, each comment thread is visible on the Wall where the story appears.

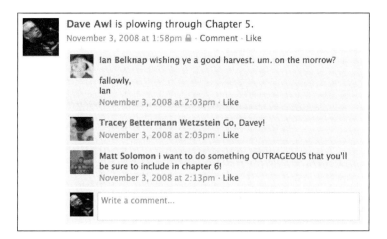

These comment threads are where you'll find some of the liveliest and most entertaining interaction on Facebook. If you're bored and looking for some banter with a friend, starting or joining in on a comment thread is always a good bet.

By default, Facebook sends you a notification each time someone comments on a story about you or something you've posted. And if you comment on a story about one of your friends, Facebook will notify you of all subsequent comments on that thread—making it easy to keep following the discussion and any responses that your own comment may have provoked.

Liking Facebook Stories

When you see a posting you like on Facebook, you can make your approval known by clicking the Like link just underneath it—Facebook's equivalent of applause. Liking a posting does four separate things:

- It sends a notification to the friend who posted it, delivering them a little warm fuzzy.
- It adds your name to the list of people who Like the posting, just above the comments.
- It subscribes you to the comment thread—you'll get notifications the next few times anyone posts a comment on that particular posting.
- It may also generate a story that can appear in the News Feed or on your Wall saying that you Liked the posting, recommending it to your friends.

 TIP: You can also Like individual comments in a thread—which sends a notification to the person who wrote the comment, but doesn't subscribe you to the thread.

 The Meaning of Like

Here's a common dilemma Facebookers face when reading their News Feeds. Suppose a friend of yours posts a news article about something tragic or disturbing—a natural disaster like a hurricane or an earthquake, or maybe a human rights atrocity like genocide in Darfur or sweatshops in China. Or maybe they post a moving status update about the loss of a loved one or an animal companion.

You want to send your friend the positive feedback that the Like link dispenses, and you want to subscribe yourself to be notified of other comments—but in this case you hesitate. Would clicking the Like link send the unintended message that you actually approve of earthquakes or sweatshops, or, you know, *death*? Do you really want it to say that you "like this" underneath that news story or status update?

Relax. Experienced Facebookers understand that Liking applies to the posting itself, not necessarily the subject matter of the posting. This is one of those cases where a word takes on a slightly different meaning in a specialized context. Where Facebook postings are concerned, *liking* really means *recommending*. (And indeed, this is why some news sites with Facebook plugins choose to have Recommend links for their stories instead of Like links.)

That said, if clicking Like for a particular story gives you the wrong-signal heebie-jeebies, you can always express your precise feedback in the comment thread instead—which will be just as effective in terms of subscribing you to follow-up comments.

Facebook and Other Websites

These days, the Facebook experience isn't confined to Facebook's own website. Facebook has introduced a variety of tools and features that make it possible to export a little bit of the Facebook magic to other sites you visit.

Facebook Connect

An example of a Facebook Connect button from the Huffington Post website

Your Facebook login information can function a little bit like a passport. In addition to verifying who you are on Facebook itself, you can also use it to take your Facebook identity with you when you visit other websites that have chosen to let you log in via a feature called Facebook Connect.

As an example, suppose you're reading a blog and you want to post a comment. If the blog offers Facebook Connect functionality, then instead of having to register for the blog separately, you'll see an option to log in with your Facebook password. Once you're logged in, any comments you post will be identified with your name and possibly your Facebook profile picture.

Facebook Badges

Facebook Badges are friendly-looking little boxes that function more or less like banner ads for a personal profile or official Page on Facebook. They say, in essence, "Hey—come check out my Facebook presence!" People can click the badge to visit the profile or Page it represents.

You can add a Facebook badge to any website or blog you manage, for any personal profile or official Page you own on Facebook. For more info, visit www.facebook.com/badges.

An example of a
Facebook Badge

Social Plugins: Integrating Facebook with Your Blog or Website

As you browse the web, you may notice special boxes or widgets on the sites you visit that display, among other things, how many people have Liked the site, or maybe certain news articles or blog posts featured on the site. And of course, you may see Like or Recommend buttons that allow you to send a News Feed story back to your own Wall giving the thumbs-up to a particular piece of content. Here's an example of a Recommend button for a news story on the CNN site:

Some of these Social Plugins may even display the names and faces of your Faceboook friends, and whether they've Liked or recommended anything recently. But don't worry—Social Plugins don't actually share any of your Facebook information with the owners of the sites that host them. To the site owners, they're just empty boxes. Your own individualized content is only visible to you.

If you want to add Social Plugins to your own site, visit developers.facebook.com/plugins for info and downloads.

Instant Personalization

When you visit a select handful of sites with which Facebook has directly partnered—currently limited to Bing, Rotten Tomatoes, Docs, Pandora, Yelp, and Scribd—you may see a feature Facebook calls Instant Personalization, whereby the site in question draws on your profile information to create a customized experience. For example, Pandora's music site may be personalized with your favorite songs already displayed, or Rotten Tomatoes might show you movie reviews by your Facebook friends.

If you access a site that's using this feature, you'll see a message that allows you to turn off Instant Personalization if you want to.

A Social Plugin box from the TechCrunch site, showing stories that have been shared on Facebook

It's important to note two other things:

1. Sites using Instant Personalization can only access your public information (including your name, profile picture, gender, and any Networks you belong to), plus any information you've made publicly available by choosing the Everyone setting, when you're currently logged in to Facebook.

2. You can opt out of all Instant Personalization if you choose by going to Account > Privacy Settings, clicking "Edit your settings" under Applications and Websites, and then clicking the "Edit Settings" button in the "Instant personalization" area. After all that, you'll arrive at a page with a checkbox you can deselect to turn it off. (See the *Privacy and Security* chapter for full info on Facebook's privacy settings.)

Downloading an Archive of Your Facebook Content

Once you've been on Facebook for a few months, let alone a few years, your profile can start to feel almost like your personal journal. You've been posting daily status updates, interesting links, and fun photos you've snapped, and having witty and/or affectionate conversations with your pals—storing away a big chunk of your daily life on Facebook.

So it's only natural you might start wishing you could back all that information up, and maybe even have a way to access it when you're not online. Facebook has you covered with a feature called Download Your Information.

Download Your Information

Get a copy of the data you've put on Facebook.

This tool lets you download a copy of your information, including your photos and videos, posts on your wall, all of your messages, your friend list and other content you have shared on your profile. Within this zip file you will have access to your data in a simple, browseable manner. Learn More about downloading a copy of your information.

Security
This is a copy of all of the personal information you've shared on Facebook. In order to protect your information, we will ask for authentication to verify your identity.

WARNING: This file contains sensitive information. Because this download contains your profile information, you should keep it secure and take precautions when storing, sending or uploading it to any other services.

Download

When you access this feature, Facebook assembles all your profile information into a single zip file that you can download to your hard drive. Inside the zip file you'll find copies of all the photos and videos you've uploaded to Facebook, as well as an HTML copy of your profile with all of your status updates, Links, Notes, and Inbox messages.

To download your info, go to the Account > Account Settings page, and click the "learn more" link next to Download Your Information. Facebook may ask you to verify your identity with your password, and then Facebook will begin gathering your information—which may take a little while. You'll get an email from Facebook notifying you when your file is ready, along with a link to start the download process.

For what it's worth, my first three years on Facebook amounted to a 21MB zip file that I was able to download in less than two minutes via cable modem.

Communicating
on Facebook

Public conversations—the ones that take place on Walls or in comment threads—are where most of the really fun interaction happens on Facebook. But there are also times when it's necessary to take the conversation somewhere private—either because you need to have a one-on-one conversation with someone, or because you want to communicate with a small group of friends without the whole world listening in.

So in this chapter, we'll look at the tools Facebook gives you for private communication, including Inbox messages and Facebook's Chat application.

But wait, there's more! Communicating on Facebook doesn't just happen in words—it happens in special nonverbal messages called Pokes, and sometimes in pictures, too, which are called gifts. So we'll take a look at some of the ways Facebook lets you substitute a Poke or a picture for a thousand words (give or take). And we'll take a peek at the future of communication on Facebook by previewing a new feature called Facebook Questions.

And finally, to round things out, we'll talk a little about the dynamics and etiquette of interpersonal communication on Facebook.

Direct Messages: The Ins and Outs of the Facebook Inbox

You can think of Facebook's Inbox as being like an e-mail account that's built right into Facebook. Just like regular e-mail, Facebook's Inbox lets you send and receive direct electronic messages addressed to specific people.

But there are a couple of important differences. For one thing, Facebook messages allow you to contact someone without knowing their e-mail address. You can send messages to anyone on Facebook that you're friends with, or anyone for whom you can see a Send a Message link when you visit their profile. This allows you to contact someone without necessarily revealing your own e-mail address, which may be useful if you don't know the person well.

Facebook messages also make it easy to attach items such as links, photos, or videos using the Facebook interface to generate handy embedded previews.

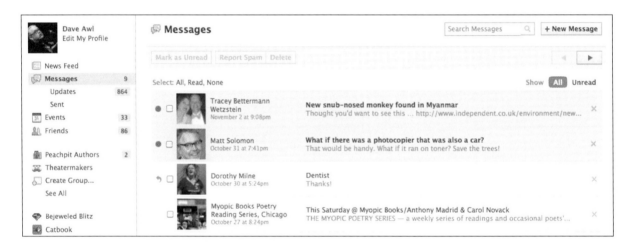

How to Check Your Messages

When you've got Facebook mail, you'll see a number appear next to the Messages icon in the blue bar, telling you how many unread messages are waiting.

Another easy way to get to your Inbox is by clicking the Messages bookmark on the Home page—which opens a submenu that displays the Updates and Sent bookmarks as well. The numbers next to the bookmarks tell you how many unread messages you have, if any.

Click the Messages icon to open its pop-up menu, and then click the See All Messages link to go to your Inbox and view your messages. Once there, you can click on the subject line of any message to read it. (You can also click on any individual message in the pop-up menu to go directly to that message.)

Message Indicators

Facebook gives you some handy indicators to let you see the status of each message in your Inbox at a glance. (See the screen shot on the facing page.)

- A blue dot next to a message means it's a new, unread message. (Unread messages will also be shaded in blue.)
- A curvy arrow next to a message means it's a message you've already replied to. (In the case of a group message, it means you were the last person in the conversation to reply.)

Managing Messages

Next to each message thread in your Inbox is a checkbox that you can use to change its status from Read to Unread (or vice versa), or delete the message. Simply select the checkboxes for one or more messages, and then click the appropriate action at the top of the page, using the Mark as Unread, Report Spam, or Delete buttons.

The Select links (All, Read, and None) let you select certain types of messages so that you can mark or delete them en masse. This is handy if you want to delete all of the messages you've already read, for example, or mark several messages as unread to remind yourself to check them again later.

> **Dig Those Crazy Threads**
> Facebook messages are organized into threads—much like the comment threads on News Feed and Wall stories. Each line in your Inbox represents one thread, which contains an original message as well as all of the replies to that message. So if you send your friend Matt a message, and the two of you get into a conversation that runs to 20 replies—possibly spread out over several days—all that back-and-forth won't take up 21 lines scattered all through your Inbox. Instead, there'll be one line for the entire thread, and when you click on it, all 21 messages will be there, in chronological order. This helps keep your Inbox organized and means you don't have to wade through so much clutter to find what you're looking for.

> **NOTE:** Although you can delete a thread from your Inbox, this action may not always be permanent. If another participant in the thread sends a new reply, the thread will appear in your Inbox again.

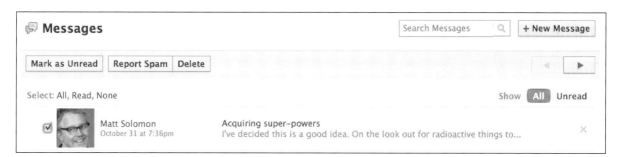

Marking a message as unread after you've read it can come in handy when you don't have time to respond right at the moment. You can display all of your Unread messages at any time by clicking the Unread link (next to the word Show in the upper-right area of the Inbox). Click All to toggle back to the regular view.

 TIP: You can also mark a message as unread, report it as spam, or delete it using the buttons at the top of the message itself after you've opened it.

The Messages bookmarks in the left-hand column

The Sorting Hat

At the time of this writing, Facebook doesn't give you a lot of tools for organizing or archiving your messages. There's no way, for example, to file your messages away into customized mailboxes or folders. You also can't flag them (other than marking them as unread), assign them levels of priority, or easily forward them. So if you're the sort of person who likes to keep a well-organized, backed-up archive of all your correspondence, you might prefer to use conventional e-mail for important messages where you do know the e-mail addresses of the other participants.

Who Can You Message?

In the To field of the Compose New Message form, you can type the name of a friend (which Facebook will attempt to recognize and autocomplete for you) or a Friend List (as long as it has fewer than 20 friends on it).

If you'd like to include a friend who isn't on Facebook in your message, you can do that, too—just go ahead and enter their e-mail address in the To field, and they'll receive your message as e-mail.

If you want to send a message to someone on Facebook whom you haven't already friended, and whose e-mail address you don't know, you can do it only by clicking the Send a Message link on their profile, or in search results.

WARNING: When you check your Facebook Inbox, be on your guard for suspicious messages, and be careful about clicking on links contained in Facebook messages. You may receive messages that appear to come from one of your friends but are actually sent by phishers who've gained access to your friend's account. Some Facebook messages may also be generated by viruses, and contain links to Trojan horses or other malware. See the *Privacy and Security* chapter for more details and some tips on how to spot suspicious messages.

Bookmarks: Updates and Sent Messages

In addition to the default view of the Inbox, which shows you messages you've received from others, you can access two other views by clicking the bookmarks in the left-hand column.

- **The Sent Messages bookmark** shows you the messages you've sent to others.
- **The Updates bookmark** shows you all of the update messages you've received from any Facebook Pages you've chosen to become a fan of. (See the *Pages* chapter for full info on updates—how they work and how to send them from Pages you create.)

Searching the Inbox

Facebook gives you a field at the top of your Inbox (for both the Inbox and Sent Messages tabs) that lets you search through your messages to zero in on what you're looking for. You can search by name (to find all the messages to or from a certain person) as well as by keyword (to find all of the messages related to summer band camp, or a Facebook Group you're a member of, or mollusks, for example).

How to Compose and Send a New Message

If you're already in the Inbox, click the New Message button at the right side of the page. From any other page on Facebook, the quickest method is to click the Messages icon in the blue bar and then choose Send a New Message from the pop-up menu.

TIP: You can also send someone a message using the Send [Name] a Message link on someone's profile page, which usually appears right below their profile picture. (If you aren't friends with the person, you may not see a Message link, depending on how they've set their privacy controls.)

 WARNING: You are allowed to send Inbox messages to people whom you aren't friends with, if their own privacy settings allow it. But be careful not to abuse this privilege. If you send too many messages to people you don't know, or Facebook receives complaints that you're sending unwanted messages to strangers, Facebook may take away your messaging privileges or even deactivate your account.

Once you arrive at the New Message form, all you have to do is fill in the To, Subject, and Message fields. You can also choose to add an attachment using the Attach buttons at the bottom of the form. From left to right:

- **The Photo button** lets you attach an image to your message by either uploading a photo from your hard drive, or taking a new photo using a camera connected to your computer.

- **The Video button** lets you add a short video clip to your message, using a camera connected to your computer.

- **The Link button** lets you attach a web link, much like using the Links application (as described in the *Sharing Content on Facebook* chapter). Enter the URL in the Link field and click Attach; Facebook will generate a preview to show you how the attachment will look at the bottom of the message. You can use the arrow buttons to cycle through the available images from the page you're linking to, and you can click the accompanying text to edit it. If you decide you want to get rid of the attachment altogether, you can click the X (Remove) link to delete it.

 NOTE: Anything you attach to an Inbox message is private, just like the message itself, and won't show up as a story on your Wall or in your News Feed.

Group Messages and Branched Threads: Who Do You Think You're Talking To?

You can address messages to more than one friend at a time—up to 20 friends per message—which is convenient if there's something you want to share with a select group of friends.

When you answer a group message, it's *verrry* important to be aware of whether you're talking to one person in the thread, or the whole group. Anecdotes abound about Facebookers who thought they were talking one-on-one, and then discovered that their flirty or gossipy messages were being read by the entire group instead of the one person they thought they had replied to.

Save Your Message So You Don't Lose Your Mind

If you find yourself writing a lengthy message (say, more than a couple of paragraphs) in Facebook's New Message dialog, you might want to open up a text editor (such as an e-mail program, TextEdit, or even MS Word) and compose your message there instead, so that you can save it as you go. Then when you're done, you can just paste your text into the Message field on Facebook. Why do I recommend this? Because Facebook's messages aren't auto-saved as you compose them, so if your browser crashes, or there's any kind of a glitch when you press the Send button, it's possible to lose the entire text you've just spent who knows how long laboriously composing. This happens all too often—I hear friends complaining about it all the time, and after it happened to me a few times early on, I developed a reflex whereby at the two-paragraph mark I automatically open up a text file and finish composing my message there. (If you don't want to mess with a text file, another good method is to periodically highlight what you've written and then copy it to your clipboard.) This technique isn't a bad idea for composing Facebook Notes, either.

TIP: You can't add someone to a group message thread once it's already in progress. So if you're talking to your friends Tracey and Stacey and you suddenly realize that your other friend Amy would totally love this conversation, you'll need to start a new group message that includes her—and then catch her up on what's been said so far.

By default, if you simply type your reply in the box at the bottom of the message thread and then click the Send button, you'll be sending your reply to everyone in the group.

If you want to reply directly to one person, you need to create a *branched thread*. You can do that by clicking the Reply link next to the person's name and the time they sent the message, just above their contribution to the thread.

Elizabeth Hoffman October 21 at 11:00pm Reply • Report
Oh, just add a gratuitous chapter about the ukulele!

A new message form will open up for the branched thread, which is now strictly between you and the person whose Reply link you clicked.

You can tell when you're reading a branched thread because at the top of the screen you'll see the notice shown below. Clicking the "View previous thread" link will let you see the group message the new thread was split off from.

This thread has been branched from a previous thread. View previous thread.

Chatting on Facebook

Facebook provides its own built-in Chat application, so you can have real-time conversations with your Facebook friends. If you've ever chatted online using an application such as AOL Instant Messenger, MSN Messenger, Yahoo Messenger, or iChat, then the mechanics of Facebook Chat will be very familiar to you. But even if you're new to Chat, it's not too tough to figure out.

Going Online (and Seeing Who Else Is Online)

The first step to chatting with a friend on Facebook is to change your own Chat availability to Online. You can do that by clicking the Chat bar that lives in the bottom right corner of your screen. Clicking the Chat bar changes your status to online, and opens the pop-up menu. You'll also see a green dot appear in the Chat bar, which tells you that your friends see you as online and available for chat; and you'll see the number of your friends who are currently online and available themselves.

Once you've opened the pop-up menu, you'll see a listing that shows you which of your friends are available for chat. A green dot next to a friend

Chat (Offline)

The Facebook Chat bar shows a gray dot when your status is offline, although the word Offline *in parentheses is probably the bigger giveaway.*

Chat (72)

When you're online for Chat, the Facebook Chat bar shows a green dot and the number of your friends who are currently online for Chat.

means they're online and have been recently active on Facebook. A half-moon means your friend is idle—which means that they haven't taken any action on Facebook within the last 10 minutes. (Which in turn is a clue that even though they've set their status to online, they might have stepped away from their computer.)

You can go offline whenever you want by clicking Options at the top of the Chat pop-up window and then choosing Go Offline.

How to Start a Chat

Starting a chat is easy. Just choose the friend you'd like to chat with in the Chat pop-up menu and click their name to open a new chat window.

The Chat pop-up menu shows you who's available to chat. Notice that Genevra's and John's names show a half-moon instead of a green dot, because they haven't been active on Facebook in the last 10 minutes. (Slackers!)

Starting a new chat: Type your first message in the field at the bottom of the Chat window, press the Return/Enter key, and wait for a response. Once your friend answers, you can continue to enter your own responses in the same field until the two of you run out of delightfully witty things to say.

Click Options at the top of the Chat pop-up window to open the Options menu.

How to Minimize or Close a Chat Window

Clicking the blue name bar at the top of the window will collapse the window down to a minimized icon at the bottom of your screen, next to the Chat bar. You can click on the mimimized Chat icon to reopen it at any time. While the Chat window is minimized, a balloon icon will appear to let you know of any new responses the person you're chatting with enters. The balloon displays a number that tells you exactly how many responses are waiting.

A minimized Chat window appears just to the left of the Chat Bar. You can click the minimized window to restore it to full size at any time.

How to Pop Out a Chat Window

If you'd like a larger Chat window (which allows you to see more of the conversation without scrolling), just click Options at the top of the pop-up menu and then click the the Pop Out Chat link. Presto, a full-size Chat window will

A number balloon lets you know how many new responses are waiting in the minimized Chat window.

open up. You can return it to the small size by clicking the Pop In Chat link that appears in the Options menu for the popped-out window.

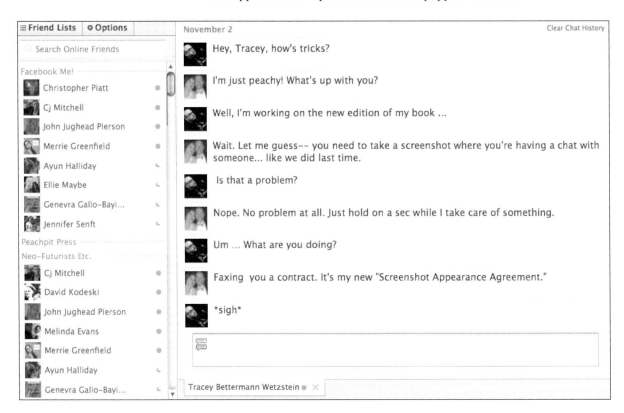

How to View and Clear Your Chat History

When you start a new conversation with a friend you've chatted with before, you'll be able to see the last few lines of your most recent conversation in the Chat window. (Currently the interface doesn't provide any way to view or access older conversations.) If you want a blank slate, you can delete that history by clicking the Clear Chat History link at the top of the window.

Using Friend Lists in Chat

If you've organized your Friends into Friend Lists like I've been urging you to do throughout this book (see the *Friends* chapter for the basics), Chat is another place where it pays off. You'll see your online friends arranged according to what Friend Lists they're on, in both versions of the Chat window.

You can rearrange the order of the Friend Lists, so that (for example) your Family list or your Favorites list comes first. Just click the Re-order Lists

You can use the search field at the bottom of the pop-up Chat menu to quickly find someone in your list of available friends. (The search field is next to the faint magnifying glass icon in the shot above, where I'm typing in the name Eli.) There's also a search field at the top of the left-hand column in the popped-out window.

command in the Options menu, and you'll be able to drag your lists into the order you want them displayed for Chat purposes.

Even better, you can turn your online visibility on and off to specific lists. So if you want to be visible to only your Family list but not your Co-Workers list, for example, you can do that. Just click the white button next to the name of a Friend List and you'll appear offline to all the people on that list.

You can also choose which Friend Lists appear in your list of online friends by clicking the Friend Lists button (just to the left of the Options button) and then clicking the names of your lists to select and deselect them. Lists without a checkmark won't appear in Chat.

The options in the Options menu

Other Chat Options

Clicking the Settings link (at the top of the Chat icon's pop-up menu) displays a few additional options you may find useful:

- **Play Sound for New Messages** allows Facebook to get your attention with an alert sound when someone sends you a new message via chat.
- **Keep Online Friends Window Open** changes the behavior of the Chat pop-up window. With this box deselected, the window automatically closes when you click elsewhere on the page. If this box is selected, the window stays open until you choose to minimize it by clicking the blue title bar of the window.
- **Show Only Names in Online Friends** hides the profile pictures in the list of online friends, which saves space and allows you to see more of the list without scrolling.

Chatting with a Group

Facebook's new-style Groups allow you to start collective chats with other members of the Group. (This doesn't work on old-style Groups, unfortunately—see the *Group Dynamics* chapter for more on the distinction between the two kinds of Groups.) Everyone in the Group who's online and available for Chat will be notified when the chat starts.

To start a Group chat, go to your Group and look for the chat link in the right-hand column. If you're not already online for Chat, it'll say "Go Online to Chat," and if you are online it'll say "Chat with Group." In your Chat window, you'll be able to see which members of the Group are currently online and available to chat.

You can leave a Group chat at any time by simply going offline. (And of course you can always minimize the Chat window.)

Click the button next to the name of a Friend List in the pop-up Chat window to appear offline to everyone in that list. (At the moment this button doesn't appear in the popped-out window.)

TIP: Facebook doesn't allow you to start a one-to-one chat with anyone who isn't in your Friends list. The only ways you can directly contact non-friends on Facebook are through Inbox messages or friend requests. However, you can participate in group chats with people you aren't friends with if you're fellow members of one of Facebook's new-style Groups.

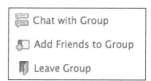

The Chat with Group link for one of Facebook's new-style Groups.

Using Facebook Chat with a Desktop Application

If you use iChat, Adium, or Pigdin as your desktop chat application, you can use it to connect to Facebook Chat via an open messaging protocol called Jabber. In iChat, for example, you can specify Jabber as the account type and then enter your Facebook username and password. Visit Facebook's Help section for more details and instructions specific to the application you're using.

Poking and Getting Poked

Caveat Poker
The ambiguity of the basic Facebook Poke makes it something of a Rorschach test. It's possible that the person you send your Poke to will read something different into it from what you intended, especially if you don't know them very well. They might think you're flirting when you just meant to say hello, or telling them to hurry up with their next Scrabble move when you actually meant to flirt. So you might want to take that into consideration before you poke, and if you want to make sure your message isn't misunderstood, use a more explicit form of communication.

Facebook has added its own distinctive entry to the lexicon of nonverbal communication: the Poke. Sending someone a Poke on Facebook is just a simple greeting—a way of saying hello without really having anything else in particular to say. You might poke someone when you want to get their attention, let them know you're thinking about them, or simply remind them that you exist. It can serve as a hug, a tickle, a tap on the shoulder, or an impatient tap of the foot.

When you get poked by someone, the Poke shows up in the right-hand column on your Home page.

You then have the option to poke the person back or simply remove the Poke (by clicking the X button). You can also leave it there for as long as you want, until you decide how you want to respond. (Sometimes I leave a Poke on my Home page as a handy quick link to the profile of someone I owe some attention to—a string-around-the-finger reminder.)

How to Send a Poke

TIP: Once upon a time, you were allowed to poke anybody you could find by searching on Facebook. But in recent times Facebook has reined in the Poke feature. These days, you can poke only those people whose profiles you're allowed to access.

When you find yourself in a poking mood, just navigate to the profile of the person you'd like to poke and find the Poke [Name] link (usually right under their profile picture). Click the link and then click Poke in the confirmation dialog that opens. Once you do that, your friend is as good as poked.

Advanced Pokeology

The basic Facebook Poke, as iconic as it is, doesn't get as much play as it used to, because a number of third-party apps have sprung up to let you poke people in more specific and less ambiguous ways. The most popular and enduring of these is probably the SuperPoke application, which lets you choose from a wide variety of things you'd like to do to your friends—from nice to silly to mock-aggressive—and then send your friend a short message telling them what you've just (virtually) done unto them. Your friend then has the option to do something back unto you.

TIP: As with any app you're interested in, you can find and install SuperPoke by typing its name in the search field in the blue bar.

○ ☹ *apologize to	○ 🐾 applaud	○ 🎂 bake a cake for
○ 🥧 bake a pumpkin pie for	○ 💬 be fabulous with	○ 👤 become BFFs with
○ 🌟 become invincible	○ 💗 blow a kiss at	○ 🕺 breakdance with
○ 🌾 build a scarecrow with	○ 🍸 buy a drink for (choose!)	○ 👖 buy designer jeans with
○ 🤒 call in sick with	○ ✂ call out	○ 🎉 celebrate Movember with
○ 💐 cheer for	○ 💥 chest bump	○ 🗣 congratulate
○ 🍜 cook pho for	○ 🍗 cook Thanksgiving dinne	○ 🫂 cuddle
○ 🕴 dance with	○ ♠ deal a flush to	○ 🏴󠁧󠁢 debate Marmite with (cho

Just a few examples of the many things you can do to your friends using SuperPoke

Dave Awl

Dave Awl took a SuperPoke! action!
Dave Awl has danced with Danielle Christoffel

🏃 18 seconds ago 🔒 · Comment · Like · Reply

An example of a Wall story announcing a SuperPoke

What Are You, a Mind Reader?

Speaking of nonverbal communications and ambiguous messages, here's a rule of thumb you may find useful: You'll have a better time on Facebook if you don't spend too much time reading between the lines, or reading things into the actions your friends do or don't take on Facebook.

Sure, it's easy to be paranoid and jump to the conclusion that someone ignored your Poke or your friend request because they dislike you. Or that a friend failed to RSVP to your Event invitation because they're trying to avoid spending time with you. Or that another friend didn't respond to the song you dedicated to them using iLike's Music app because they secretly loathe your taste in music.

But it's just as possible that your friend is merely having trouble keeping up with all the invitations and Pokes

they're receiving these days. Maybe they had a bad day, aren't feeling well, or are traveling at the moment and don't have reliable Internet access. Maybe they're having difficulty figuring out the semiotics of Facebook. Or maybe they just accidentally clicked the wrong button.

The point is, unless someone tells you point-blank that you're on their D-list or you've ticked them off, you can't reliably deduce that from their Facebook behavior. Assuming the worst will only get you ulcers, and maybe wind up doing real damage to a friendship that is perfectly healthy.

So cut your friends plenty of slack. And spend your Facebook time focusing on the Facebook friends who *do* return your Pokes.

Why Send Someone a Picture of a Cupcake?

Although they aren't nearly as ubiquitous as they used to be, especially since Facebook retired its own official Gifts application, Facebook still has a few third-party apps kicking around that allow you to send a picture of something to a friend as a "gift." So it's probably still worth mentioning here, since newcomers to Facebook are occasionally thrown by the image-as-gift concept, at least until they get used to the idea.

Take my friend Susan, who one day, shortly after joining Facebook, changed her status to read, "Susan doesn't really understand the sending of cupcakes on Facebook and won't be participating until it make sense to her." Susan's friends had been greeting her using a then-popular app called Send Cupcakes, which lets you create a customized cupcake (pick one of several cupcakes, choose a frosting, add a topping)—and then send an image of the final cupcake to a friend.

To Susan, it made no sense whatsoever to send someone a picture of a cupcake they couldn't actually *eat*.

If you share Susan's bewilderment, it may help to think of Facebook's gifts not so much as gifts, but as greeting cards. After all, if you send a friend a card with a picture of a funny kitten on it, you're not sending them an actual kitten—you're sending them the *idea* of a kitten, just to say hello and give them a little lift.

Ultimately, this is all just a variation of what the transactional analysis gurus call *warm fuzzies*. Friends and loved ones are generally looking for ways to send and reinforce the message that they care about each other. If they can entertain each other or make the other person laugh in the process of sending a warm fuzzy, that adds value to the message.

One of the best things about Facebook is that it gives you innumerable interesting ways to send warm fuzzies to the people you care about—and the sending of picture-gifts can be part of that.

So, if you know that your friend Amy is a big coffee fanatic and you use a gift app to send her the idea of a grande cappuccino, in addition to letting her know you're thinking about her, you've demonstrated that you know what she likes—a sign of true friendship.

And by the same token, if your brother is a huge fan of the Muppets and you use an application to send him a picture of, say, Beaker, then in addition to telling him you love him, you've also sent him the vitally important message "*Meep meep meep meep meep meep.*"

Facebook Questions

As I'm writing this, Facebook is developing and beta testing a much-anticipated new feature called Questions. Facebook hasn't announced an official date when Questions will become available to everyone on Facebook, but says it'll happen "within the next few weeks." So by the time you read this, Facebook Questions may already be part of daily life under the blue bar.

Like Quora or Yahoo! Answers, Facebook Questions is a tool that allows you to post your burning questions and get answers to them from other users.

Of course, you can do that right now on your own Wall—posting questions for your Facebook friends using your status update, and discussing their answers in the comment thread. But the twist with Facebook Questions is that you'll be able to make your questions public, presenting them to the entire

Facebook community—and drawing on the brainpower of more than half
a billion potential question-answerers.

Ask Any Question

Anyone can answer your question, which
means you can tap into the collective
knowledge of the millions of people on
Facebook. And because your question appears
right in your friends' News Feed, you'll also
get answers personalized just for you.

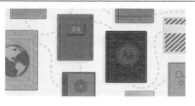

Explore Any Topic

Gardening? Politics? Physics? Get lost in your
favorite subject. See what people are asking
right now and explore related themes. Browse
answers from people with deep knowledge on
a topic or follow a question and wait for
answers to roll into your News Feed.

Get Quality Answers

You can contribute to making Facebook a
positive experience for everyone. When you
mark answers as helpful or unhelpful, the best
answers rise to the top and are seen by the
most people. Have a great answer yourself?
Publish it! Learn more about Facebook
Questions.

Info from Facebook's preview page for Questions at facebook.com/questions

When you ask a question, you'll have the option to add a photo—so if you
want to know what kind of bird is singing outside your window, or what the
sign says outside a restaurant in a foreign city where you're traveling, you can
take a picture of it and attach it to your question.

You can also attach a poll, in case your question can be most effectively
answered by a survey.

And you can tag your question with a category like "Cycling" or "Photography," which will help bring it to the attention of people who are interested in
those topics.

Answers will also be marked as helpful or unhelpful by those who read them,
allowing the best answers to get the most attention.

You can follow questions you find particularly interesting, so that you get
notifications when new answers are posted.

And of course, you'll be able to browse through Facebook's archive of previously asked-and-answered questions by topic, to find out the answers to
questions you haven't gotten around to asking just yet.

The Fine Art of Not Being Obnoxious

 Let's get one thing clear: Facebook etiquette can be murky territory. After all, people of diverse ages, backgrounds, levels of computer proficiency, political leanings, and religious perspectives use Facebook, in countries around the world. So there are bound to be some colliding expectations and assumptions about what constitutes polite interaction. But it seems reasonable to start with the assumption that you join Facebook to have fun with your friends, not to annoy them. So here are a few basic tips for playing well with others:

1. Know your friends.

The golden rule says that you should do unto others as you would have them do unto you. But here's the rub: On Facebook, not everyone wants to be done unto the same way. You can't assume that just because you enjoy being sent pictures of cupcakes, Muppets, and funny kittens every day of the week, all of your friends do, too. On Facebook, different folks enjoy different kinds of pokes. Some people like word games. Some people like adversarial games that involve pretending to turn each other into vampires, kickboxing, or recruiting each other into the mob. Others prefer gentler, more cooperative pursuits like sending each other sea creatures, or dedicating songs and videos to each other. So it's worth taking a little time to consider your audience before you fire off an invitation or a request. Think before you click.

2. Know how to take a hint.

On a related note, sometimes silence speaks louder than words, so it's important to pay attention to the responses you *don't* get from your friends, as well as the ones you do. If you keep sending a particular friend Event invitations to come to your performances or seminars or weekly book club meetings, and you get no response, take the hint and stop badgering them.

If responses are slower than you expect, take that into account, too. Some people are naturally more active on Facebook than others. Some people have more time in their day for playing games and socializing, whereas others have to wedge it into a half-hour they've stolen between the time the kids fall asleep and hitting their own wall of exhaustion.

If you pay just a little bit of attention, you'll soon get a sense of which friends want to play regular games of Scrabble with you, which pals are always quick to reply to a Wall post, and who generally needs a few days in order to check in and respond. Once you have a good idea of how much time and attention your individual friends can spare, you can tailor your level of interaction to theirs.

Of course, a corollary is that the closer you are to someone, the more you may be able to get away with stretching those boundaries. If it's an old friend you've been through thick and thin with, you may be able to deliberately annoy them with impunity—and they may even find it funny. But that's strictly a swim-at-your-own risk scenario.

3. **Treat new friends with extra restraint.**

If someone who doesn't know you very well accepts your friend request, they're engaging in an act of trust—taking a chance on you. Don't make them regret their decision by abusing that trust.

That means treating them with kid gloves until you get to know them. When you make a new friend, don't immediately start bombarding them with Inbox messages, app requests, and invitations to Events. Take things slow. Wait until you have a sense of their likes and dislikes before you start nudging them on a regular basis.

Here's a good rule of thumb: Don't send a new friend a second invitation or request before they've replied to the first one. If you strive for a harmonious 1:1 ratio of requests to responses, you'll most likely avoid ticking your new friend off.

4. **Be sensitive to your friends' feelings.**

Some people are very private, while others are downright exhibitionists. You may be completely comfortable posting pictures of yourself cavorting on the beach in your Borat thong, or dancing on a table with a bleary grin and a plastic cup in your hand—but some of your friends may be shyer about such things, or have uptight in-laws and bosses to worry about. They may be trusting you to understand that what happened in Vegas was supposed to stay there, rather than happening all over again on Facebook the next day.

Wall posts work the same way. Your friend may love your ribald repartee when you're hanging out one-on-one, but may not be so thrilled to have it posted on their Wall where co-workers, parents, or teenage kids can see it.

So—if you're not sure whether your friend will be comfortable with a photo you'd like to post, take the initiative and ask them about it ahead of time. And if a friend asks you to take a photo down, or they remove their name from its tags, you should respect that unless you have a very good reason not to.

Before you write on someone's Wall, take a moment to remember that it's not a private one-to-one text message—it's more like sticking a note on their front door that the whole neighborhood can see. And if your friend deletes something you wrote on their Wall, cut them some slack. They may very well have laughed out loud, right before they clicked the Delete button.

5. Facebook is not LinkedIn—dress down for success.

It's fine to use Facebook for business purposes—but remember that Facebook is first and foremost a *social* space. Here's what I mean: Suppose you get an invitation to a Hawaiian-themed party. And suppose that you show up to a room full of people in floral shirts and leis dressed in a navy blue business suit, and while the other attendees are learning hula moves and drinking fruity cocktails, you circulate among them thrusting your business card under their noses and attempting to sell them life insurance.

It's fairly likely that after ten or fifteen minutes of that, you'll find yourself propping up a wall by your lonesome, while the other guests scramble to put as much furniture as possible between themselves and you.

That's not to say you can't sell insurance and find willing customers at a party. But you need to use a subtler approach, turn on the charm, and enter into the spirit of the shindig. Once you've chatted with someone for a while, made them laugh a little and gained their trust, you can casually mention what you do for a living and gauge their level of interest without so much risk of being stabbed through the heart with a pineapple-topped toothpick.

The foregoing may not sound like social-skills rocket science, but it's amazing how many people show up to Facebook dressed in their navy blue suit and brandishing their business card—metaphorically speaking.

So do a little reality check. If the Info tab of your profile consists mostly of phrases like "my new teleseminar," "entrepreneurial market niche position- ing," and "make money!!!" you might want to humanize it a little by also listing some of your favorite TV shows and bands and things, so you seem a little less like a profit-driven zombie.

Just sayin.'

Applications and Other Add-Ons

As a public transportation rider, I don't resort to car metaphors very often. But in this case, it fits: If Facebook is a car, then applications are the options. You can get where you're going using the tools that come with Facebook by default, but adding applications may make the ride more fun, and possibly even more productive.

Some Facebook apps are practical, like the GPS navigator in your dashboard; some add entertainment to the ride, like a built-in stereo; some are for self-expression, like the plush toy dangling from your rearview mirror; and some are games (let's say those are the equivalent of playing 20 Questions or doing word puzzles on a long car trip).

In this chapter, we'll look at how to respond to invitations you get from your friends to use applications; how to tell the worthwhile applications from the worthless ones; how to manage settings and options for the applications you do choose to embrace; and how to remove and block applications you don't like.

And after we've covered all that, we'll finish with a brief roundup of some of Facebook's most popular and entertaining apps.

Applications 101: The Basics

There are certain applications that are part of your Facebook account by default, and most of these have been at least mentioned in the preceding chapters: Notes, Links, Groups, Events, Photos, Videos, and Chat are all basic Facebook applications. But there are countless other optional applications available to you. Some are made by Facebook, but most are by a host of third-party developers, which allows Facebook to benefit from the creativity and inventiveness of many minds.

It's completely up to you which of these third-party applications (if any) you decide to authorize and how much attention you want to give them. If you don't like an application after trying it out, you can remove it from your account, and if you find an application especially annoying, you can block it completely so you never get any invitations to use it from your friends.

You can find new applications using Facebook's search tool as well as the Application and Games dashboards, and the Application Directory, which we'll look at later in this chapter.

Accessing Your Applications

Facebook provides two special pages that serve as central locations for accessing your apps: the Games dashboard and the Applications dashboard. The former is where you can check out recent activity for any app that's considered a game, and the latter is for all the rest. Both dashboards are accessible via handy bookmarks in the right-hand column on the Home page.

The Games Dashboard

At the top of the Games dashboard, you'll see any recent requests you've received from friends who'd like to play games with you.

The bookmarks for the Games dashboard and the Applications dashboard appear on the Home page. The numbers next to them tell you how many outstanding requests you currently have. Lower down you may see bookmarks for some of your recently used applications.

The next area, a little further down on the page, shows you stories related to games you've recently played. (You can use the menu in the upper right and the links along the top to filter which games you see stories for.)

And down at the bottom of the page is the Friends' Games area, which shows you some of the games your friends have been playing lately. This can be a great way to find new games, as well as figure out which of your friends you can get a game going with by checking out an app they like.

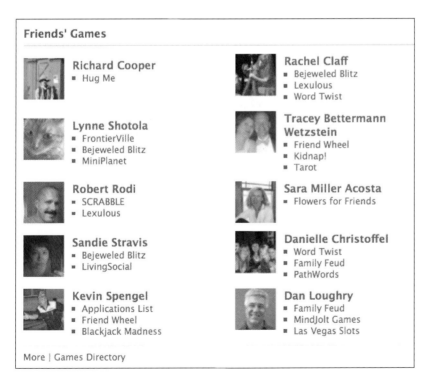

The Applications Dashboard

Like the Games dashboard, the Applications dashboard shows you recent requests at the top, from friends who are inviting you to participate in the non-game apps they use.

In the middle of the page is the Your Applications area, which shows you some of the apps you've used recently.

TIP: If you want to access a particular application and you don't see it on either of your dashboards, or a bookmark for it on your Home page, you can find it by searching in the blue bar, or by visiting the Applications You Use page—see the section "Managing Applications (and Application Privacy)" later in this chapter.

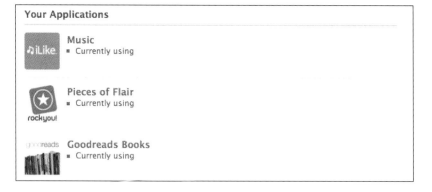

And just like the Games dashboard, the Applications dashboard shows you some of the apps your friends have been using recently.

Responding to Requests from Applications

When a friend of yours wants to interact with you using an application, the app sends you an application request—a little message letting you know that you've been invited to participate in whatever the app does. As mentioned in the previous section, you can see your recent app requests at the top of the Applications dashboard or the Games dashboard, depending on which category they fall into.

Each application request looks something like this—a request I got for one of Facebook's many quiz applications.

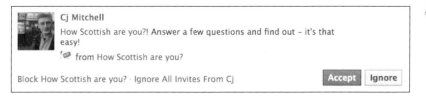

Clicking the Accept button will take you into the application itself. (For Games, this button currently says "Accept and Play.") Clicking the Ignore button makes the request disappear from your life.

NOTE: The first time you accept a request from an application you've never used before, you'll be asked to authorize the application—giving it permission to access your Facebook account for the basic info it needs in order to work. The authorization process is described in the upcoming "Authorizing Applications" section.

How to Block Unwanted App Requests

If you decide that an application just isn't for you, and you don't want to get any more requests from that particular app, you can easily block it from communicating with you in the future. Just below every app request is a Block [Name of Application] link. Click that, and you'll get a dialog telling you that in the future the app will be prevented from sending you any requests and from accessing any info about you. (However, you'll still be able to see the app on your friends' pages if they have it displayed.)

TIP: You don't have to respond to application requests right away; there's no time limit or expiration date. So feel free to let them sit for a while if you think you might get around to exploring them later.

The Block [Name of Application] and Ignore All Invites From [Name of Friend] links live down at the bottom of an application request.

> **Don't Panic!**
> Facebook apps are social in nature, and they're supposed to be fun—most of them, anyway. So there's no reason to let them stress you out. If you're getting more requests than you can handle, and your mood ring is turning an ugly shade of brown, breathe, relax, and remember that you're not obligated to accept any Scrabble challenges or tend to anyone's virtual pets or crops if that's not your thing. And if your friends are really your friends, they won't judge you for it.
>
> You can remove or block apps, of course, but you can also simply click the Ignore button on any requests you don't have time to deal with until you get caught up.

If you ever change your mind and want to stop blocking an app, you can overturn the restraining order. Just choose Privacy Settings from the Account menu in the blue bar, and at the bottom of the page, find the Block Lists area.

Block Lists
Edit your lists of blocked people and applications.

Click the "Edit your lists" link and you'll be taken to the page where you'll find the list of blocked applications. Click the Unblock link next to the app(s) you want to stop blocking, and you're done.

How to Block App Requests from Specific Friends

If you have a Facebook friend who sends you lots of requests you aren't interested in, you can choose to ignore all application requests from that particular friend.

Click the Ignore All Invites From [Name of Friend] link below any request sent to you by that person. You'll see a dialog asking you to confirm this action, and once you do that, presto—any requests from the friend in question will be automatically ignored before they even reach you.

And don't worry—your friend won't get any kind of notification that you've taken this action, so you don't have to worry about hurting their feelings.

If you change your mind at some point in the future, you can remove your friend's name from the list of people whose requests are ignored by the same process you use to unblock an application, as described in the preceding section. Look for the Block Application Invites area on the Block Lists page, and click the Unblock list next to the name of the person(s) whose inviting privileges you'd like to restore.

Authorizing Applications

Authorizing an application is a little bit like adding it to your Friends list—you're giving it permission to access your basic Facebook info, so the two of you can get to know each other a little, and the app knows enough about you to function.

When you access an application for the first time—whether you're accepting a request or clicking on an app you found in search results, the Application Directory, or a link on someone else's profile—you'll get the Request for

Permission dialog shown below. Notice that the dialog tells you exactly what information from your profile the developers of the app will be able to access if you give it permission. This full disclosure is a relatively recent addition, in response to growing concerns about privacy.

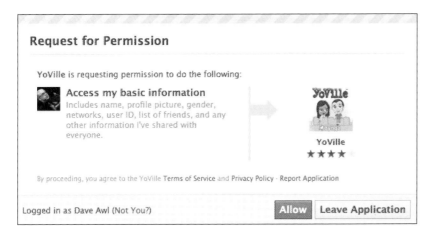

Clicking the Allow button authorizes the app and allows you to go ahead with using it. Clicking the Leave Application button lets you skedaddle without giving the app any info.

How to Decide Which Apps Are Worthwhile and Trustworthy

When you get a request from an application you haven't used before, you're presented with a bit of a dilemma. Some Facebook applications are loads of fun, very useful, or both. Others are pointless time-wasters that will annoy you with endless requests, and in some cases even pester your friends in your name, without your permission.

So how do you tell the good apps from the bad? How do you decide which ones are worth authorizing and which ones you should kick to the curb?

Fortunately, there's no need to install apps blindly. If you're on the fence, you can do the Facebook equivalent of a background check on an app to help you decide whether you want to authorize it or not.

The first step in evaluating an app is to take a look at its official Facebook Page—every app on Facebook has an informational Page with basic information about the app and its makers. You can access the Page for any app by clicking the name of the app in the Request for Permission dialog (as shown at right), or by searching the app's name in the blue bar's search field, and then clicking the words View Application next to the search result.

TIP: Some apps claim to raise money for charity or political causes—and some have been very effective at it. The now-defunct (Lil) Green Patch app, for example, raised more than $100,000 for the Nature Conservancy during its life on Facebook. If you have questions about an app's fundraising claims, check the Page for the app. You can usually find details there about exactly how much money has been raised in the past, and where it's been donated.

Click the name of the application in the Request for Permission dialog to visit the official Facebook Page for that app and learn more about it.

Once you reach the app's official Page, there are several key things to look at:

Information

★★★★ (4.0 out of 5)
Based on 27,720 reviews

Users:
6,908,616 monthly active users,
49 friends

Category
Games

This application was **not** developed by Facebook.

The star rating at the top of the Information box is a reasonably good indicator of how its users feel about it.

1. **Star rating.** In the right-hand column of the Page, you'll see an Information box, just like the Info box on a personal profile. The Information box for an app always includes a rating from one to five stars based on user reviews for the app. That gives you a quick visual gauge of how happy its users are. If the rating is four stars or better, that's a good sign. If it's two stars or below, that may be a red flag.

2. **Friends.** Under the Users heading in the Information box, you'll see the number of friends of yours who are currently using the app—in blue, meaning it's a clickable link. Clicking that link will show you a listing of exactly which friends have authorized the application. If a lot of friends whose judgment you trust are pictured there, that's a good endorsement. (You can also contact those friends to ask them whether they recommend the app or not.)

3. **User reviews.** Click the Reviews tab at the top of the Page to read direct feedback from people who've already used this app. If you see a lot of negative reviews, you might want to steer clear—especially if the reviewers give you specific and convincing reasons as to why they're unhappy. On the other hand, glowing praise from fans of the app might convince you that it's worth your time. (One downside to this: on Pages for some of the more popular apps, you might have to wade through a lot of postings

from people who are simply asking other users to add them as friends, among other spam.)

4. **Wall and Discussion Board (if enabled).** You'll also find feedback from the app's users in these areas of the Page. Scan them for recurring complaints or hearty endorsements.

And of course you can also peruse the Info tab and Wall to read what the app's makers have to say about the app and how it works.

Now you've got some input to go on, and can make an informed decision about whether to app or not to app.

Managing Applications (and Application Privacy)

Although many applications have their own specific settings that you can access from inside the apps themselves, there are some general settings that apply to any app you install.

If you decide an app isn't for you after you've been using it for a while, you can send it packing by deauthorizing it. And in response to privacy concerns, these days Facebook gives you the ability to see exactly what profile information apps are accessing. In some cases you can grant and deny permission for specific kinds of information. You can also control whether apps your friends are using can access information about you via your friends' profiles.

How to Edit the Privacy Settings for an Application

Whenever you want to take a look at what the applications you've authorized are getting up to, and maybe rein them in a little, you can pay a call on the Applications You Use page in the Privacy Settings.

Start by choosing Privacy Settings from the Account menu in the blue bar. Down at the bottom, under the Applications and Websites heading, click the "Edit your settings" link.

 Applications and Websites
    Edit your settings for using applications, games and websites.

From there you'll arrive at the Applications, Games and Websites page. Up at the top, in the Applications You Use area, you'll see a handful of recently used applications.

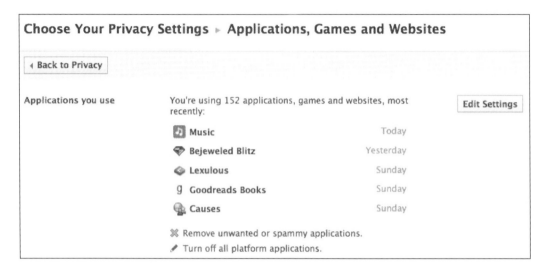

To see the full list, go ahead and click the Edit Settings button next to this area. That will take you to the Applications You Use page, where you'll be able to view and manage settings for all of the applications currently authorized to access your Facebook account.

Here you'll see the applications listed in order of how recently you've used them, with the most recently used at the top. By clicking the Edit Settings

link on the right side of the listing for any specific app, you can see exactly
what profile information it's currently allowed to access.

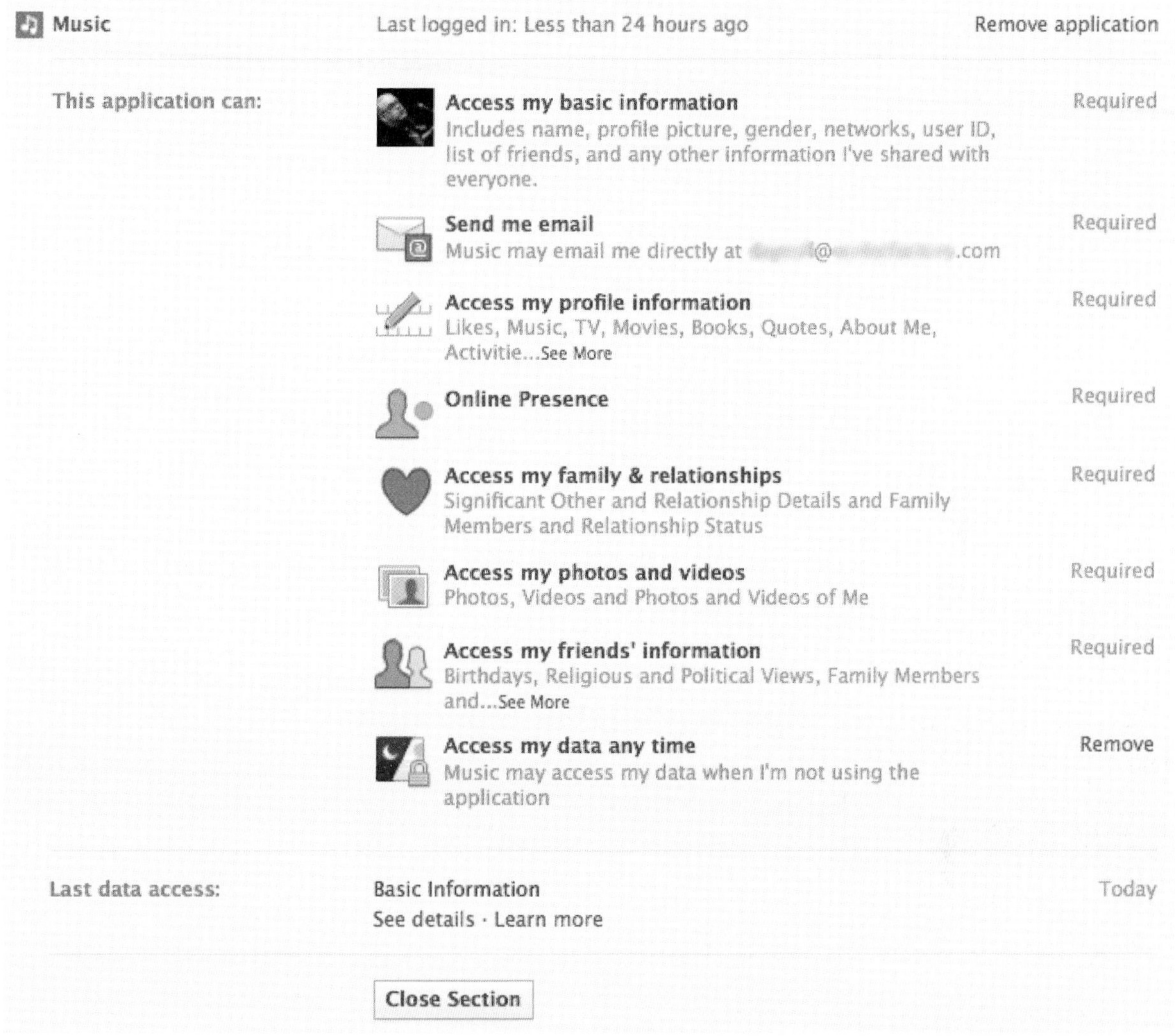

🎵 Music	Last logged in: Less than 24 hours ago	Remove application

This application can:	**Access my basic information** Includes name, profile picture, gender, networks, user ID, list of friends, and any other information I've shared with everyone.	Required
	Send me email Music may email me directly at ████████@████████████.com	Required
	Access my profile information Likes, Music, TV, Movies, Books, Quotes, About Me, Activitie...See More	Required
	Online Presence	Required
	Access my family & relationships Significant Other and Relationship Details and Family Members and Relationship Status	Required
	Access my photos and videos Photos, Videos and Photos and Videos of Me	Required
	Access my friends' information Birthdays, Religious and Political Views, Family Members and...See More	Required
	Access my data any time Music may access my data when I'm not using the application	Remove

Last data access:	Basic Information See details · Learn more	Today

Close Section

On the right side, next to each category of information, you'll see whether that information is required in order to use the application or not. If there's a Remove link instead of the word Required, you can click that to remove the app's access to that data.

Down at the bottom, in the "Last data access" area, you can find out what kind of data the app requested last time it accessed your profile. Click the "See details" link to open the Access Log dialog, with all the details.

💬 **Define "Anytime"**

What's the "Access my data anytime" area (visible in the screen shot above) all about? If enabled, it means that even when you're logged out of Facebook, a friend can still use an app to interact with you, such as SuperPoking you or starting a word game with you.

8

TIP: Given that the applications you've used most recently are at the top of the Applications You Use page, that means that if you decide you want to do a little spring cleaning and get rid of the apps you don't use anymore, you'll find them gathering dust down at the bottom of the page. It might be a good idea to make use of the Page Down key and then work your way up from the bottom.

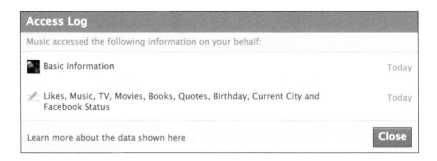

Access Log

Music accessed the following information on your behalf:

Basic Information — Today

Likes, Music, TV, Movies, Books, Quotes, Birthday, Current City and Facebook Status — Today

Learn more about the data shown here **Close**

When you're done looking at the info for an app, click the Close Section button toward the bottom of its settings area to return to the regular list view.

How to Remove Applications

While you're viewing the expanded info for an application, you can click the "Remove application" link at the top. If you're in the regular list view, you can click the X at the far right side of the listing for any application. Doing either of those things opens a dialog that lets you remove (deauthorize) the app in question. Once you do that, it's gone from the list and no longer has direct access to any of your profile information. (But see the following section for how it might have indirect access.)

How to Keep Applications You Don't Use from Accessing Your Information

In addition to the applications you've authorized yourself, applications that your Facebook friends are using may be able to access some of the basic info from your profile. For example, some of your friends might be using an app that displays all of their pals' birthdays on a calendar. That app will access your profile to get your birthday in order to include you in the display.

Facebook gives you the ability to control which information is available to apps via this indirect method. Choose Privacy Settings from the Account menu in the blue bar, and then click "Edit your settings" under Applications and Websites as shown earlier to go to the Applications, Games and Websites page. In the "Info accessible through your friends" area, click the Edit Settings button.

| **Info accessible through your friends** | Control what information is available to applications and websites when your friends use them. | **Edit Settings** |

This opens the "Info accessible through your friends" dialog.

Info accessible through your friends

Use the settings below to control which of your information is available to applications, games and websites when your friends use them. The more info you share, the more social the experience.

☐ Bio   ☐ My videos
☐ Birthday   ☐ My links
☐ Family and relationships   ☐ My notes
☐ Interested in and looking for   ☐ Photos and videos I'm tagged in
☐ Religious and political views   ☐ Hometown
☐ My website   ☐ Current city
☐ If I'm online   ☐ Education and work
☐ My status updates   ☐ Activities, interests, things I like
☐ My photos   ☐ Places I check in to

Your name, profile picture, gender, networks and user ID (along with any other information you've set to everyone) is available to friends' applications unless you turn off platform applications and websites.

[Save Changes] [Cancel]

By selecting or deselecting these checkboxes, you can choose to make such info as your education history, your photos, or whether you're online or not (just to pick a few examples) off-limits to applications you haven't authorized.

There's a clear trade-off here: The more of these checkboxes you deselect, the more you protect your privacy—but the less your friends will be able to interact and communicate with you using applications on Facebook. (For example, they might be prevented from sending you a message or starting a game with you using their favorite application.) It's a little like making your phone number unlisted—it protects you from bill collectors and crank callers, but it may also make it harder for the people you actually like to give you a jingle.

How to Control Who Can See Your Applications and Games Activity

In the section on the dashboards for applications and games, I pointed out how you can see which apps your friends have been using lately. Facebook gives you the ability to control whether your own activity appears on your friends' dashboards—and if so, who can see it. You'll find this setting on the Applications, Games and Websites page shown earlier (Account > Privacy Settings > Edit your settings) under the heading "Game and application activity." Use the menu to choose the visibility level you want.

The options in the menu for controlling who can see your game and application activity. If you want to be really precise about it, you can choose Customize and select a Friend List you've created that contains only the people you want to share your activity with.

| Game and application activity | Who can see your recent games and application activity. | |

Turning Off Platform: How to Banish Third-Party Applications Completely

There's one other step you can take, if you decide you want to ban all apps, games, and third-party website access from your Facebook account entirely: turning off Platform access. (Platform is the software that allows apps to run on Facebook.) But beware: If you do this, you'll lose any settings and data in apps you've used previously, and your friends will no longer be able to communicate with you using apps (although they can still interact with you using normal Facebook channels like the Wall or the Inbox, of course). But turning off Platform access will prevent third-party apps and websites from accessing your profile information—effectively pulling up the drawbridge.

If you decide you want to turn off Platform access, go to the Applications, Games and Websites page (Account > Privacy Settings > Edit your settings) and find the link that says "Turn off all platform applications."

TIP: The "Remove unwanted or spammy applications" link in the shot at right simply takes you to the Applications You Use page, as discussed earlier.

Note that although you can restore Platform access from this location if you change your mind at some point in the future, you won't be able to get back any settings or data you lost by turning it off.

Adding Extra Tabs to Your Profile

We've already talked about the three tabs that appear on your Profile page by default (assuming you have the necessary content to make them all appear): Wall, Info, and Photos. But you can also add optional extra tabs for official Facebook applications (such as Notes, Links, Events, and Video), and rearrange the order of those tabs. (Sadly, Facebook no longer allows tabs for third-party applications on personal profiles, so the days of having a Catbook or Goodreads tab on your personal profile are now in the past.)

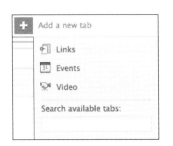

The menu for adding an extra tab to your profile

To add a tab, click the plus (+) button to the right of the other tabs at the top of your profile. Then choose the app you'd like to promote to its own tab from the pop-up list that appears. (If you don't see the app you want in the menu, you can type its name in the search field to see if it's available.)

TIP: You can rearrange the order of your tabs by dragging them. But note that only six tabs can appear above your profile; any others you create are shifted to an overflow menu marked with a >> symbol, right next to the plus button.

Facebook Credits

Facebook Credits are Facebook's own virtual currency. They serve as the coin of the realm for a variety of different apps and games on Facebook. You can use them to buy virtual goods within certain apps—everything from greeting cards and gifts for friends to buildings for your imaginary farm. In some games, you can use them to enhance your playing ability: for example, in the game Bejeweled Blitz, you can use Facebook Credits to buy "boosts" that give you extra time at the end of the game or to add special gems to the game board that increase your scoring ability.

To buy Facebook Credits, go to Account > Account Settings and click the Payments tab. You'll see the number of credits you currently have (if any) displayed under the Credits Balance heading.

Your current Facebook Credits balance is visible from within most Facebook apps, and you can use the Get More link to replenish them if you find yourself running low.

If you need to purchase additional credits, click the "buy more" link. A dialog opens that lets you buy credits using an existing payment method (such as a credit card or PayPal account), or by entering a new one.

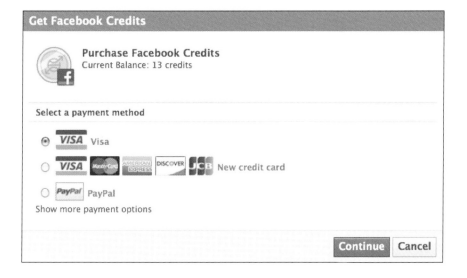

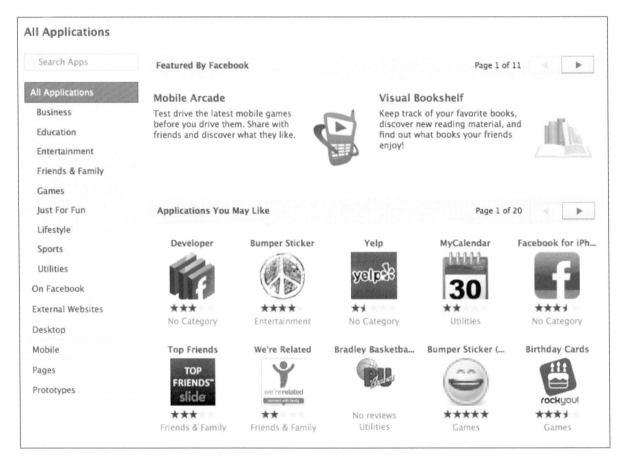

More | Applications Directory

The Applications Directory link at the bottom of the Applications dashboard page

Finding Apps: The Application Directory

If you'd like to browse for interesting new apps without waiting for a friend to send you a request, Facebook makes it easy—you can go app hunting any time you want using the Application Directory. To access it, go to your Application dashboard and click the Application Directory link at the bottom.

All Applications

Search Apps

All Applications
Business
Education
Entertainment
Friends & Family
Games
Just For Fun
Lifestyle
Sports
Utilities
On Facebook
External Websites
Desktop
Mobile
Pages
Prototypes

Featured By Facebook   Page 1 of 11

Mobile Arcade
Test drive the latest mobile games before you drive them. Share with friends and discover what they like.

Visual Bookshelf
Keep track of your favorite books, discover new reading material, and find out what books your friends enjoy!

Applications You May Like   Page 1 of 20

Developer — ★★★ — No Category
Bumper Sticker — ★★★★ — Entertainment
Yelp — ★★ — No Category
MyCalendar — ★★ — Utilities
Facebook for iPh... — ★★★★ — No Category

Top Friends — ★★★ — Friends & Family
We're Related — ★★ — Friends & Family
Bradley Basketba... — No reviews — Utilities
Bumper Sticker (... — ★★★★★ — Games
Birthday Cards — ★★★★ — Games

TIP: You can use the search field at the top of the Application Directory to search for applications by name (if you're looking for an app you already know the name of) or by keyword (if you're looking for apps related to cats or cooking or Lithuania or kayaking, for example).

The default page for the directory shows you a selection of apps that Facebook thinks you might like, based on actions you've taken in the past. The categories along the right side of the page let you browse apps that relate to (for example) business, education, entertainment, sports, and other niches.

A Brief Guide to Some Popular Facebook Apps

There are thousands of apps on Facebook, and it would be impossible to do more than scratch the surface of them—so the roundup that follows is shamelessly subjective and arbitrary. My goal here isn't to present a definitive catalog of Facebook's best apps, but just to show you a little of the range and variety of apps that are available, and encourage you to do some exploring to find your own favorites.

Culture-Sharing

One of the best parts of life on Facebook is the ability to share with your friends what you're reading, listening to, and watching, and keep track of what's on their cultural radar as well. There are lots of apps that make it easy to display your current recommendations, and find out about new books, music, and films by your favorite artists (as well as new discoveries).

Music (by iLike) is a perfect example of this. Although the iLike Music app wasn't developed by Facebook, it's the closest thing Facebook has to an official music application.

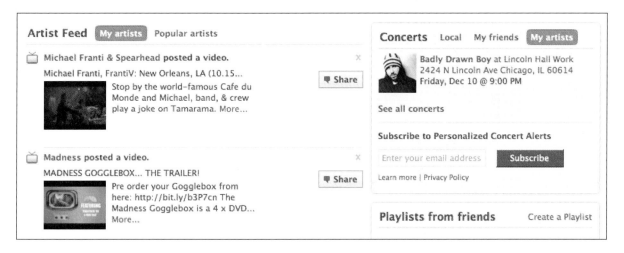

iLike's Music app Home page (shown above) helps you keep track of the artists you're a fan of, check out their new releases, find out when they're touring in your area, and make plans to meet up at concerts with friends. You can also use iLike Music to share playlists with your friends and challenge your friends to music trivia quizzes.

Albums by LivingSocial is another useful music app that's geared to showing off your album collection. You can display, rate, and review the albums you're currently listening to, as well as your old favorites.

For book lovers, **Visual Bookshelf by LivingSocial** (shown below) lets you display the books you're currently reading, books you've already read, and books you want to read. You can rate and review books, and check out what your friends are reading.

My Profile

Dave

MY BOOKS

112 books
0 reviews

View messages

Reading now
See all 9 in my collection

The Berlin
Stories: The
Las...

The Selected
Poetry of Rain...

The Left Hand
of Darkness

Turtle Diary

My Top Rated Books

 On the Great Atlantic Rainway: Selected
Poems 1950-1988
☆☆☆☆☆

 Changing Planes
☆☆☆☆☆

Already read
See all 101 in my collection

Great
Expectations

Nicholas
Nickleby

A Wizard of
Earthsea (The
E...

The Lathe of
Heaven: A
Novel

If you're already a member of the Goodreads book-sharing site, you'll find that the **Goodreads** app conveniently syncs your book list to the Goodreads box you can place on your Facebook profile.

The **Movies** app by Flixter is geared toward movie buffs. It lets you catalog and rate the movies you've seen, and compare your rankings with those of your friends. From the app's Home page you can also watch trailers, check showtimes for local theaters, play film trivia games, and more.

Activism

The **Causes** application makes it easy to support the causes you believe in. Choose from a diverse selection of charitable and political organizations. Once you click the link to "join" a cause, you can recruit other supporters and help raise donations for the organizations you've chosen to support.

Causes

Active member in 1 of 21 causes.

Bit-O-Heaven Ranch Horse Rescue

Stop Plastic Pollution: The Great Garbage Patch

Amnesty International

See All

Self-Expression

Pieces of Flair lets you collect and display small round buttons on a virtual bulletin board. You can spend hours obsessively browsing through the catalog of thousands of pins created by the Pieces of Flair users, and then arranging them into the perfect expression of your personality. You can even create your own button images and send them to your friends.

Profiles for Pets

Let's face it—those of us with animal companions think of them as our friends. So it's only natural that lots of Facebook users have the urge to create Facebook accounts for their cats, dogs, ferrets, and other nonhuman roommates. But technically, these are against Facebook's rules (because you're not supposed to create an account on someone else's behalf), so they can be deactivated as "fake profiles" if Facebook discovers them.

Fortunately, there's a great set of related apps that come to the rescue. You can create a profile for your cat on **Catbook** (shown below) or for your dog on **Dogbook**, listing their favorite activities and interests.

Your pet's profile comes complete with its own Wall and status update, and the ability to make friends with other pets and human beings. In addition to Catbook and Dogbook, there's also **Ferretbook**, **Horsebook**, **Rodentbook**, and **Fishbook**. (One can only hope that Reptilebook is in development.)

Virtual Farms, Gardens, Homes, and Pets

A character in the FarmVille game

If creating profiles for your real-world pets isn't enough for you, don't worry—there are plenty of opportunities to nurture virtual plants and animals on Facebook, too.

Possibly the most wildly popular game on Facebook in recent times has been **FarmVille**, which lets you build an nurture your own set of green acres—growing and planting crops and harvesting livestock. Players can interact by sending each other gifts and helping each other accomplish various farm-related tasks. **FrontierVille**, another popular game by the same maker, puts you in the role of a pioneer in the old west.

Yoville is a virtual world where players choose an avatar to live in a home they design and decorate according to their own taste. Players can throw virtual parties, exchange gifts, and shop for clothes and furniture among other activities.

Pet Society lets you create a custom-designed pet—choosing its name, color, gender, and other features—and then care for it. Friends can visit each other's pets, give each other gifts, play games, and more.

Sea Garden is an old favorite that provides a little patch of virtual ocean to tend. Friends send each other whales, dolphins, stingrays, and other sea creatures. Friends can also hide gifts inside each other's treasure chests, and send each other messages in bottles. Sea Garden helps raise funds for ocean protection organizations, including the Surfrider foundation.

Pet Society

Word Games

Word games are an ever-popular pastime both online and off, and Facebook has a thriving lexicon of them.

The most famous of these is **Lexulous**, which began life as an online version of Scrabble called Scrabulous that quickly became the most popular game on Facebook. Unfortunately, the developers of Scrabulous didn't own the rights to Scrabble, and after a much-publicized legal dispute they were reluctantly forced to reinvent the application as Lexulous, with some small differences

The Otter character from the Sea Garden application

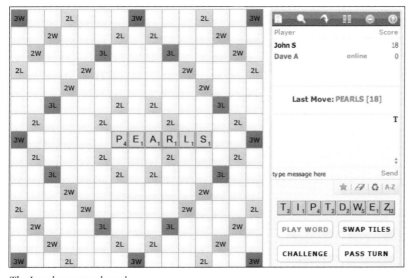

The Lexulous game board

There's now an official, authorized **Scrabble** application available on Facebook as well.

Other popular Facebook word games include **Word Twist**, which lets you challenge a friend to see who can create the most words out of a series of random letters. You earn points for speed as well as the length of the words you find. In **Scramble**, the goal is to find words in a grid of letters, playing solo or against friends. **Pathwords** is similar, but keeps things active by adding new letters to the board as you play, and removing letters you've used.

Other Games

Facebook is a never-ending arcade that lets you play every kind of game imaginable: from card games to board games and beyond. You can play poker with your pals using the **Texas HoldEm Poker** app, or match wits with your friends using the animated **Who Has the Biggest Brain?** game. You can even play a Facebook version of the **Family Feud** game show.

One of Facebook's most popular games at the moment is the disturbingly addictive **Bejeweled Blitz**, in which players score points by arranging animated gems into patterns on a grid while racing against the clock. If you're doing well, the gems burst into flames, explode, or turn into strange spinning cubes, and when you've recovered from all that excitement, you can compare your score with your Facebook friends.

Some gems that might explode—if you're lucky—in the Bejeweled Blitz game

For Bloggers

If you've got a blog outside of Facebook, there are plenty of ways to import and promote your blog's content on Facebook. As discussed in the *Sharing Content on Facebook* chapter, you can use Facebook's Import function to turn your blog posts into Facebook Notes automatically. But there are some great third-party apps for bloggers, too.

One of the best of these is the **NetworkedBlogs** app, which helps you promote your blog by adding it to a directory of Facebook blogs and connecting it to your friends who have blogs of their own. Using this app allows you to easily import blog posts to your Facebook Wall (as an alternative to using Facebook's Notes application).

The Facebook Toolbar

If you use Firefox or Internet Explorer as your web browser, Facebook has a nifty toolbar you can install that gives you quick access to much of Facebook's functionality even when you don't have Facebook itself open in your browser.

You can find the toolbar easily by navigating to Facebook.com/toolbar.

Click on the listing and follow the easy instructions to install the toolbar.

Once the toolbar is installed, you'll be able to see at a glance your current number of new pokes, friend requests, and Event and Group invitations. The toolbar also includes a handy Facebook Share button, a search field, a Home button, a Quick Links menu that gives you access to key Facebook pages, and a status update field (not shown above).

Photos and Videos

Photos are a huge part of life on Facebook. With more than 2.5 billion photos uploaded each month, Facebook is the web's largest photo-sharing site—bigger than Flickr or Photobucket.

Uploading your photos to Facebook does more than just give you a place to put them. Photos posted on Facebook get attention, because sharing photos on Facebook is an active process. Facebook's News Feed ensures that when you post photos on Facebook, other people will know about it and check them out.

Facebook is also an ideal place to host and share original videos, which benefit the same way photos do from Facebook's News Feed.

In this chapter, we'll start by looking at the various ways to view photos and videos on Facebook, and then we'll cover how to upload, organize, and tag your own photos and videos.

And because Facebook photos and videos are great vehicles for promoting creative projects, events, and causes, we'll talk a little about how you can use them to help get attention for whatever you've got that needs an audience.

Sharing Photos on Facebook

In a sense, posting photos on Facebook is the opposite of the slide shows my older relatives used to put on when I was a kid. With a slide show, you'd invite everyone to gather in one place to look at some photos together. With Facebook, on the other hand, the photos you post seek out their audience, finding their way to your friends in all sorts of different places.

Facebook's News Feed and notifications mean that when you publish photos on Facebook, people notice. And because each photo you post has its own comments thread, you'll get feedback too, as lively conversations spring up about each picture. (Maybe even livelier than the conversations my aunts and uncles used to have at those old-fashioned slide shows.)

Facebook gives you a bunch of useful tools to help you post your photos easily and organize them into albums. But before we talk about posting photos, let's look at how you can view your friends' photos on Facebook. That way, when you're ready to upload your own photos, you'll have a sense of how and where they'll be visible to others.

Viewing Photos

There are three easy ways to view photos on Facebook: check them out via the News Feed on the Home page, browse them from within the Photos application, or drop by a particular friend's profile to see all their photos.

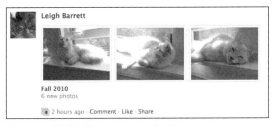

An example of a Photo story on the Home page

The Photos Application

Facebook's Photos app is its central hub for both viewing and posting photos. Photos is one of the basic Facebook applications that are part of your account by default, so you should find it already bookmarked in the left-hand column of the Home page. When you click the Photos bookmark, you'll be taken to the home page for the Photos app itself.

 What Is This Thing Called "Tagging"?

Each time you upload a new photo or video to Facebook, you have the option to *tag* the people who appear in it. Tagging involves clicking on the faces of the people in the picture and then choosing their names from a pop-up list of your friends. Anyone you tag will get a notification from Facebook, letting them know that a new photo or video of them has been posted, so they can go take a look at it.

Tagging someone also means that a story will appear on their Wall about the photo or video, and News Feed stories may appear on the Home pages of their friends as well.

You can tag people who aren't on Facebook, too, and Facebook will send a notification message to the e-mail address you specify for them.

Tags can be added and removed at any time. And you always have the option to remove your own name from any photos or videos where you've been tagged. See "Detagging Photos and Videos," later in this chapter.

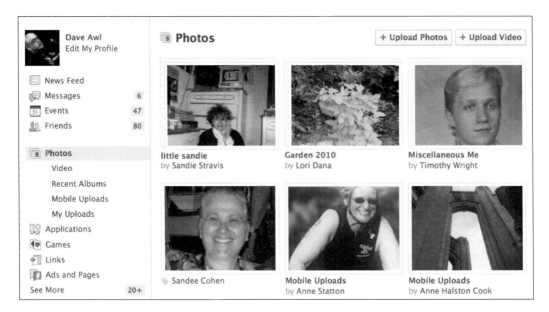

The Photos home page shows you a selection of photos your friends have recently uploaded, or in which they've been tagged, and also provides handy buttons for uploading photos or videos of your own.

Friends' Profiles

If you want to view photos of a particular friend, you can swing by their profile, where there are a few different ways to access their photos. The most obvious is to click the Photos tab, if it's visible.

The Photos tab shows you photos in which your friend has been tagged in the top part of the page, and your friend's photo albums in the bottom part. (And of course, your own Photos tab works the same way for your own photos.)

If the Photos box is visible on your friend's profile, you can click the See All link to go the page that shows all of their photo albums.

If the Photos box isn't displayed, you can click the View Photos of [Name] link just under your friend's profile picture, which will take you to the same selection of photos as the Boxes tab.

Adding Photos

Uploading your photos to Facebook is a quick and painless process. Facebook gives you a number of tools to make it easy, including several choices for uploading.

Creating an Album

Facebook photos are organized into albums, so before you upload any photos to Facebook you need to create at least one album. Start by going to the Photos application, and then click the Upload Photos button in the upper-right corner of the page.

You can also go to the Photos tab on your profile and click the Create a Photo Album button to achieve the same results.

TIP: When you look at a friend's Photos tab, you may see a link that says "Photos of [Your Friend's Name] and Me." Clicking that will display any photos in which you and your friend are both tagged.

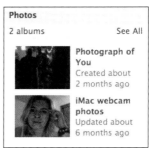

The Photos box

Click the link under a friend's profile picture to see their photos.

NOTE: If you've already created an album that you'd like to add photos to, you can bypass this step. See the upcoming section "Editing and Adding Photos to Existing Albums." And if you're uploading from your mobile phone, you can upload to the automatically created Mobile Uploads album.

TIP: If you're planning on posting a lot of photos, you might want to do some advance planning. Come up with a short list of categories that your photos fall into, such as Travel, Pets, Family, Holidays, and so on, and then create an album for each category.

Either way, you'll arrive at the Create Album page, where the first step is to name the album—pick something descriptive.

Next, type the location where the shots were taken. (This step is optional.)

Finally, use the Privacy menu to decide who will be allowed to see the photos in this album. If the photos you're posting are promotional, then you'll want to choose Everyone to give them the widest possible audience. On the other hand, if they're personal—photos of a family gathering, for example—you might want to limit the album to Friends Only, or even choose the Customize setting to restrict access to a particular Friend List. (See the *Friends* chapter for info on creating Friend Lists.) When you've completed those steps, you're ready to click the Create Album button.

Uploading Photos

Once you've created your album, you'll arrive at the Upload Photos page.

TIP: Before you start the upload process, take some time to prepare the photos you want to upload and organize them into one or more folders on your hard drive so they're easy to find—this will help the upload process go more smoothly. Keep in mind that each album is allowed to hold up to 200 photos, so if you've got more than that, you'll need to break them up into multiple albums. (Your first Mobile Uploads album holds 100 photos, and if you go over that the next one will automatically be created.)

Note that if Facebook's main photo uploader gives you any problems, you can also try using its stripped-down Simple Uploader, or its Java Uploader applet, via the text links underneath the Upload Photos button.

But let's try the regular uploader first. Click the Select Photos button to start the upload process. A dialog will open that lets you navigate to the folder where the photos you want to upload are located on your hard drive and select them.

Once you're done selecting the photos you want in the dialog, you'll return to the Upload Photos page, where you can click the Upload Photos button to import the photos you've selected to Facebook. Once the upload is complete, you'll arrive at the Edit Album Page where you can begin organizing your photos and adding captions to them.

Using the Java Uploader

If you decide to use the Java Uploader applet (by clicking the text link on the Upload Photos page), you'll need to click the Allow button to authorize it in the dialog that opens. Then you can use the left side of the uploader window to navigate to the folder on your hard drive that contains the photos you want to upload and select them. Once you've made your selection, click the Upload button to proceed.

Using the Simple Uploader

If you prefer to use the Simple Uploader, once again you can access it using the text link on the Upload Photos page. The Simple Uploader may be the most glitch-proof option, but its downside is that you'll have to browse for each individual photo you want to add—which isn't a problem if you're only adding a few but can be a real pain if you're uploading dozens of pics.

TIP: After you've uploaded your photos, you may see a message at the top of the page asking you if you'd like to publish the photos now or wait until you've finished working with them. If you choose to publish them now, a story will appear on your Wall and in your friends' News Feeds letting them know you've posted some new photos. But there's no hurry—if you'd rather wait until you've added captions and put your photos in order, there'll be plenty of opportunities to publish them later on in the process.

Once you've opened the Simple Uploader, use the Browse buttons to navigate to each of the first five photos you'd like to upload. (If you have more than five photos, you can upload them in separate batches.)

Once you've specified the photos you want to upload, click the Upload Photos button to proceed.

Editing Photo Information

Once you've uploaded your photos, you'll arrive at the Edit Photos page, where you can add or change the basic info for each individual photo.

Type a caption in the caption box that will appear on the page with the photo it applies to. Click the button that says, "This is the album cover," next to the photo you'd like to appear on the Albums page as the icon for this album. You can also select the "Delete this photo" checkbox to remove the photo from the album, and use the "Move to" menu to transfer it to a different album (assuming you've already created others to choose from).

The Flick Picker Upper (and Other Easy Ways to Facebook Your Photos)
There are lots of handy tools for getting your photos onto Facebook besides the uploading process described here. If you use Flickr, Photobucket, or iPhoto to manage your photos, for example, you'll find tools for sharing your pictures with Facebook built right in. With a little digging, you can also find a variety of desktop applications and web browser extensions that provide still more options for transferring photos to your Facebook profile.

The Future of Tagging?
In addition to the manual method of tagging photos described on the next page, Facebook is currently testing a facial recognition feature to make tagging photos even easier. Facebook automatically scans for faces in the photos you upload, puts a box around them, and asks you, "Whose face is this?" By the time you read this, the feature may be live.

You can also tag people who are in the photos while you're on this page—see the following section for details. When you're all done editing this info, click the Save Changes button at the bottom to continue.

Tagging Photos

You can tag photos either from the Edit Photos page or on the page for any individual photo. To tag someone in a photo on the Edit Photos page, move your pointer over the person's face. (If you're on the page for an individual photo, you'll need to click the Tag This Photo link first.) You'll see your cursor change to a crosshair. Click the face, and the tagging dialog will open, allowing you to type the person's name. Facebook will provide a list of friends whose names match what you type, and you can click the appropriate name.

If the person isn't on Facebook, you can simply finish typing.

> **TIP:** If you're on the page for an individual photo when you do the tagging, and you type the name of a person who isn't a Facebook member, Facebook will give you the option to send the person an e-mail notification at an address you specify.

Adding an Album Description

When you click the Save Changes button on the Edit Photos page, Facebook takes you to the main Album page so that you can see its contents at a glance.

Glastonbury
By Dave Awl · View Photos

Add More Photos

The next thing you'll want to do is add a description for the album. This will serve as introductory text on the album's main page—you can think of it as a caption that applies to the group of photos as a whole. To do this, scroll down to the bottom of the Album page and click the link that says Edit Album Info. You'll be taken to the Edit Info tab on the Edit Album page.

> **TIP:** When someone else adds a tag to one of your photos or videos, you'll get a request to approve the tag before it actually appears. (And of course, if you click Ignore, the tag will never appear.) The same thing happens the other way around if you add a tag to someone else's photo or video. Tag requests show up on the Requests page, just like friend requests or app requests.

> **Detagging Photos and Videos** If someone tags you in a photo or video and you're not happy with it, you always have the option to remove the tag yourself. Just go to the photo or video in question and click the Remove Tag link next to your name in the list of tags.
>
> Only friends are allowed to tag you in a photo or video on Facebook. So if someone keeps tagging you in pictures you find embarrassing, try asking them to stop tagging you. If they ignore your wishes, then you're well within your rights to defriend them—which will prevent them from tagging you in the future.
>
> On the flip side, if someone detags themselves in a photo or video you've posted, try not to take offense. It may not mean they dislike the picture, but simply that there are people on their Friends list who shouldn't see it.
>
> Finally, if a friend asks you to remove a photo or video of them from Facebook, you should honor that request unless you have a very good reason not to—respecting your friends' feelings is part of friendship, after all. And note that Facebook will remove photos and videos that violate its Terms of Use, once they're brought to its attention.

Edit Album Info
Share This Album
Post Album to Profile

The Edit Album Info link at the bottom of the Album page

TIP: Facebook will include the text you enter in the album's Description field as part of the News Feed story it generates whenever you add photos to the album or post it to your Wall. That's why it's good to include a snappy description that provides a little context for the photos your friends will see in their News Feeds.

TIP: The box for the Photos app generally appears on your profile by default once you have some photos for it to display. Same goes for the Photos tab at the top of your profile. If you've previously removed the box, you can easily restore it. Go to the Edit Settings dialog for the Photo app on the Application Settings page, click the Profile tab, and then choose the option to add a box.

There, in the Description field, you can type your introductory text for the album. (You can also edit the album's name, location, and privacy settings from this page.) Click Save Changes when you're done.

Organizing Photos in an Album

Now it's time to arrange the photos in your album. Click the Edit Album Info link at the bottom of the Album page to go back to the Edit Album page if necessary, and this time click the Organize tab.

On the Organize tab you can drag the photos in the album into the order you'd like—to make them tell a story, for example. You can use the Reverse Order button to make the first photo the last and the last photo the first, flipping the sequence in which the photos were uploaded.

When you're all done arranging, click the Save Changes button at the bottom of the page. You can click the Edit Photos tab to return to the page where you can change captions and other attributes at any time, and clicking the Edit Info tab takes you to the page where you can change the description, location, and privacy settings for the album. The Delete tab allows you to delete the entire album if you decide you want get rid of it.

Additional Photo Controls

On the Album page, click any photo to go to the page for that photo. Down at the bottom of the page, you'll see some additional controls. You can change the photo's orientation using the rotate buttons, tag people (as discussed earlier), edit the photo's individual caption and other options, delete the photo, or designate the photo as your current profile pic. And of course you can click the Share link to post it to your Wall or send a message to friends.

The additional controls that appear at the bottom of the page for each individual photo. The rotate buttons are just above the Share link, with the curvy arrows.

Photo Comments

Photos are the ultimate conversation starters, so every photo you post gets its own individual comments thread. Down at the bottom of the page you'll see the area where viewers can enter their comments and click Like. Facebook will notify you each time someone Likes or adds a comment to one of your photos (or any photo you've been tagged in, even if it's part of someone else's collection).

Sharing Your Album

Once your album is ready for viewing, if you haven't already published it you can click the Post Album to Profile link at the bottom of the Album page to create a story that will appear on your Wall and in your friends' News Feeds. Or click the Share This Album link to open a dialog that lets you send an In-box message to friends you'd like to come take a look at it.

The Share This Album and Post Album to Profile links

Editing Existing Albums

Once you've created an album, you can go back to it anytime to edit its info, delete photos, or add photos (up to the limit of 200 per album). Go to the Photos tab on your profile, and in the lower part of the page you'll see the various albums you've created. (Or click the See All link in the Photos box on your profile.) Then click on the album you'd like to work with, and when you get to the album page, click the Edit Album Info link.

From there you can access all the same tools and options you used when creating the album, as covered in the previous section.

If you'd like to add photos to the album, just click the Add More Photos button at the top of the album page to access the various options for uploading.

Public Images, Unlimited

Down at the bottom of the page for each photo you upload, as well as for each album as a whole, Facebook gives you a public URL that can be accessed without signing in to Facebook. You can send this URL to anyone you'd like to see your photos who isn't a member of Facebook, and you can also use it to link to Facebook photos on blogs or other web sites. (But note that this will only work if your privacy settings allow the photo or album in question to be seen by whoever clicks on the link. So if you're posting it on a public blog, for example, you'd need to set the privacy setting to "Everyone.")

Sharing Video on Facebook

Facebook's Video app does for video what Photos does for still images. Like its counterpart, Video gives you multiple easy ways to post original content to your profile. And once you've done that, Facebook provides you with a built-in audience thanks to its News Feed and notifications, which ensure that your friends will see your work—and maybe your friends' friends, too, depending on the privacy settings you choose. (On the other hand, because each video you post gets its own specific Privacy control, if you want to post something just for family or a small group of friends, you can do that, too.)

And just like YouTube videos, Facebook videos can be embedded on blogs and other outside sites—making your potential audience as worldwide as the web itself.

Viewing Videos

As with photos, Facebook gives you a variety of ways to see videos created by your friends, or videos in which your friends are tagged. Here are some of the key places to watch Facebook's never-ending video festival.

The News Feed

Like photos, Facebook videos show up as News Feed stories, so you might spot them on the Home page or on a friend's Wall.

The Video Application

You can access the Video application via its bookmark on the Home page, in the left-hand column. These days it's hidden underneath the bookmark for the Photos app—when you click the Photos bookmark, four other bookmarks appear below it. The Video bookmark is just below Photos in that submenu.

When you click the Photos bookmark, the Video bookmark appears just underneath it.

The Home page for the Video app shows you the latest videos posted by your friends, as well as videos in which your friends have been tagged recently. Click on the thumbnail for any video to go its page, where you can watch the video and comment on it.

Viewing Videos by a Specific Friend

To see all the videos that a friend of yours has uploaded or been tagged in, you can go directly to their profile and click the View Videos of [Name] link under their profile picture. (If the friend in question hasn't posted or been tagged in any videos, the link won't appear.)

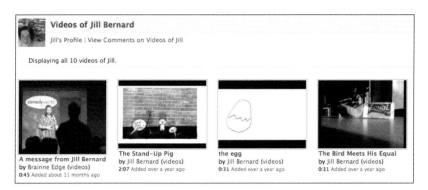

Click the link under a friend's profile picture to see their videos.

Posting Original Videos

Facebook gives you three convenient ways to post your original videos. From within the Video application (one of the basic Facebook apps that's part of your account by default), you can post an existing video file from your hard drive, record a new video from scratch using your webcam (or other video camera that's connected to your system), or upload a video from your mobile phone. (See the *Going Mobile* chapter for info on mobile uploads.)

Remember that videos you upload or record to Facebook need to be less than 20 minutes long, with a file size of less than 1024 MB. (If your account is new, Facebook may limit you to 2 minutes and 100 MB until you verify it. In that case, click the "Verify your account" link in the upload dialog for further instructions.) If your file exceeds those limits, Facebook won't let you upload it.

TIP: If you have longer videos or films already hosted on other sites, you don't necessarily need to duplicate that content on Facebook. Instead you might consider posting a short teaser or trailer to whet viewers' appetites, and then direct them to a URL where they can view the entire work.

Uploading a Video from Your Computer

On the home page for the Video application, click the Upload Video button, which will take you to the dialog where you can select a video. (For that matter, you'll find the Upload Video button on the home page for the Photos app, too.)

NOTE: In order to emphasize that you should upload only original videos you've created yourself, Facebook stipulates that any videos you upload should be made by you or one of your friends, and should feature you or one of your friends.

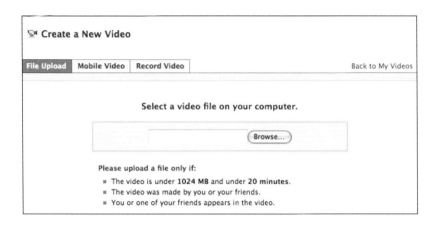

In the File Upload dialog, use the Browse button to navigate to the video file you'd like to upload. Facebook will begin uploading your file, and the Video Data form will appear where you can enter basic info about your video during the upload and after it's complete.

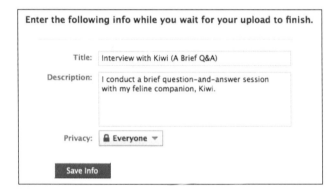

Give your video a name and type a brief description, and then use the Privacy menu to choose who will be allowed to see the video.

When you're done entering the info, click the Save Info button to proceed to the page for your new video.

Recording a Video

To record a brand-new video using any video camera attached to your computer, go to the Video application and click the Upload Video button. Then, on the Create a New Video page (as shown in the previous section), click the Record Video tab. On the Record Video tab, you'll see the Adobe Flash Player Settings dialog displayed.

If you haven't already granted Facebook access to your camera, you'll see the privacy settings below. Click the Allow button to proceed.

The Camera settings for Adobe Flash Player

Click the Camera button at the bottom right and use the Camera menu to choose the camera you'd like to use, if it isn't already selected. Click through the various other settings to make sure everything's ready to go, and then click the Close button to exit the Flash Player Settings.

Facebook will open the video recorder window—click the circle button to begin recording, and the same button (which changes to a square) to stop.

Left: The Record button. Right: The playback controls.

The Display settings for Adobe Flash Player

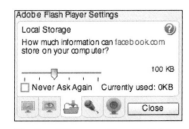

The Local Storage settings for Adobe Flash Player

You can play back your video to see how it turned out. If you don't like it, you can click Reset to delete it and start over. If it's good to go, you can click Save to proceed.

Once you click Save, you'll arrive at the Edit Video page, where you can tag people, assign a title and description, and set the Privacy controls. You can also click through various frames of the video to choose a thumbnail image that will represent the video when it appears on Facebook pages.

When you're all done setting these options, you can click Save to finish. You can also click Skip for Now to save the video without setting any options, or Delete to erase the video. If you click Save or Skip for Now, you'll proceed to the page for your new video.

The Microphone settings for Adobe Flash Player

Additional Video Controls

Once you've uploaded or recorded your video, you'll arrive at the page for the video, where you'll see some additional controls. You can tag people who appear in the video, use the rotate buttons to change the video's orientation, edit it, delete it, or embed it somewhere else.

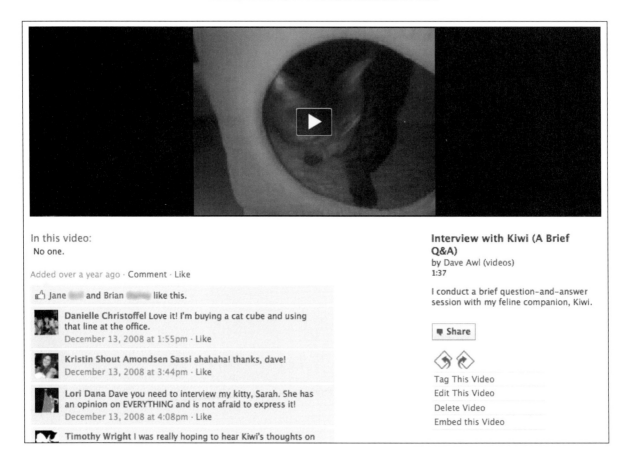

Video Comments

Just like photos, each video you post gets its own comments thread, with a field down at the bottom of the page for viewers to enter their comments. Facebook will send you a notification each time someone posts a comment about one of your videos (or any video you've been tagged in) or Likes it.

Tagging Videos

Tagging videos works much like tagging photos. Click the Tag This Video link on the video's page, and type the names of the people you want to tag in the box. When you're finished, click Done Tagging.

Embedding Facebook Videos

Any video you've posted to Facebook using the Video application can be embedded on other sites, just like YouTube videos. On the video's page, click the "Embed this video" link. The "Embed your video" dialog will open, with the Embed code displayed.

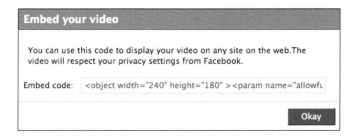

From there, all you have to do is copy and paste the code. Click the Okay button to close the dialog once you've got what you need.

Adding a Video Box or Tab

If you haven't already done so, you can add a box for the Video application to your profile. You can also assign the Video app its own tab if you want to give your videos some extra prominence on your profile. Go to the Application Settings page, choose the Profile tab in the Edit Settings dialog for the Video app, and click the option to add a box, a tab, or both.

Using Photos and Videos Promotionally

One of the interesting things about both photos and videos is that while they're creative works in their own regard, they're also ideal media for showcasing *other* creative works. And when you factor in the way Facebook's News Feed pushes photos and videos out to the people in your network—with the passive endorsement effect to increase their reach and impact—they become highly effective tools for promoting projects, events, and even ideas.

So in addition to posting funny pictures of your cat, your kids, or your most recent trip to Mexico, it's worthwhile to think about how you can use Facebook photos and videos to tap into an audience for whatever else you use your talents to create.

If you're in a theater company with a show about to open, for example, you might post some shots of rehearsals in progress, headshots of the cast, or flyers and posters for the show itself. If you make handcrafted jewelry or furniture, post some samples of your work. If you bake, show everyone your latest cake; if you're a knitter, show off your latest scarf or sweater. You get the idea.

Facebook videos can be a great promotional tool, too. Conduct short interviews with your collaborators, or have a friend interview you about your latest project, event, or cause. You can use Facebook to video blog, or to get your message out through short films, sketches, or original songs.

This is not meant to encourage anyone to blatantly spam Facebook's News Feed, by the way: To be effective, you need to make sure that what you post is genuinely engaging and appealing to your Facebook friends. If it feels too much like crass advertising, instead of enlarging your audience you'll wind up alienating people and encouraging them to defriend you.

On the other hand, if you give people something compelling and worthwhile to look at, Facebook will help make sure they see it.

Group Dynamics

Most of the interactions covered so far in this book have been between people who already know each other. But there's a whole big Facebook world out there beyond your Friends list, and Facebook's Groups are the common areas—the cafés and clubs, if you will—where you can mix with people you don't know yet, and maybe get to be friends with them eventually.

Facebook's Groups are also useful for enabling communications among subsets of your Friends list, or tracking down old friends you haven't yet connected with on Facebook.

These days, there are two different kinds of Groups on Facebook: the new model and the old model. So in this chapter, we'll start out by looking at both kinds of Groups and how they differ. Then I'll fill you in on the new-style Groups: how they work, how to use them, how to create them, and how to manage them. At the end of the chapter I'll include some information on old-style Groups, because you can still join, interact with, and manage the ones that were created before the changeover.

Groups: Free-Associating on Facebook

TIP: Facebook's Friend Finder (discussed earlier in the *Friends* chapter) lets you automatically search for members of your graduating class. But suppose you specifically want to track down members of your old marching band, including friends who were older or younger than you? One strategy is to create a Group for the band and then keep an eye on its members list. Some of the friends you're looking for may find their way to the Group before you find them individually on Facebook.

On the surface, the idea of Facebook Groups is simple. Facebookers with a common interest form an online club, with its own page where members can mingle and socialize. This provides a convenient way to meet new people outside your geographical area and real-world social scene. And Groups are an ideal forum for geeking out—they allow fans of someone or something to connect with their fellow devotees, sharing information, photos, videos, and general chitchat about the object of their obsession.

But there are other ways you can put Groups to work, above and beyond those obvious uses. Groups can help you track down old friends, for example. (See the tip at left.) They also make an excellent tool for communicating with collaborators on creative endeavors, as well as work groups and project teams. (As I was writing this book, I created a Group to help me keep track of the people who graciously gave me permission to use their names and faces in these pages.)

New-Style Groups and Old-Style Groups: What's the Diff?

Late in the process of preparing this edition of *Facebook Me!*, Facebook launched a brand-new version of its Groups feature—changing the way Groups work in certain fundamental ways.

The result is that there are now two different kinds of Groups on Facebook—which, for the sake of clarity, I'll be calling new-style Groups and old-style Groups.

Old-style Groups are still around—any Groups that were created before the change still exist, and still work the old way. You can still join them, and run them if you're a creator or admin for an old-style Group. But old-style Groups can't be created anymore—any new Groups that are created on Facebook take the new form, and follow the new rules.

New Groups, New Look

There are some big visual differences between the two kinds of Groups: Old-style Groups look similar to Pages and personal profiles, with tabs along the top for the Wall, Info, Photos, and possibly others. New-style Groups, on the other hand, have a shared content area that looks something like a Wall, but no tabs along the top.

Bypassing Invitations: New-Style Group Members Can Add Other Members

The feature that makes new-style Groups especially useful is also their most controversial aspect: Your Facebook friends have the ability to add you to new-style Groups without your prior approval.

With old-style Groups, you had to join a Group before you were a member of it. People who were already members or admins of the Group could invite you to join it, but you weren't an official member until you clicked the Join button.

With new-style Groups, on the other hand, existing members of the Group have the ability to add any of their friends to the Group whom they feel would make a good addition. This helps new-style Groups form and grow much more quickly and easily than the old Groups did.

Of course, not everyone is wild about this change: To some people, these new-style Groups sound a little like the Borg from *Star Trek*. ("You have been added to a Group. You will be assimilated.") And there is some potential for mischief, since people can add you to Groups that you wouldn't choose to join yourself, and might even consider objectionable.

But it's important to remember two key facts that help mitigate the Borg factor:

1. You'll be notified by Facebook as soon as you're added to any new-style Group, and
2. You can leave the Group immediately if you don't want to be a member, just by visiting the Group and clicking its Leave Group link.

The Idea Behind New-Style Groups: Another Way to Choose Your Audience

Why did Facebook change the Groups feature? The main reason was to give Facebook users a new way to choose exactly who sees the content you share. Facebook's new-style Groups are intended to make it easy to share certain content with (for example) only your friends from college, or only your family members, or only the members of your local scooter club.

Throughout this book I've been encouraging you to create and use Friend Lists for this purpose—and Friend Lists are still the best way to do it, because they give you more precise control than new-style Groups, and can be

Open, Closed, or Secret
In the real world, some clubs are open to the public and others are private. That's true of Facebook Groups, too. Facebook's new-style Groups come in three degrees of privacy:

Open Groups are the most public. The Group's page, its members, and all Group content are visible to everyone, even people who aren't members.

Closed Groups are a little more private. The Group's page and members are visible to the public, but the Group's content is visible only to members.

Secret Groups fly below the radar for maximum privacy. Nobody but members can see the Group, its members, or its content.

All three kinds of Groups allow members to add their Facebook friends as new members.

TIP: In case you're wondering, as of this writing there's no setting that allows you to prevent anyone from ever adding you to a new-style Group without your prior approval. The best you can do is leave Groups immediately if you don't want to be a member—and if someone is adding you to Groups you don't want to be a part of, politely ask them to cease and desist. If they persist, then they might be a good candidate for defriending.

Houston, We Have Achieved Group Chat

New-style Groups make it possible to have chat sessions with multiple people for the first time on Facebook. Group members can launch Group chats that include any members of the Group who are currently online. See the section on Facebook Chat in the *Communicating on Facebook* chapter for all the details.

Using New-Style Groups as E-Mail Lists

One other useful feature of new-style Groups is that you can use them as e-mail mailing lists. Every new-style Group can have an e-mail address assigned to it, chosen by the admins who run the Group. Any member of the Group can send e-mail to that address (using the e-mail address associated with their Facebook account), and the e-mail message will be added as a posting to the Group's page. Members of the Group will be notified of the new posting via Facebook's notifications (including e-mail notifications, for those who have them enabled). See the upcoming section "How to Post Content to a New-Style Group" for more on posting to Groups via email.

plugged into Facebook's privacy settings in all sorts of useful ways (as covered in previous chapters).

But here's the problem: Most Facebook users don't bother to create Friend Lists, either because they don't know how or don't want to take the time to do it. (According to Facebook, at the time they rolled out the new Groups feature, only 5% of Facebook members were using Friend Lists.) So Facebook's solution was to reinvent Groups as a kind of collaborative Friend List. One person creates the Group, various members add other members, and *voilà*—the Group takes shape without most of its members having to go to any special effort. You have just a few highly motivated people doing the organizing, but (in theory) everyone benefits.

Of course, the down side to that benefit is that because other members can add people to the Group, you don't have the same precise control over the audience you're posting to that Friend Lists give you. When you post to a Friend List, you know exactly who's on it—whereas with a group, any number of strangers might have been added since the last time you checked it.

Instant Notifications

A major advantage that new-style Groups have over old-style Groups is that Group members get notifications of activity within the Group from Facebook—for example, when someone posts something new on the Group's page. My friend Jason says the level of participation in the new-style Group he started is "quadruple" what it was for old-style Groups, simply because of the notification factor.

How to Join, Leave, and Add Friends to New-Style Groups

There are two ways to join a new-style Group: the passive way, in which a friend adds you to the Group, and the active way, in which you make the decision to add yourself to the Group.

In the first case, if a friend adds you to a Group, you'll get a notification from Facebook in your Notifications menu, looking something like this:

Laura Pexton Ross added you to the group Peachpit Authors.
51 minutes ago

If you find your way to a Group you haven't been added to by a friend, just look for the Ask to Join Group button. (At the time of this writing, it lives over to the right of the Group's name at the top of the page.) New members have to be approved by an admin before they can join, so after you click the button, be patient—it may take a while before an admin has a chance to review your request.

The Ask to Join Group button at the top of the page for a new-style Group

To leave a new-style Group at any time—whether you were added to it by a friend or joined it deliberately—just go to the Group's page and click the Leave Group link in the right-hand column.

To add friends to a new-style Group, click the Add Friends to Group link just above the Leave Group link. A dialog will appear that lets you enter the names of the friends you'd like to add.

The links for adding friends to a new-style Group and leaving the Group

TIP: Once you leave a Group, your friends can't re-add you to it. (So you don't have to worry about your smart aleck buddies continually adding you to the same Group as a prank.) But you can request to join again if you change your mind.

How to Edit Your Settings for New-Style Groups

Once you've joined or been added to a new-style Group, you'll see the Edit Settings button at the top of its page. Clicking it opens the Edit Settings dialog. From this dialog you can control:

- What notifications you get from the Group,
- Whether you get notifications by e-mail or not,
- Whether a bookmark for the Group appears in the left-hand column of your Home page, and
- Whether you get notified when a member starts a Group chat.

The Edit Settings button for a new-style Group you belong to lives at the top of its page.

The choices in the "Notify me when" pop-up menu let you control exactly what triggers a notification from a Group. If you choose "Only posts I am subscribed to," you'll only get notifications from postings you've Liked or commented on.

What's Up, Docs?
There's one brand-new kind of content you can post that's currently only available in Facebook's new-style Groups: Facebook Docs. Docs are online documents that can be written collectively and edited by multiple Group members. You can create a new Doc by clicking the Doc button on the Publisher, and view or edit existing Docs using the Docs area on the Group's page.

Docs (1)	See All
Who Are You? 8 hours ago	

The Docs area on a new-style Group page lets you access and edit existing Docs.

Creating Group Events
Clicking the Create Event button on the Publisher for your Group lets you set up a calendar item that's linked to your Group. The name of your Group will appear as the host of the Event, and all members of the Group will automatically be invited. See the *Facebook Calendar* chapter for more info on creating Events.

How to Post Content to a New-Style Group

New-style Groups give you two options for posting content: by using the Publisher at the top of the Group's page, or by e-mail (if the Group has an e-mail address set up).

Posting via the Publisher

New-style Groups have the newer looking version of the Publisher (also called the Share Menu in Facebook documentation) at the top of the page. Just click the button for the type of content you'd like to share, and the appropriate controls will appear.

Posting via E-mail

If you're a member of a new-style Group with an e-mail address assigned to it, you'll see the address up at the top of the Group's page. You can send e-mail messages to that address from the e-mail address that's associated with your Facebook account, and they'll appear as postings on the Group's page. Members will be notified of your posting (subject to their personal notification settings) just like postings made using the Publisher.

How to Create a New-Style Group

Prior to creating a group, you might want to prep the materials you'll need ahead of time. You'll want to:

- Choose a photo or graphic to use on the Group's page.
- Write a brief description of the Group: its nature, purpose, and mission. Keep this to a short summary—just a couple of sentences.
- Decide whether the Group will be open, closed, or secret.

As mentioned earlier, you have three choices for the Group's level of privacy:

- **Open** means that the members and all Group content will be visible to the public, even people who aren't members.
- **Closed** means that members are visible to the public, but the Group's content is visible only to members.
- **Secret** means nobody but members can see the Group, its members, or its content.

When you're ready to create your Group, you can get started by clicking the Create Group bookmark in the left-hand column of Facebook's Home page. The Create a Group dialog will open.

You can type the name you've chosen for your Group in the Group Name field, and enter the names of friends you want to add in the Members field. Down at the bottom, you can choose the level of privacy for the Group.

Also, if you click the Group Icon button at the left side of the Group Name field, you'll open a menu of little icons you can choose in place of the standard Group icon. (This icon will appear next to the bookmark for the Group in Facebook's left-hand column, among other places.)

Click the Create Group button in the left-hand column of the Home page to start the process of creating a new-style Group.

WARNING: Facebook explicitly forbids the creation of Groups that "attack a specific person or group of people (e.g., racist, sexist, or other hate groups)," and says that "creating such a group will result in the immediate termination of your Facebook account."

NOTE: Don't forget that because this is a new-style Group you're creating, any friends whose names you enter in the Members field will be added to the Group immediately. They won't be sent an invitation asking them to accept— they'll get a notification telling them you've added them to the Group.

An example of a couple of bookmarks for Groups in the left-hand column, showing the icons chosen by the Groups' creators next to the names of the Groups

Once you click the Create button, you'll see a confirmation that the friends you chose have been added, and once you click Okay, you'll arrive at the page for your brand-new Group.

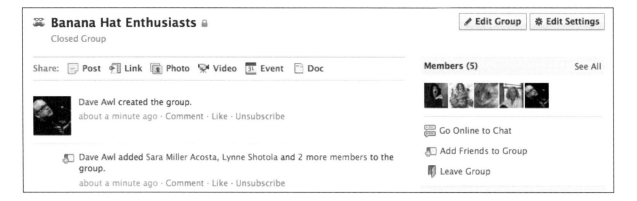

Adding a Picture, Description, and E-mail Address

The first thing you should do is spruce up your Group a little: add a photo and description so that when the members you've added arrive they can see what the Group's all about. So your next step is to click the Edit Group button at the top of the page, which takes you to the Edit Group page.

Type or paste your description in the Description field and add a picture by clicking the "Add a profile picture" link in the upper-left corner. (This works the same way as adding a photo to your personal profile—you can choose to upload a picture or take one using a connected camera.)

Finally, from this page you can choose an e-mail address for your Group by clicking the Set Up Group Email button. The Create Group Email dialog will open, with a field where you can enter your desired address, in the form *[name]@groups.facebook.com*. (It's probably best to just use the name of your Group itself, with no spaces or punctuation, as the first part of the address.)

WARNING: Your Group's e-mail address is one thing you can't change after you've set it up—so think carefully about what you want it to be, and for heaven's sake proofread it three times for typos before you finalize it.

Managing New-Style Groups

First off, the Group's creator and anyone who's been given admin privileges can click the Edit Group button on the Group's page to update its name, description, profile picture, and so forth at any time. You can even change the privacy level if you want (in which case all members of the Group will receive a notification that the privacy level has changed). The one thing you can't change, as noted in the warning at right, is the e-mail address.

TIP: As creator or admin of a Group, you have the responsibility of keeping an eye on your Group to make sure it grows and thrives. Think of your role as similar to that of the host at a party: You want to make sure new arrivals feel welcome, help keep the conversation flowing, and serve as a buffer if arguments break out.

Promoting Members to Admin

Every Group starts out with one admin: the person who created it. But it's helpful to have more than one person to keep an eye on things, especially if it's a popular Group or one that's topical enough to provoke debate. You can add new admins to your Group by clicking Members in the left-hand column of the Edit Group page, and then clicking the Make Admin link next to the name of the person you want to promote on the Members page. You can remove an admin by clicking the Remove Admin link next to their name.

TIP: Anyone you promote to admin will be allowed to edit the Group's info, remove or ban members, and add and remove other admins for the Group. But note that seniority applies: You can only remove an admin who was appointed more recently than you were.

Removing or Banning Members

If you find yourself charged with the unpleasant task of removing or banning a member, you can do so by clicking the X link following their name on the Members page. A pop-up menu will appear that lets you choose whether you want to remove the member or ban them permanently. Removed members can request to join the Group again in the future, but banned members won't even be able to see the Group's page or find it in search (banning is the equivalent of blocking). Admins can reverse the banning process, however, by clicking the appropriate link next to the banned person's name in the list of Members.

Joining an Old-Style Group

Becoming a member of an old-style Facebook Group is as easy as clicking a button or a link. The main difference from new-style Groups is that you have to do that clicking yourself: No one else can add you to an old-style Group.

Generally, you'll be doing the clicking in one of two places: the Requests page, because you've been invited to join a Group; or the home page for a Group you've found on your own. If you get an invitation, you can click Confirm to join the Group or click Ignore to make the invitation go away without joining.

If you find your way to a Group you haven't been invited to, just look for the Join button. (If the button says "Request to Join," that means it's a closed Group, and one of the Group's admins has to approve new members before they can join.)

Leaving an Old-Style Group

If you join an old-style Group and then decide later on that you need to make an exit, don't worry: It's easy to check out. Just click the Leave Group link on the Group's home page (currently located at the bottom of the left-hand column). Nobody is notified when you leave a Group, and no News Feed story is generated, so you don't have to worry about offending the other members (unless and until Facebook adds a Leave in a Huff option).

Communicating in Old-Style Groups

Most old-style Groups have two main ways for members to communicate with each other: the Wall and the discussion board. The Wall for an old-style Group is similar to the Wall on an individual profile: Members can post comments, and (depending on how the Group's settings have been configured by its creator or admins) possibly other content such as links, photos, and videos too. For slightly more organized conversations, the discussion board organizes comments by topic. Group members can create new topics, kicking off the conversation with a question or provocative comment, to which other members can respond.

NOTE: The discussion board is an optional feature, so some Groups you join may not have one. Groups can also be set so that only admins are allowed to post to the Wall. If both of those options apply to a Group you belong to, and you're not an admin, then the only way to communicate with your fellow members is by sending them Inbox messages.

Within the discussion board, you can use the pop-up menu to filter the list for topics you've created, or topics created by your friends. Clicking Start New Topic opens a simple form that asks you to name the topic and then kick it off with an initial post.

TIP: By default, Facebook sends you a notification whenever someone replies to a post you make on a discussion board, so you can keep up with the conversation without having to obsessively check the board every ten minutes.

Managing Old-Style Groups

If you're the creator of an old-style Group, or you have admin privileges, you can easily update or change the basic info for the Group. On the Group's home page, click the Info tab and the Edit Information link, and then make changes as desired. To edit settings such as members' posting privileges and whether the Group is open, closed, or secret, click the Edit Group Settings link on the home page for the Group.

Message All Members
Promote Group with an Ad
Edit Group Settings
Edit Members
Invite People to Join
Create Group Event

The links on the Home page for a Group as they appear to an admin. These links aren't visible to ordinary members, with the exception of Invite People to Join.

TIP: The quickest and easiest way to access the Groups for which you're an admin is to simply type the name of whichever Group you want to visit into Facebook's search field.

Admins
▪ Elizabeth Hoffman
▪ Dave Awl (creator)

Officers
Elizabeth Hoffman Banana Hat Provocateur
Dave Awl Banana Hat Fanatic [remove]
Sara Miller Acosta Banana Hat Savant
Richard Cooper Theoretical Wearer of Said Hat

The Admins for a Group are listed in the left-hand column, with the Group's creator identified in parentheses. Below that, any Officers are listed. If you're an Officer, you can resign your post at any time using the "remove" link next to your name.

NOTE: As with new-style Groups, admins for old-style Groups do have the power to remove other admins, but seniority applies— you can only remove an admin who was appointed more recently than you were.

Promoting Members to Admin

You can promote Group members to admin status by clicking the Edit Members link and then clicking Make Admin next to the name of the person you want to promote. Admins gain the ability to edit the Group's info and settings, promote or remove members, create officers, delete Wall posts, delete discussion board topics and posts, and create Group Events.

Removing Members from the Group

To remove a member, click the Edit Members link and then click the X (Remove) link next to the name of the person you want to eject (shown to the right of the Make Admin button in the image above).

Adding Officers

Officers for old-style Groups are purely ceremonial figureheads—the position doesn't come with any special duties or privileges. But people you designate as officers for the Group are displayed in a list on the Group's page—and listing these prominent members can give the Group credibility, or help convey a sense of who its movers and shakers are. If your Group has formal officers such as a president, vice president, treasurer, and so forth, this is the place to list them. On the other hand, if you want to anoint key members with whimsical titles drawn from the works of Dr. Seuss, feel free.

To add or edit officers, click the Edit Group Settings link on the Group's Home page and then click the Officers link at the top. Click the Make Officer link next to the name of each person you'd like to designate. Enter a title in the Make Officer dialog that appears and click the Make Officer button to confirm. Your updated Officers list will appear on the Group's main page. You can return to the Edit Officers page anytime to add or remove officers.

Make Officer?
Please enter a position for Elizabeth Hoffman:
Make Officer?   Cancel

Sending a Message to Your Group

You can use the Message All Members link on the page for your Group to send an Inbox message to everyone in the Group's member list. (However, this option is limited to Groups that have fewer than 5,000 members.) The Message All Members link is visible only to admins.

Moderating Posts and Discussions

As admin, you have special powers you can use for good—to help keep your Group's discussions on-topic and spam-free, and to squelch flame wars and other unpleasant distractions. You can delete any inappropriate Wall comment by clicking the Remove button for that post. For discussion boards, you have the option to mark posts as irrelevant in addition to deleting them. Marking a post as irrelevant hides the post but doesn't remove it: Members can still view a hidden post by clicking the Show Post link next to it. (An admin can restore a post marked as irrelevant to full visibility by clicking the "Undo Irrelevance" link that appears next to it.)

Creating Group Events

Clicking the Create Group Event link on the Home page for an old-style Group lets you set up a calendar item that's linked to your Group. The name of your Group will appear as the host of the Event, and the Event itself will appear in the Events box (and under the Events tab, if it's enabled) on the Group's page. See the *Facebook Calendar* chapter for more info on creating Events.

 Moderating in Moderation
If you're used to moderating groups on other services, such as Yahoo Groups or Google Groups, you'll find that the moderation options for Facebook Groups are somewhat limited in comparison.

Although you can delete individual postings, or hide them on a discussion board (using the "Mark as Irrelevant" feature), there's no way to set a Facebook Group so that all posts must be approved by a moderator before they appear, and you can't assign different levels of posting privileges to different members of the Group. That means moderation of Facebook Groups is an after-the-fact activity, and you may need to keep a fairly close eye on your Group's Wall and discussion board if you want to keep the conversation on-topic and in bounds.

Everything's a trade-off, of course. Despite the limited moderation controls, creating Groups on Facebook pays off by allowing you to take advantage of Facebook's News Feed to draw attention to your Group and help it grow.

---

3 hours ago · Mark as Irrelevant · Report · Delete Post

The links that are available to admins underneath each post on a discussion board

---

Post Marked as Irrelevant
9 hours ago · Show Post

The Show Post link allows you to see for yourself what's so darned irrelevant about it.

The Facebook Calendar

Call it "the social butterfly effect": Social networking sites have triggered a pleasant metamorphosis in the process of organizing social events. In the old days—not so long ago—keeping track of the invitations and RSVPs for a large gathering could be a real headache for the host. And as a guest, you often had no idea whether there'd be lots of groovy people you knew at a particular event, or whether the high point of your evening would be something wrapped in phyllo dough you snagged from a passing hors d'oeuvres tray.

But over the last several years, sites like Evite have made it easy for hosts to manage guest lists online and for attendees to see who else is planning to show up. Facebook ups the ante even further by connecting Events to its News Feed, making it easy to spread the word and assemble a crowd for public events like performances, benefits, grand openings, or club nights—as well as more intimate gatherings.

All of which means that one social butterfly flapping its wings—or rather, clicking its mouse—can cause a fabulous party to erupt just a few days later. And you can find out about it just by clicking your own mouse on Facebook's Events app.

In this chapter, I'll show you how to use Facebook's Events application to find upcoming Events in your social network, as well as how to create and promote your own. We'll also look at how Facebook helps you keep track of your friends' birthdays, and some of the fun ways you can use Facebook to send birthday greetings. And while we're on the subject of calendars, I'll cover a few third-party calendar apps you can choose to install.

The Events Application

When in the course of Facebook events it becomes necessary to invite your friends to a swell soirée, let your fans know about your band's next gig, or drum up a crowd for any other kind of get-together—well, that's when the Events app comes in mighty handy. The Events app (which is one of Facebook's basic applications) also serves as a resource for finding out about fun things to do when you're planning your own social itinerary—it's a little like a hip friend who knows where all the best parties, concerts, gallery openings, and poetry readings are. All you have to do is ask it.

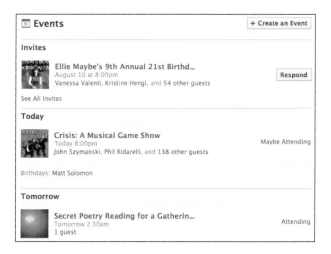

The Events bookmark in the left-hand column of the Home page, with the three subordinate bookmarks that appear underneath when you select it. The number in parentheses is the number of outstanding invitations you have. Yes, I'm a little behind on those, too.

The Events bookmark in the left-hand column on Facebook's Home page gives you quick access to the main page for the Events app, which shows you an overview of upcoming Facebook Events you've been invited to and friends' birthdays. When you click the Events bookmark, three other bookmarks appear underneath it. Friends' Events shows you Events your friends are planning to attend, so that you can scope out what's on their social radar. Past Events is an archive of Events you were invited to that have already taken place. (This comes in handy for remembering what you did last weekend—especially if you had such a good time that it's all a blur.) The Birthdays bookmark shows you all of your Facebook friends who have birthdays coming up in the near future. (More about that toward the end of this chapter.)

TIP: You can also access the Events app by clicking "See All" in the Events area on the Home page.

TIP: After an Event is over, it doesn't disappear in a puff of smoke—you can visit its page the next day, or even weeks later, to post photos and videos from the event itself and talk about what a hoot it was with the other attendees. The Past Events bookmark is one easy way to get there.

Profile of an Event

Each Event that's created on Facebook gets its own page with its own Wall, where the host and guests can post messages as well as photos, videos, and links related to the Event.

Along the left side of the Event page, you can see the people who have RSVP'd "Yes" to this Event, so you know who's currently planning on showing up, as well as the other invitees—those who said "Maybe," those who haven't replied yet, and those who have declined, if any.

TIP: At the top of an Event page, you can see your current RSVP status, who invited you (if anyone), and whether the Event is public or private.

Responding to Event Invitations

Invitations to Events are flagged out in the Events area on the Home page, and appear on the main page of the Events app. Click the Respond button, and then choose Attending to tell the host you'll be there with bells on; or Maybe Attending if you'd like to go but you're not so sure about the bells just yet. Click Not Attending to tender your regrets.

If you want to include a message with your RSVP, type it in the optional field; it will appear as a posting on the Event's Wall. If you want to find out more about the Event before you RSVP, just click on the name of the Event to go check out its page.

NOTE: If you're viewing an Event invitation on the Requests page, the buttons you click to RSVP say Yes, Maybe, and No instead of Attending, Maybe Attending, and Not Attending. Tomayto, tomahto.

Once you respond, you'll show up in the appropriate category of guests on the page for the Event. The Event itself can be accessed via the Events application or by searching, and you should see a reminder in the Events area of your Home page when the Event is a few days away.

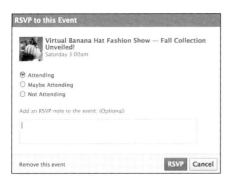

The RSVP dialog that opens when you click the Respond button

> **TIP:** You can also RSVP directly from the Event page itself—which is especially handy if you found an Event through a listing in the Events app rather than an invitation on your Requests page. Just click the appropriate button at the top of the Page for the Event.

> **NOTE:** If you're not interested in an Event and you don't want any reminders about it, you can remove it from your Facebook calendar entirely. Just click the "Remove this event" link at the bottom of the RSVP dialog, or the bottom of the page for the Event.

Keeping Track of Events

As mentioned earlier, you can always check the Events application to see what's going on in the near future. But in case you're not that proactive, don't worry—Facebook has you covered.

The Events Area

For starters, as long as you check in on your Home page on a regular basis, you'll see reminders for your upcoming Events appear in the Events area in the right-hand column. Events show up in this area up to three days before they take place and then disappear the following day. (If you're really booked up, you may need to click the See More link to display the whole list.)

Events that appear on your Home page include: (1) any Event you've confirmed your attendance for, and (2) any Event you've been invited to but haven't responded "No" to or removed from your Events.

Exporting Events

You can also export your Facebook Events as an ICS (iCalendar) file, which can be imported into many calendar applications such as Microsoft Outlook, Apple iCal, Google Calendar, and more.

To export all your Events, go to the Events app and click the Export Events link at the bottom of the page. To export any specific Event, go to its page and click the Export link at the bottom of the page.

When you Export a single event, a dialog will open that gives you the choice of either downloading the file directly or having it e-mailed to you.

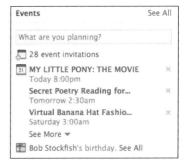

The Events area of the Home page. Clicking the See All link takes you into the Events application—so it's really just a shortcut to the app.

TIP: Before you start creating your Event, you might want to prep a few items ahead of time, so that you have them handy as you're working:

1. A photo or graphic for your Event page.
2. The basic facts: time, date, and address.
3. A short description of the Event that will appear in the More Info area of the page.

Creating an Event

Ready to create a Facebook Event? Go to the Events app and click the Create an Event button at the top of the page. You'll arrive at the Create an Event page, where you enter the basic data about your Event.

Creating Events on the Fly

You don't necessarily have to go into the Events app itself in order to create a new Event. If you're in a hurry to get the word out, you can create an Event by clicking the Event button on the Publisher, or by clicking in the "What are you planning?" field in the Events area of the Home page.

Public or Private?

Events come in two types: public or private.

Public Events allow anyone to add themselves to the guest list, whether or not they've been invited, and send invitations to their friends. Anyone can see its info and content, as well as News Feed stories about the Event.

Private Events require an invitation in order to RSVP, and only admins can send invitations. Events that are private can't be found by searching, and none of the Event's info, content, or News Feed stories will be visible to people who haven't been invited.

Start by specifying when your Event takes place. In the "When?" area, use the controls to choose the date and start time for the Event. If you want to specify an end time as well, so your guests know when to clear out, click the "Add end time" link to display the relevant controls.

In the "What are you planning?" field, type the name for your Event—make it snappy and succinct. (You don't need to include the date or the place in the name itself, because you've already entered that info above.)

Now it's time to add a location in the "Where?" area. Enter the name of the location in the field provided, and if you'd like to add precise coordinates, click the "Add street address" link to display additional fields for that info.

Type the Event's description in the "More info?" field—this information will be displayed on your Event's Wall. (You probably want to be generous here: this is your main sales pitch to persuade your invitees that their lives will be empty if they don't attend your festivities.) To add an image for your Event, in the upper-left corner, click the Add Event Photo button. A dialog will open that lets you browse for a photo or graphic on your hard drive.

If you'd like to invite your first guests immediately, you can click the Select Guests button. A dialog will open that lets you select friends by clicking on their photos, and also invite friends who aren't on Facebook by entering their e-mail addresses. You can also hold off on this step if you prefer, and invite guests later in the process.

The Select Guests dialog. Note that you can use the Filter Friends menu to choose a Friend List you've previously created, and zero in on people from that list. So, for example, if you're throwing a party for people you work with, you could choose your Co-Workers list. You can also choose from past events, and invite the same people who attended your previous shindig. This is an especially convenient trick for recurring events such as a weekly book group, a monthly club night, or an annual holiday party.

TIP: If you'd like to display contact info such as a phone number or e-mail address on the Event page, you can include that in the More Info field. But don't feel obligated to disclose that information if you don't want to. This is Facebook, after all, so anyone who wants to get in touch with you can send you an Inbox message (unless you've changed your privacy settings to disallow that—in which case they can still post a message for you on the Event's Wall).

Click the Add a Personal Message link at the bottom of the Select Guests dialog to type a short greeting to the people you're inviting. Click Save and Close to send your invitations and return to the Create an Event page.

Then set the options below. Select or deselect the checkbox that says "Anyone can view and RSVP (public event)" to specify whether the Event should be public or private. (This option is selected by default, so if you want the Event to be private, don't forget to deselect it before you move on from this page!)

Next, decide whether you want the list of people you've invited to be displayed on the Event's page or not, and select or deselect the checkbox next to "Show the guest list on the event page."

Once you've set all those options, click Create Event to proceed.

Creating Related Events

If the Event you're creating will be hosted by a person or organization who has a Page on Facebook, you can create it as a Related Event (assuming you have admin privileges for the Page). This means that the Event will show up in the Events area of the Page that it's related to, and the Page will be listed as the creator of the Event on its page.

The easiest way to create a Related Event for a Page is to go to its Events tab and click the Create Event button. (If you've never created an Event from your Page before, you may need to first add the Events tab by clicking on the plus sign menu to the right of the other tabs and then choosing Events.)

Note that there's no way to go back and add a Page as host for an Event after you've already created it—so if it's important, don't overlook this step when you're creating the Event.

Also note that if the Event is related to a Page, it can't be set to private; all content related to Pages is public.

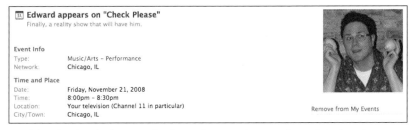

Don't be afraid to think creatively about what constitutes an "event"—it doesn't necessarily have to involve people getting together in the same location, for example. My friend Edward created a Facebook Event to let friends know about his appearance on Check, Please!, *a TV show on which customers review local restaurants.*

💬 **Party Out of Bounds**

"Who's to blame when parties really get out of hand?" the B-52's wondered back at the dawn of the '80s. In recent years there have been a number of news stories blaming Facebook for that phenomenon—such as the horror story in the UK press about a family whose home was trampled by 300 gatecrashers who turned up at their daughter's 16th birthday party. According to news accounts, the birthday girl had originally sent the invite to 100 friends on Facebook.

Of course, Facebook isn't the only medium used to spread the word about parties online—MySpace, e-mail, mobile phones, and instant messaging play a role, too. Still, in the age of rapid-messaging technology, before you advertise any event online you should ask yourself how you'll handle things if the crowd that turns out is bigger than expected.

If you choose to promote your event in public, make sure the venue can accommodate the number of people you're inviting and their guests. Set contingency plans in place in case the crowd exceeds expectations—make sure you have people you can trust to cover the door if necessary, and turn away guests who can't be accommodated once the venue is at capacity.

And as those news stories underscore, you should be *very* cautious about publicly promoting parties on Facebook that take place in someone's home. Consider setting the Event as private, and avoid posting your home address in the invitation itself. Remember that you can always send that info to the invited guests separately, as an Inbox message.

Promoting Your Event on Facebook

If the Event you've just created is open to the public and you're hoping for a large turnout, there are a number of ways to promote it on Facebook. Of course, the first and most important step is to send out invitations—not only to let the people you're inviting know about the Event, but also because each time one of them accepts your invitation, a News Feed story may be generated that tells their friends about the Event, thus expanding your audience.

And ultimately, that's the key to promoting your Event on Facebook—getting its name to appear in Facebook's News Feed as often as possible (without overdoing it in a way that annoys your friends).

Here are some other good strategies:

- When you create your Event, make sure the name is snappy and engaging. The name may be all your invitees will see in the invitation itself, so you want it to get their attention and convey the Event's appeal. Try to inject a little humor if possible.

- When you send out your invitations, I highly recommend using the Personal Message field to include a short greeting. This will help you grab your invitees' attention and increase the odds that they'll respond (or at least check out the Event's page).

- Mention the Event in a status update.

- Write a Note about the Event.

- Post the Event to your profile using the Share button on the page for the Event. Remember that when you post something to your profile, the story also appears in your friends' News Feeds. If there's a long lead time of several weeks, you can probably even get away with doing this once a week or so without seeming too pushy.

- Post photos, videos, and links on your Event's page, and start a conversation on the Wall for your Event. News Feed stories get generated each time people comment on your Event's photos, videos, and posted links, as well as when they post on your Event's Wall—and each of those stories will contain the name of your Event and a link to its page. When someone else comments on something that's part of your Event's page, make it a point to answer or thank them with a comment of your own—thus keeping the conversation going.

You'll be most effective if you space these actions out in time, so that they don't seem like overkill—or desperation.

Finally, if you decide you'd like to advertise your Event on Facebook, it's easy to do. Just click the Advertising link at the bottom of any page on Facebook to start the process. See the *Advertising and Promoting on Facebook* chapter for more info about Facebook Ads.

Managing an Event

Once your Event has been created, you can manage its guest list and various options from the Event page itself. By clicking the Edit Event link at the top of the Event page, you can cancel the Event if necessary, invite more guests, and change the Event's info, settings, and image.

By clicking the Message Guests link, you can send an Inbox message to all of the guests. (If the Event is hosted by a Page, instead of a message you can send an update to the Page's fans. See the *Pages* chapter for more information about updates.)

Clicking the See All link next to the guest list on the Event's page allows you to manage your guests. If you'd like some help with your hosting duties, you can add admins to an Event by clicking Make Admin next to the name of the person you'd like to promote. You can also remove or block guests in the same dialog, if necessary.

The admin links on the page for an Event. Visitors who aren't admins won't see these.

" " Pace Yourself
Is there a limit to how many invitations you can send out at one time? Why, yes, there is. Although technically you're allowed to invite an unlimited number of people to a Facebook Event, you can only invite them in batches of 100 at a time, and you can only have 300 pending invitations at a time. Once you hit 300, you'll have to wait for some people to RSVP before you can send out more invitations.

Birthdays on Facebook: The Year-Round Birthday Party

NOTE: Facebook does allow you to change the name of an Event if you need to. If you change it after guests have already confirmed, Facebook will send your guests an automatic notification of the name change.

If you ask me (and since you're reading this book, I suppose you did), one of the most fun aspects of life on Facebook is that it's almost always someone's birthday. After all, it's always satisfying to let your friends know how much they mean to you when their birthdays roll around, and Facebook gives you a number of easy ways to do that.

But let's face it: The older you get and the more friends you acquire, the harder it gets to keep all those dates rattling around in your cranium. Fortunately, with Facebook on your side, you no longer have to—all you have to do is keep an eye on the Events area of your Home page, and Facebook will tip you off when your friends are celebrating another lap around the sun.

TIP: If you're really into birthdays and don't always check the Events area of your Home page, you can also choose to get reminders from Facebook via e-mail when one of your friends has a birthday on the horizon. Go to Account > Account Settings > Notifications to edit your e-mail notifications. Under the first category, Facebook, select the "Has a birthday coming up" checkbox.

Something from the YouTube Gift Shop?

If you want to post a greeting that's a little more animated than just writing "Happy birthday" on your friend's Wall, searching up a YouTube video to post in their honor makes for a fun Facebook-style gift.

Start by identifying someone or something you know your friend is a fan of: a band, a TV show, a comedian, a cartoon character. (Scanning the Info tab on their profile might give you a clue if you're drawing a blank.) Then go to YouTube and type the relevant name in the search field, along with the word *birthday*. Very often you'll turn up something fun and surprising. You can then use the Link button in the Publisher on your friend's profile to post the video to their Wall.

For example, my friend Herman is a devoted Smiths fan. So for his birthday I typed *Morrissey* and *birthday* into YouTube's search field and found a live video of the crowd singing "Happy Birthday" to Morrissey at one of his concerts. Typing *birthday* and *Doctor Who* into the search field turned up a fan-made video of a Dalek singing "Happy Birthday," which was perfect for my friend Steve, a fellow Whovian. (He didn't even mind being threatened with extermination before the toy Dalek self-destructed ...)

When your own birthday arrives, you can expect your Wall to fill up with greetings from your friends—even the ones who don't normally remember your birthday—thanks to the fact that Facebook has tipped them off. And the rest of the year, you get to be the one who remembers all of your friends' special days. Of course, not everyone chooses to make their birthday public on Facebook, so most likely you'll have some friends who won't show up in Facebook's birthday notifications. But for those who do, here are a few fun ways to give them a shout-out:

1. Write a message on their Wall. This is the simplest and most direct option. Creativity is always appreciated—as are heartfelt declarations of admiration and affection—but on the other hand, if you can't think of anything clever, there's nothing wrong with a simple "Happy Birthday."

2. Use SuperPoke to "throw a birthday cake at" your friend. (See the *Communicating on Facebook* chapter for more about SuperPoke.) Other apps have birthday features you can take advantage of as well, such as the ones mentioned below.

3. Post a video. Dedicate a song or a find a video you know will make your friend laugh. (See the sidebar "Something from the YouTube Gift Shop?")

Other Calendar Applications

In addition to the Events app, there are several third-party applications that can help you with calendar and scheduling functions. Here are three of the most popular (all of which you can find in the Applications Directory or by searching):

- **Birthday Calendar**, as you might guess from the name, is focused on birthdays. Inside the app you can view all of your Facebook friends' birthdays laid out in a printable calendar-page format, month by month for the coming year. A selection of electronic greeting cards and gifts is built right into the app.

- **Hallmark SocialCalendar** also creates a graphic calendar display, and in addition to birthdays it lets you track anniversaries, get-togethers, and other social occasions. An activity feed lets you keep an eye on what events your friends are adding to their own calendars.

- **Weekly Schedule** lets you create a graphic schedule of your activities, so your friends can see at a glance when you might be free to get together. My pal Shaina says this is one of the best apps on Facebook for college students who are trying to keep track of each other's complicated class and work schedules.

Pages

Welcome to the chapter on Pages—and please notice the capital *P*. There are thousands of pages on Facebook, but only some of them are Pages.

As I've mentioned a few times in earlier chapters, a Facebook Page is a special kind of profile that allows public figures, organizations, and businesses to communicate easily with throngs of fans, supporters, or customers. Pages (which Facebook also refers to as *public profiles*) offer valuable demographic information and traffic statistics to let Page administrators (*admins* for short) know what kinds of visitors have been checking out their Pages and what those visitors are interested in.

There are other advantages to Pages, too, which we'll address in the course of this chapter. First we'll look at how you can find Pages for people and organizations you admire and follow their postings in your News Feed. Then I'll take you through the process of creating, managing, and promoting Pages of your own.

The key point to keep in mind as you read this chapter is that a well-run Page is the cornerstone of any successful Facebook promotional strategy. So we'll be building on the basics covered here when we get to the next chapter, *Advertising and Promoting on Facebook*.

Pages vs. Groups and Profiles
Pages are one of the most useful tools on Facebook—but not everyone understands what they're for or how to create them. Often, people who want to set up a presence for a band, a comedy group, or even a bookstore create a personal profile (or in some cases a Group) when what would really serve their needs best is a Page.

One reason for this confusion is that people who are more familiar with MySpace expect Facebook to work similarly. On MySpace, people create profiles to represent all kinds of entities, and fans create MySpace profiles in honor of bands or other public figures they're not personally affiliated with. But as mentioned in earlier chapters, on Facebook the rules are different. Profiles represent individual people, whereas organizations are best represented by Pages (or in some cases, Groups). And nobody is allowed to create a profile for a person other than themselves, or a Page for an entity they don't officially represent.

As discussed in the *Group Dynamics* chapter, however, there are a few circumstances where Groups may suit your needs better than Pages: for example, if you're looking to create a gathering place for fans of a public figure, but you aren't an authorized representative of that public figure. (See the sidebar "Fake Pages: Swim at Your Own Risk.")

Pages vs. "Fan Pages"
These days, lots of people refer to Facebook Pages as "fan pages." But that term is technically inaccurate and possibly misleading, because it sounds too much like it means "pages created by fans." Whereas Facebook Pages are intended to be exactly the opposite—they're supposed to be official pages created by authorized representatives of a public figure or organization, in order to communicate *with* fans.

Facebook Pages 101

On the surface, Facebook Pages look a lot like the pages for personal profiles. There's a place for an identifying image or graphic up top; tabs for the Wall, Info, Photos, and optional apps; the Publisher at the top of the Wall; and various boxes in the left-hand column. The Page's fans can interact with each other using the Wall (and the discussion board if it's enabled).

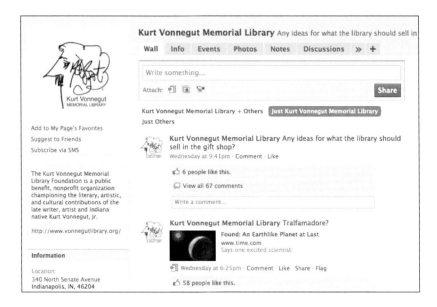

But Pages offer a number of special advantages for the people who maintain them:

- With Pages, you can communicate directly with your Page's fans via the News Feed. The status updates, Links, Notes, photos, and videos you post on your Page's Wall can appear on in the News Feed just like postings from friends.

- Admins for Pages don't have to approve friend requests. When people choose to become a fan of your Page, they're automatically approved—which can be a real time-saver if your Page attracts hundreds or even thousands of fans.

- Admins have access to statistics on the traffic and activity for their Page.

Becoming a Fan: Finding and Liking Facebook Pages

If you keep an eye on the News Feed and your friends' profiles, you'll see stories about Pages popping up regularly—telling you that a certain friend "likes" a band, film, TV show, local restaurant, charity organization, or what have you.

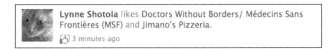

Lynne Shotola likes Doctors Without Borders/ Médecins Sans Frontières (MSF) and Jimano's Pizzeria.
⟁ 3 minutes ago

You can click on the name of the Page in the story to go check it out, and become a fan (or "liker") of the Page yourself if you choose. But you don't necessarily have to wait around for a News Feed story to tip you off. If you're wondering whether there's a Facebook Page for someone or something you admire, you can search for it using the blue bar's search field.

Once you find your way to a Page you'd like to become a fan of, all you have to do is click the Like button at the top of the Page.

Becoming a fan of a Page does four things: First, it generates a News Feed story, as mentioned above. Second, it adds the Page to the Likes box on your profile (and the appropriate area(s) of your Info tab). Third, it adds you to the People [Who] Like This box on the Page itself, which displays the Page's fans.

And fourth, it means you can see postings from the Page in your News Feed, and receive Updates from the Page in your Inbox. (See the "Following Pages" section.)

🔍 **TIP:** Breaking up with a Page is easy. If you decide you no longer want to be a fan or supporter, just go to the Page and click the Unlike link down at the bottom of the left-hand column.

✏ **NOTE:** Not so many moons ago, the Like button at the top of Pages used to say "Become a Fan," and the People [Who] Like This box was the Fans box. Although Facebook has renamed these elements, the word "fans" is still the most convenient way to refer to the people who choose to connect with a given Page—so I'm sticking with it, gosh darn it.

✏ **NOTE:** When you become a fan of a Page, the creator and admins for the Page don't gain access to your e-mail or other contact info—so your privacy isn't compromised.

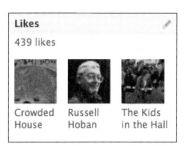

The Likes box on a personal profile

The People [Who] Like This box on a Page

✏ **NOTE:** Two years ago, when I wrote the first edition of this book, Facebook limited the number of pages you could become a fan of to 500. In the time since, however, that limit has either been eliminated or raised dramatically: I have one friend who currently has more than 2,600 Pages listed in his Likes box. The majority of people I know, however, have less than a few hundred Likes. So go ahead, Like away—you probably aren't in danger of hitting the limit anytime soon.

Following Pages

TIP: Individual Pages can be hidden from and restored to your News Feed, just like individual friends. (See the *Sharing Content on Facebook* chapter for all the skinny on how you can control what you see in your News Feed.)

Once you've become a fan of a Page, you'll be able to see content posted by the Page in your News Feed—just like the content you see from your Friends.

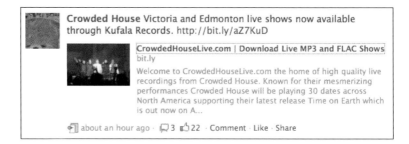

If the Page is for a band, you may see postings about upcoming concerts or music releases. Pages for TV shows might post about the new season or DVD releases, while politicians' Pages are likely to focus on campaigns, political issues, or fundraising. You get the idea.

Additionally, when you Like a Page you'll be subscribed to the Page's Updates, which are messages sent by the creator of the Page or its other admins. Updates appear in the special Updates area of your Inbox. To access them, go to your Inbox and then click the Updates filter. You'll see all your recent Updates in chronological order. If you'd like to stop receiving updates from a Page you're subscribed to—without removing yourself from its fans—you can click the Unsubscribe button at the top of any Update from that Page.

To view your Updates, click the Messages bookmark in the left-hand column on the Home page. Then click the Updates bookmark that appears just below the Messages bookmark.

Updates, Schmupdates
Although plenty of Pages do still send them out, Updates are really a holdover from the time before Pages had the ability to communicate directly to the Home pages of their fans. I'll be honest—these days, I never remember to check the Updates area of my Inbox, because I get information from the Pages I follow right in my News Feed.

Creating a Page

The easiest way to begin the process of building your brand-new Page on Facebook is to navigate to any existing Facebook Page, and then click the Create a Page link at the bottom of the left-hand column. (In some cases the link may say "Create a Page for My Business," but it takes you to the same place.) Once you click the link, you'll arrive at the Create a Page page, which presents you with a form (shown on the next page) to start the process.

Step 1: Decide Whether You Want to Create an Official Page or a Community Page

If the Page you're planning to create is intended to be the official Facebook presence for a public figure, organization, or other specific entity, you can go ahead and use the Official Page form on the right-hand side of the page.

Fake Pages: Swim at Your Own Risk

In theory, Facebook forbids the creation of Pages by anyone who isn't an authorized representative of the entity that the Page represents. Facebook is about real identities, after all, so the policy for Pages is consistent with the policy for personal profiles: no impersonations, aliases, or pseudonyms allowed.

In practice, however, Facebook's directory is crowded with Pages that were created by fans eager to have a place on Facebook for their favorite writer, musician, or artist. Complicating matters, it isn't always easy to tell an authentic Page from a fake one—although one dead giveaway (pun intended) is if the Page is for a long-departed writer like Shakespeare or Emily Dickinson. (Well, that's assuming the writer in question hasn't been authorizing the Page and dictating updates via Ouija board.)

In fact, part of the reason Facebook created Community Pages was to address this problem—so that fans can express their affection for public figures and other entities that don't have official Pages on Facebook.

If you choose to create an unauthorized Page, or become a fan of one, be aware that Facebook may choose to invoke the rules and deactivate the Page (and the accounts of its creators) without warning, at any time—especially if Facebook has any reason to believe that the admins for the Page are using it to deliberately impersonate someone else.

Your best option, if you want to express your love for a public figure or organization who doesn't have a Page yet, is to create a Group where you and your fellow fans can geek out together in a nondeceptive, peer-to-peer kind of way.

Official Page

Communicate with your customers and fans by creating and maintaining an official Facebook Page.

Please note that you will not be able to edit the name of a Page after it has been created.

Create a Page for a:

○ Local business

○ Brand, product, or organization

○ Artist, band, or public figure

Page name: [_____]

(examples: Summer Sky Cafe, Springfield Jazz Trio)

☐ I'm the official representative of this person, business, band or product and have permission to create this Page.
Review the Facebook Terms

[**Create Official Page**]

TIP: Before you start creating your Page, you might want to prepare a few items ahead of time, so that you have them handy:

1. The name for your Page.
2. A primary photo or graphic to illustrate your Page.
3. Info: Look at other Pages in the same category as the one you'll be setting up to see what kind of information you'll need.
4. Content: You might want to prepare some initial Wall postings—status updates, Link posts, pictures, or video clips—to post on your Page. If the Page is for a band, you might want to prepare some songs to upload to the Music Player, and information on releases for the Discography app.

But Facebook's position is that you should create a create a Community Page instead (using the simple one-step form on the left-hand side) if the Page you want to set up will represent a generic topic, activity, or interest (like, say, "Existentialism" or "Sleeping" or "Paintings of Children with Unnaturally Large Eyes"), or a cause (such as a political protest or a grassroots campaign to get your favorite classic TV sitcom star a gig hosting *Saturday Night Live*).

Setting Up a Business Account

If you're only on Facebook for work reasons—to set up a Facebook Page or other advertising on behalf of your employer or client—you don't necessarily have to set up a personal profile. You can set up a kind of limited account called a *business account* instead.

Business accounts don't have profile pages, aren't visible in search results, and can't send or receive friend requests. You also won't be able to view other users' profiles using a business account.

Note that you can create a business account only if you don't already have a personal account on Facebook.

To create a business account, first you'll need to begin the process of setting up the Page or ad that you're on Facebook to administer. You can do this by clicking the Advertising link on your Facebook Home page, which is visible without logging in. Once you've entered the basic info for your Page or ad, you'll be offered the option to create your business account and instructions on how to proceed.

Finally, if at some point you decide you'd like to convert your business account into a regular user account with a profile, you can do so by clicking the Create Your Profile button that's visible when you log in to your business account.

WARNING: Unlike the names of Groups and Events, the name of a Page can't be changed once the Page has been published. So proofread it carefully and make sure it's correct before you click the Create Page button. If at some point you absolutely have to change your Page's name, your only option is to create a new one, encourage your fans to migrate, and then delete the old one. Quelle headache.

Community Page

Generate support for your favorite cause or topic by creating a Community Page. If it becomes very popular (attracting thousands of fans), it will be adopted and maintained by the Facebook community. Learn more.

Please note that you will not be able to edit the name of a Page after it has been created.

Page name: _____

(examples: Elect Jane Smith, Recycling)

Create Community Page

Facebook's thinking is that people connect to those kinds of Pages primarily to express support on their profiles for whatever the Page represents—but they don't want a steady stream of content in their News Feed from the Page in question. Needless to say, not everyone agrees with this analysis. But it's Facebook's playground, so they get to make the rules. And they do enforce this policy: In some cases, Facebook has been known to convert these kinds of Pages from Official Pages to Community Pages, stripping their admins of the ability to post new content to the Page's Wall.

Naming Your Page

Names for fan-based Groups on Facebook are often long declarative statements, such as *Lloyd Cole Is My Guru*, or *The Puppet Bike Makes My Heart Smile!!* Constructions like *Friends of DJ Dave Roberts and Planet Earth Chicago*, or *Tracey Ullman Fan Club*, or *An Appreciation Society for Edward John Moreton Drax Plunkett: Lord Dunsany*, are common, too.

Pages are different in this regard. The name for a Page should be the simple, unadorned name of the entity it represents. So if you're setting up the official Facebook Page for the B-52's, for example, you want the name of the Page to be simply *The B-52's*, rather than *Fans of the B-52's* or *The Facebook Love Shack and Wig Emporium of the B-52's*.

Think of it in terms of the News Feed story that will be generated when someone becomes a fan. You'll want that story to say "Dave Awl likes The B-52's," rather than "Dave Awl likes Fans of the B-52's"—which may be true but isn't really the point.

Step 2: Choose a Category and Name Your Page

Assuming you decide to go ahead and create an Official Page, your first task is to decide what category your Page belongs in. Choose one of the three top-level categories: "Local business" (for businesses such as restaurants, hotels, and cafés); "Brand, product, or organization"; or "Artist, band, or public fig-ure." Selecting one of those buttons will cause a pop-up menu to appear with a variety of more specific subcategories to choose from.

What's in a Category?

You also can't change the category for a Page once it's created, so choose carefully. If you decide later on that you want a different category, the only option is to delete the Page and re-create it using the new category—and of course, you'll lose any current fans in the process and have to start from scratch. (For this reason, you should take a look at the Page before you click the Publish button, and if you need to delete it and start over, do it before the Page has been publicized.)

This does matter, because different categories of Pages are set up with different informational fields and apps by default. A Page for a restaurant, for example, has fields for information that diners may be looking for, such as customer attire, parking availability, payment options, price range, and culinary specialties. A Page for a film offers fields for the director, cast, and screenwriter as well as a plot synopsis. A Page for a politician lists party affiliation, as well as the offices the politician currently holds and is campaigning for.

Your best bet is to do a little comparative category shopping before you create your Page—take a look at some Pages that fall into specific catego-ries and choose the type that best suits your needs.

Admittedly, Facebook's selection of categories for Pages is less than complete—or satisfying. There are Film and TV Show categories for example, but no Book category. (There is a Writer category, but if a writer wants to create a separate Page for a specific book, they're stuck using a general category like Product or Other Public Figure.) There's also no specific category for theater companies—Other Public Figure is the best bet at present (although I know of one Chicago performance group that chose to classify itself as a "religious organization," apparently hoping to inspire religious fervor among its fans).

Once you've chosen a category (and possibly a subcategory), enter the name of your Page. Click the checkbox to affirm that you are indeed authorized to create an official Page for whomever the Page will represent, and then when you're ready, click the Create Official Page button.

Step 3: Add Content

Once your Page has been created, you'll arrive at a blank template for your brand-new Page. The Get Started Tab (which is visible only to admins for the

Some of the Local Business categories

Some of the Brand, Product, or Organization categories

The Artist, Band, or Public Figure categories

Page) gives you a number of handy links and buttons to start adding content to your Page quickly and easily.

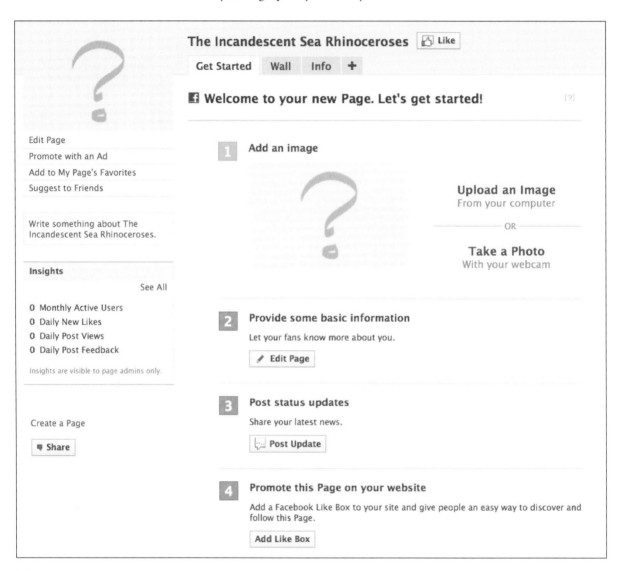

TIP: One tweak you'll probably want to make as soon as you've uploaded an image for your Page is to adjust the thumbnail version that will appear next to all of your Page's Wall stories. This works the same as it does for a personal profile pic—see the sidebar "Thumbnail and I" in the *Signing Up and Setting Up Your Profile* chapter for the details.

Your first step should be to add a photo or graphic to illustrate your Page. Choose something eye-catching and appealing that conveys the essence of the person or entity that your Page will represent. Click either the "Upload an Image" link or the "Take a Photo" link (in the step 1 area of the Get Started tab) to proceed. (These controls work pretty much the same as the ones for a personal profile.)

Your next step should be to click on the Edit Page button (step 2 on the Get Started tab) to begin adding information that will appear under the Info tab. (You can also do that by clicking the Info tab itself, of course.) The available fields will vary depending on the category you chose for your Page earlier. Fill out as much info as you'd like, and then click the Save Changes button and the Done Editing button to finish.

Managing a Page

Once your Page is created, you can accomplish most of its care and feeding from the repetitively named Edit Page page. To go there, click the Edit Page link just under the profile image in the upper-left corner.

From this page (which contains many more controls than are shown below) you can control the Page's settings, add and remove admins, add and customize applications, post various kinds of content, send Updates, and more.

TIP: The "Write something" box underneath your Page's image is another content holder that works the same way it does on your personal profile. This is one of the first places visitors may look when they come to your Page, so write something snappy to grab their attention.

Edit Page
Promote with an Ad
Add to My Page's Favorites
Suggest to Friends
Remove from My Page's Favorites

The Edit Page link is at the top of the list of links visible to Admins just below the profile image on a Page.

TIP: If you'd like to work on your Page behind the scenes for a while, to get it shipshape before the rest of the Facebook world comes to gawk at it, you can set its status to Unpublished. Go to the Settings area on the Edit Page page, click the word *Settings*, and then choose Unpublished from the Published pop-up menu. Once you've done that, your Page will become invisible to all Facebook users except for the Page's admin(s), until such time as you change the menu back to Published. And you can use this trick anytime in the future that you need to take your Page offline temporarily.

NOTE: Page admins and creators are not visible to the Page's visitors or fans. (Pay no attention to the admin behind the curtain!) Any comments you post on the Page or its threads will appear as comments from the Page itself, rather than your personal account. (However, one exception to this pattern is that if you click Like on any Page content, the Like will show up under your own name rather than the name of the Page.)

WARNING: One reason to be careful about whom you add as an admin is that once you've given them admin privileges, they'll have the ability to remove you—even if you created the Page originally. So make sure whoever you add is worthy of your trust.

TIP: One possible approach to targeting different information to different geographical areas would be to create country-specific Facebook Pages. For example, you could create separate Facebook Pages called Acme (US), Acme (UK), Acme (India), etc. and then restrict their visibility to those countries. You could also create Pages for entire regions, or other groupings of countries. For example, you could create an Acme (Europe) Page and an Acme (Asia) Page and restrict them to the countries located in those continents. But note that any such targeting is subject to the accuracy of the locations identified in users' personal profiles.

Adding and Removing Admins for Your Page

If you'd like to give admin privileges to others so that they can help you manage the Page, you can do so from the Edit Page page. Scroll down to the Admins area in the right-hand column and click the Add link. A dialog will open that allows you to select friends you'd like to add as admins. (You can also add people whom you're not friends with on Facebook by entering their e-mail addresses in this dialog.)

Once your Page has multiple admins, if you need to remove someone you can click the Remove Admin link next to that person's name in the Admins area.

Restricting Access to Your Page by Country or Age

If you'd like to limit who can access your Page, you can do that on the Edit Page page. Scroll down to the Settings area, and click the Edit link to reveal the controls.

The controls in the Settings area of the Edit Page page

To set the countries from which people can visit your Page, type the names of one or more countries in the Country Restrictions field. To set the minimum age required to visit your Page, use the Age Restrictions pop-up menu.

Note that instead of restricting access to the entire Page, you can choose to control the visibility of specific posts. (See the upcoming section, "Targeting Wall Posts by Age or Location.")

Setting a Gender for Your Page

You can also choose how your Page is referred to in News Feed stories. Use the Gender pop-up menu in the Settings area of the Edit Page page to choose the correct pronoun for your Page. For example, if your page is for a female writer, you'd want stories to use the pronoun *her* ("Dorothy Parker updated her profile"); for a band you'd probably want *their* ("The B-52's updated their profile"); and for a movie, TV show, company, or product you'd probably want *its* ("Arrested Development updated its profile").

Adding Applications to a Page

One of the advantages of a Facebook Page is that you can add applications to Pages. In fact, some kinds of Pages come with apps pre-installed: A Page in the Band category, for example, comes with a music player and the Discography app, which is designed to display a listing of all the recordings the artist has released so far.

To add an app to your page, go to the Page for the app (which you can find by searching or by browsing the Applications directory). Not all apps can be added to Pages, but if an app is Page-friendly, you'll see an "Add to my Page" link underneath the profile image in the upper-left corner of the app's Page.

When you click the link, you'll see a dialog asking you to confirm that you want to add the app to your Page. (If you manage more than one Page, you'll see a menu to select which Page you're adding the app to).

Choosing What Visitors to Your Page See by Default

First impressions count—so now that you've set up your Page, you may want to make some choices about what the people who arrive there see first. You have two key decisions to make: 1) which tab visitors see first, and 2) whose postings they see when they visit the Wall tab.

Setting the Default Landing Tab for Your Page

The default landing tab is the first tab that visitors see, by default, when they arrive at (or "land on") your Page for the first time. Some Page owners want newcomers to arrive first at the Info tab, so they see basic background information about the Page. Others want visitors to see the Page's Wall first, so they're drawn in by the Page's content and conversations (this is the default setting). Still others may want to choose the tab for a custom application that allows the Page to display special content to its visitors (see the sidebar "Custom Tabs for Pages").

You can control which tab visitors see first by accessing the settings for your Page's Wall. Click the Wall tab and then click the Options link just underneath the Publisher. At that point the Settings link will appear—click that to open the settings for your Wall.

Once the settings appear, choose the tab you'd like visitors to see first from the Default Landing Tab for Everyone Else menu.

To access all the Pages for which you're currently an admin, just choose Manage Pages from the Account menu in the blue bar.

TIP: You can remove an app from your Page by clicking the Remove Application link next to its name on the Edit Page page.

The Options link appears below the Publisher on your Page's Wall.

The Settings link appears after you click the Options link.

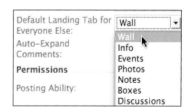

Choose the tab you'd like visitors to arrive at first from the Default Landing Tab menu.

Custom Tabs for Pages
Just like you can with a personal profile, you can add tabs and rearrange tabs for the various applications on your Page. In fact, one popular strategy for commercial Pages is to develop a custom application that displays exactly the content you want visitors to see when they stop by your Page—and then make the tab for that custom app the default landing tab for the Page. This gives you the ability to design any message you want and make it the first thing people encounter when they arrive at your Page. I'll talk more about this approach in the next chapter, *Advertising and Promoting on Facebook.*

You can access the Default View for Wall menu by clicking Options and then Settings under the Publisher on your Wall. Choosing All Posts (the default setting) means posts by fans will be visible on your Page's Wall by default. Choosing Only Posts by Page from the menu hides fan postings.

TIP: You can also access your Wall settings on the Edit Page page, by clicking the Edit link under "Wall Settings."

The Filters link lives in the upper-right corner of the Wall, underneath the Publisher.

Choosing the Default View for Your Wall

If your Page has a lot of fans—and they're a talkative bunch—they may quickly fill up your Wall with postings and comments of their own. This can be both a blessing and a curse.

On the one hand, if your fans shower your Wall with praise, enthusiastic reviews, and declarations of their undying loyalty, this can make a huge positive impact on newcomers who visit your Wall. And even if your fans sometimes post complaints or negative feedback, you have the opportunity to show off your customer service skills by solving their problems and making them happy. Pulling off that kind of turnaround in public view can be a powerful way to persuade new customers that you're worth doing business with. (I've seen this effect first-hand on my clients' Pages—and it's amazing how quickly customers' grievances can turn to gratitude after a little direct attention.)

The downside of course, is that your own postings may get lost in the midst of all the content your fans are posting—the age-old problem of signal versus noise. So Facebook's Wall settings give you two choices (as shown in the Default View for Wall menu at left): You can choose to set your Wall so that visitors see only the official posts from your Page by default, or you can set it so that postings from your fans are visible alongside your own.

Most social media gurus seem to agree that it's smart to put your fans' postings front and center—because social media is about conversations, about engagement, about demonstrating that you're listening as well as talking. By showcasing your fans' interactions, you put that dynamic to work for you to draw others in. Whereas if you hide your fans' postings by default, that can send a signal that you don't value or trust their input—and make them feel dramatically less inclined to participate on your Wall. (Which in turn means dramatically less News Feed stories generated about your Page.)

And of course, what we're talking about here is only the default view: Fans who want to focus on postings from the Page itself can always do that by clicking the appropriate filter at the top of the Wall to change their view, as shown below.

Fans can change what they see on a Page's Wall by clicking the Filters link in the upper-right corner of the Wall (shown at left), and then choosing one of the three options above. The [Page] + Others filter displays postings from the Page along with postings by fans; the Just [Page] filter shows only postings from the Page itself; and the Just Others filter shows only postings by fans.

Posting to Your Page's Wall

Whenever you have content to add to your Wall, you can use the Publisher on the Wall tab to post status updates, Links, Notes, photos, or videos—just like you would on a personal profile.

Select Customize from the padlock button's menu to choose the audience for your post.

Targeting Wall Posts by Age or Location

Even if your Page itself isn't restricted to specific countries, Facebook allows you to choose which fans will see each posting, on post-by-post basis, according to two factors: Location and Language. Underneath the Publisher at the top of the Page is a button with a Padlock icon on it. Clicking that button reveals a menu that lets you select the option to customize the audience for your post (instead of having the post be visible to Everyone, which is the default). Once you select the Customize option, the dialog shown below opens, containing two fields: Location and Languages.

You can type the names of one or more countries in the Location field, and the post will be visible only to users in the chosen countries (subject to profile accuracy). If you enter the names of one or more languages in the Languages field, only users who currently view Facebook in that language will see the posting—allowing you to target Spanish-speaking users, for example.

Sending Updates to Fans

As discussed earlier in the "Following Pages" section, Facebook allows you to send Update messages to your Page's fans, which appear in the Updates area of the Inbox. And as I mentioned in the "Updates, Schmupdates" sidebar, Updates are really kind of passé—they're easy to overlook these days, and I rarely bother to send them out for my own Pages. As a Page admin, your most effective communication tools are the ones in the Publisher: status updates, Links, Notes, photos, and videos.

The Favorite Pages Box
The Favorite Pages box (shown above) lets you display a selection of other Facebook Pages you like. You can use it to give a sense of your Page's identity, showing off who you like and who you're allied with. You can use it to recommend other artists, causes, or products you think your fans would be interested in. And you can use it as a kind of link-exchange back-scratching tool: Adding someone else's Page to your Page may inspire them to return the favor, thus potentially sharing your fan bases with each other.

To add a Favorite Page to your Page, go to the Page you want to add and click the "Add to my Page's Favorites" link in the upper-left area.

Promoting Your Page

The key strategies for promoting a Page are very similar to the tips for promoting an Event discussed in the previous chapter. The key is content, content, content: Customize your Page with timely info as well as photos, videos, music, and appropriate apps to make it a destination your fans want to come back to. Encourage conversations on your Wall, discussion board, and comment threads to keep generating News Feed stories.

You can also choose to promote your Page with a Facebook ad as discussed at the end of this chapter.

If you've got a web site or blog, you can link directly to your Facebook Page. Facebook Pages are visible to all visitors, even the ones who don't have Facebook accounts or aren't logged in. (However, logging in to Facebook is required to post comments on the Page.) And of course, linking to your Page from another site will be much easier if you set a username for your Page (see the section at right).

Sending Page Suggestions

If you'd like to send an automatic message to someone suggesting that they might want to Like your Page, you can do that using the Suggest to Friends link that appears underneath the profile image on your Page (and is visible only to admins). However, I recommend that you use this feature *very* judiciously—lots of folks get annoyed when they're barraged with automatic Page suggestions, and then you can wind up creating enemies (or at least frenemies) rather than fans. Besides: If you really want to persuade someone to check out your Page, you may have better luck by sending them a friendly, personal Inbox message, explaining why you think they'll be interested. It's the difference between suggesting *to* someone and suggesting *at* them.

That said, if you've got the time and the inclination, there's certainly no harm in sending out occasional Updates to your Page's fans. To do so, visit the Edit Page page, and under the Promote Your Page heading in the right-hand column, click the Send an Update link. The Update form will open—and from there the process is similar to sending an Inbox message. You can select the "Target this update" checkbox to display controls that will let you specify who receives the Update—filtering by location, age, or gender.

Setting a Username for Your Page

Setting a username for your Page is similar to the process of setting a username for your personal profile (as discussed in the *Signing Up and Setting Up Your Profile* chapter). And the advantage of doing it is the same: Setting a username for your Page gives you a handy, easy-to-remember URL for your Page that you can link to and share with others to help them find you. (Arguably, this is an even more important benefit for a Page than for a personal profile, since Pages are promotional in nature.)

There is one key difference from profiles, however: Facebook won't allow you to set the username for a Page until it's acquired a minimum of 25 fans. Once you've met the 25 fans requirement, you can set the username for your Page by navigating to facebook.com/username.

On the Username page, choose the name of the Page you'd like to set a username for (assuming you manage multiple Pages). Then enter the username you'd like and click the "Check availability" button to make sure it hasn't already been claimed by someone else. (If it has, you'll need to come up with something else—although if it's case where someone else is squatting on a name for which you hold the legal rights, you can contact Facebook via the link provided in the response and request help in resolving the situation.) If the name you want is available, just click the Confirm button and it's yours.

Importing Content from an External Site or Blog

If you already have an official website or blog for the entity that your Page represents, you might want to automatically import blog posts from that site as content for your Page. Fortunately, it's easy to do using Facebook's Notes application. Start by going to the Edit Page page, scroll down to the area for the Notes application, and click the Edit link.

> **What's in a Username?**
> Facebook usernames can't be changed or transferred once you've clicked the Confirm button—so think carefully about what you want your username to be before you finalize it, and for heaven's sake, proofread it half a dozen times for typos. In general, you want something short, simple, and easy to remember—and as close to the real name of the entity your Page will represent as possible. So if you were setting the username for say, Sterling Cooper's Page, you'd want facebook.com/sterlingcooper.

☐ **Notes**
Edit · Application Settings · Link to this Tab · Remove Application
With Facebook Notes, you can share your life with your friends through written entries. You can tag your friends in notes, and they can leave comments.

You'll be taken to the Notes page (where you can write and publish Notes from your Page in addition to importing external content). Click the link that says "Edit import settings" at the bottom of the left-hand column. From there, you'll arrive at the Import a Blog page, where you can enter the URL or RSS/Atom feed for the blog from which you'd like to import content.

Subscribe
📶 The Partly Dave Show's Notes
Edit import settings

The "Edit import settings" link

📶 **Import a Blog**   Back to The Partly Dave Show's Notes

Import an External Blog

You can import posts from one external blog so that they appear along with your notes. Facebook will automatically update your notes whenever you write in your blog. Imported blog posts cannot be edited.

Please only import your own blog. If you import too many blog posts in a day, you could be blocked from writing or importing new notes, and this could result in your account being disabled.

You are not importing from an external blog to your notes.
Enter a URL below to import to your notes.

Web URL: Enter a website or RSS/Atom feed address

☐ By entering a URL, you represent that you have the right to permit us to reproduce this content on the Facebook site and that the content is not obscene or illegal.

Start Importing

Insights

See All

348 ⬆ Monthly Active Users
  4 ⬆ Daily New Likes
  0   Daily Post Views
  5 ⬇ Daily Post Feedback

Insights are visible to page admins only.

The Insights box on your Page gives you a quick snapshot of recent Page activity. Click the See All link to go to the main Insights Page where you can access much more data.

Once you click the Start Importing button, whenever you post a new entry to your blog, Facebook will import its content as a Facebook Note. Each new Note will appear on the Wall for your Page, as well as under its Notes tab.

Viewing Insights for Your Page

One of the great advantages of setting up a Page is that Facebook gives you access to a robust set of data regarding your Page's traffic and user activity, so you can see how much attention it's attracting, and how effectively the content you're posting is engaging your fans and other visitors. To access this data, find the Insights box on your Page (which is visible only to admins) and click the See All link. You'll be taken to the main Insights page, where you can access data for all of your Pages.

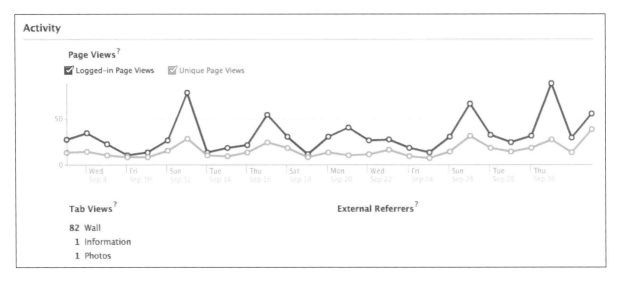

The chart shown above is just one sample of the kind of data available on the Insights page—you can track everything from page views to the number of new fans your Page attracts each day, as well as demographic breakdowns of your fans by age, gender, city, and country. This is useful for gauging the effectiveness of content added to your Page, as well as advertising, promotions, and other activity.

As a bonus, the data on your Insights page can be exported by clicking the Export button at the top of the Page. You can choose to export the data as either an Excel (XLS) or comma-separated (CSV) file.

Advertising and Promoting on Facebook

In the early '90s, when I first started organizing fringe theater and performance events, I didn't even own a computer. Promoting shows was a tedious process involving endless phone calls, stuffing press releases in envelopes, and slapping address labels on hundreds of postcards.

Then e-mail and the web came along, and things got easier. You could send out dozens of press releases, and promo announcements to hundreds of fans, with a single click of the Send button. Instead of spending the rent on glossy printed promo materials, you could stick it all up on the web and then just send out the URL. A giant leap forward for starving artists and shameless self-promoters everywhere.

Facebook represents a similar "Mother may I" moment. Tools like status updates, Notes, Pages, photos, and videos make it easy to grab the attention of your friends and fans—and, as we've seen, give you the opportunity to reach out to *their* friends as well, without being pushy or annoying about it.

In this chapter, we'll look at how to use these various tools together, as part of a grand unified Facebook promotion strategy. I'll also cover some of the ABCs of social media marketing, how to keep your Facebook presence engaging, and the basics of Facebook's paid ads.

Don't Sell It—Share It

The subtitle of this book is "A Guide to Socializing, Sharing, and Promoting on Facebook." I don't want to understate the importance of the socializing part, but sharing and promoting are the real icing on the Facebook cupcake—and they work hand in hand, because on Facebook, the best way to promote your creativity is to share your creativity.

Or to put it another way: The most effective way to advertise on Facebook is *not* to advertise. I know that may sound like a Zen riddle, but bear with me—this particular pebble isn't so hard to snatch. To be really effective at promoting on Facebook, you need to step outside the standard promotional mindset.

Facebook is first and foremost a social space, which means that traditional, direct-sell advertising is greeted with about as much enthusiasm as a life insurance commercial in the middle of an action movie. On the other hand, thanks to the News Feed's ripple effect, if you post content that amuses, entertains, informs, or otherwise engages people, you'll attract friends and fans. So instead of merely advertising what you have to offer, share it and let people see it for themselves. From your Facebook Page, you can post photos, videos, long and short messages, invitations to events, and more, all in a way that enters into the spirit of the party. By doing so, you can become part of the friendly Facebook conversation instead of interrupting it.

This is especially true for creative folks of all stripes—designers, photographers, writers, filmmakers, musicians, theater people, crafters, cupcake artists, you name it—as well as any business where you can show people samples of the products you offer and the work you do. Think of each of the Facebook tools discussed in the following section as opportunities to show off your talent, your craftsmanship, your innovation, your sense of style— whatever qualities make up the essence of your brand.

Ultimately, this is really just a variation of that old creative writing rule, "show, don't tell." Instead of using Facebook to tell people how inventive you are, post samples of your inventiveness and show them. (Of course, once you've done that, Facebook's paid ads can play a helpful role in drawing attention to what you've posted—which I'll discuss later on in this chapter.)

Promoting on Facebook—by the Numbers

Throughout this book I've been pointing out how Facebook's various tools can be used to get your message out. Now it's time to put all the pieces of the puzzle together—to look at how Facebook's various tools can be used most effectively in combination with each other, so that the whole effect is greater than the sum of the parts.

1. **Create a Page.** As I mentioned at the beginning of the *Pages* chapter, a well-run Page is the cornerstone of any successful promotional campaign on Facebook. Whatever you're publicizing, you'll need a home base for it on Facebook—a central location for all the basic info, announcements, events, and other content that you'll be posting. Pages are the perfect tool for communicating with—and thereby building—your army of loyal fans, supporters, and/or customers.

2. **Feed the News Feed.** As we've seen, the key to spreading the word about something on Facebook is generating News Feed activity. If you create a Page, an Event, or any other content on Facebook, don't just let it sit there. Add content to its Wall and use the Share button to post it to your own Profile. If someone comments on something you've posted, be sure to reply, in order to keep the conversational ball rolling.

3. **Use status updates** for short, timely messages. Status updates are a perfect medium for broadcasting whatever news you have to share, as well as asking questions or starting discussions with your fans in order to stay on their radar and encourage them to make regular visits to your Page.

You can also use your status update as a pointer to draw attention to other kinds of content you've posted— a "hey, check this out" message when you upload a video or create a brand-new Event, for example.

4. **Use Notes for messages that are too long for a status update.** Like photos and videos, Notes can be used to draw attention to other things—and you can go into more detail than status updates allow for, given that status updates are currently limited to 420 characters. You can use Notes to post journal-style entries about projects in progress, or events in the planning stage, whetting interest and building anticipation for the final product.

You can also use Notes to ask questions, soliciting input that can help you create a stronger version of whatever you're working on. For example, when I was working on the *Applications and Other Add-Ons* chapter of this book, I wrote a Note asking my friends to tell me about their favorite Facebook apps—and got a number of useful suggestions as a result.

5. **Use Events to draw attention to time-sensitive happenings, build enthusiasm about them, and track your potential audience.** Posting public Events on Facebook helps you reach not only the people on your invitation list, but potentially their friends, and friends of friends, as well—thanks to the ripple effect of Facebook's News Feeds. Remember that you can use Events to promote not only performances, get-togethers, and meetings in the physical world, but also TV and radio appearances, scheduled chat room meetings, or anything else with a start and end time you'd like your audience to be aware of.

6. **Use photos and videos to show off your projects in an eye-catching and entertaining way.** As discussed in the *Photos and Videos* chapter, posting photos and videos on Facebook is a visual way to grab attention for projects, performances, and events of all kinds. (And of course if you're a photographer, you can just show off your photos.)

7. **Use Links to direct attention to content posted elsewhere.** If you post content elsewhere on the web, such as a video on YouTube, a new entry on your blog, or a new podcast on your web site, be sure to post the link to your Facebook Page or profile so your fans and friends see it in the News Feed.

8. **Use Groups to network with fellow fans, professionals, and other peers.** Use Groups to facilitate communication among people with whom you share a common interest or goal. As discussed in the *Group Dynamics* chapter, Facebook Groups are great for project teams and group collaborations.

9. **Make use of Facebook ads.** If you'd like to embrace actual, bought-and-paid for advertising, Facebook makes it easy to advertise the Pages and Events you've built on Facebook, targeting the people most likely to be interested in what you're doing. See the section on Facebook Ads later in this chapter for more info.

Here's a hypothetical example to tie it all together. Suppose you're in a band with a gig coming up toward the end of the month, and you're looking to set up your Facebook presence. How should you proceed?

Answer: Start by setting up a Page for the band, and then use Page suggestions (or Inbox messages) to invite your friends to come check it out. You and your fellow band members should also post it to your personal profiles, so it shows up in the News Feed on your friends' Home pages. You can also mention the new Page in your status updates.

Wait a few days till your Page has had time to attract some fans. Once you've hit the 25-fan mark, you can set a username for your Page, so that you can easily link to your Page from your main website (assuming you have one) or blog, and also include the link in any promotional e-mails you send out.

Then create an Event, with your Page as host, for the upcoming performance. Send out Event invitations to your friends, letting them know about the Event, and encouraging them to pass along the invitation to their friends. Be sure to also post the Event to your Page's Wall, to get the attention of your Page's fans.

As the Event draws near, you can continue to generate interest by posting photos and videos to the page for the Event itself. Upload shots of the posters or flyers for the gig, if you have them, and pictures or video clips from previous performances. If you get comments, be sure to comment back to keep the discussion going, let your fans know you appreciate their support, and keep your Event showing up in the News Feeds. And if you've got the budget for it, consider taking out a Facebook ad to promote your Event.

There are lots of variations on the foregoing scenario, of course—but the key is to figure out how to use these tools in combination with each other.

Finally: As I mentioned in the *Communicating on Facebook* chapter, Facebook isn't LinkedIn. Facebook is first and foremost a social space, so it's important to strike a healthy balance between personal communications and promotional messages. As a word of warning, Facebook is ever-vigilant about spam, and moves aggressively to shut down users who seem to be over-promoting. If you send out too many Inbox messages or Event invitations from your personal profile, or join too many Groups in a short space of time, you may get a warning from Facebook that you're on thin ice.

So pace yourself. Don't be pushy—instead, make it your business to post information and content that's catchy, engaging, and appealing enough that other people want to share it with their friends. Then sit back and let Facebook's News Feeds carry your message to the outer edges of your social network, and beyond.

Strengthening Emotional Attachments with Customers

An experiment conducted by the *Harvard Business Review* (HBR) in early 2010 found that Facebook Pages can be very effective at creating stronger "emotional attachments" between businesses and their customers. HBR e-mailed a survey to thousands of customers on the mailing list for a Houston-based bakery called Dessert Gallery (DG), then set up a Facebook Page for DG and invited everyone on the mailing list to become a fan of the Page. They updated the Page several times a week with news, positive reviews, info about contests and specials, profiles of DG employees, and of course, lots of photos of scrumptious desserts. (I want to click the Like button just reading about it.)

Three months later, HBR surveyed DG's customers again. They found that becoming fans of DG on Facebook "changed customer behavior for the better": Customers visited the store more often after becoming fans, were more likely to recommend DG to their friends, were most likely to say that they preferred DG to its competitors, and reported a greater emotional attachment to DG (3.4 on a 4-point scale, compared to an average of 3.0 for customers who weren't Facebook fans).

Cheat Sheet: Key Principles of Social Media Marketing

I've discussed many of the following ideas in other parts of this book (or even within this very chapter), so some of this is review—but I thought it might be useful to give you a checklist of some of the most important do's and don'ts of social media marketing in one handy bulleted list.

- **Don't advertise—engage!** People come to Facebook to socialize, to be entertained, and to get useful information, but almost nobody comes for the deliberate purpose of being advertised to. To reach people on Facebook, you need to grab their attention by giving them something they need. See the section "Free Ice Cream: Delivering Value to Your Fans" for more on this.

- **Show, don't tell.** As discussed at the beginning of this chapter, remember that the best way to persuade Facebookers that you have something great to offer is to use Facebook's sharing tools to give them a taste of how great that something is, rather than just telling them about it.

- **Don't just talk—listen.** The great value of social media is that it creates a two-way connection: an opportunity to build a stronger bond with your audience by listening to what they have to tell you and responding to them directly. In a world where customers who try to contact companies are routinely greeted with, "Please listen carefully because our voice menu options have changed," genuine communication is a killer app. If fans know they can get your ear by visiting your Facebook Page, that can do wonderful things for your traffic.

- **Responsiveness matters.** One of the worst things you can do is set up a Facebook Page and then neglect it. Make sure that you have one or more people keeping an eye on the Page on a daily basis to respond to comments and questions in a timely fashion. You want your customers to feel like there's a real live person on the other end of the metaphorical line when they post on your Wall (as opposed to the feeling of talking to, you know, an ordinary wall).

- **Practice good customer service.** In one of my early retail jobs, a wise manager pointed out to me that when customers complain, the main thing they often want is an opportunity to voice their frustration and know it's been heard—a chance to vent. It's amazing how quickly you can turn their frowns upside down (or at least smooth them out a little) if you give people a sympathetic ear, acknowledge their frustration, and demonstrate your desire to make things better.

Free Ice Cream: Delivering Value to Your Fans

It's easy enough for people to become a fan of your Page on Facebook: All they have to do is click the Like button. But the other edge to that sword is that it's also easy for people to tune you out if they find the content you're posting uninteresting or even annoying. All any fan has to do is click the Hide button next to one of your postings on the Home page, and poof!— your postings are no longer reaching their News Feed.

For this reason, fan counts on Facebook can be deceptive. Sure, you may have several thousand or more smiling faces in your People Who Like This box. But Liking isn't the same thing as listening, and you can't be sure that those people will continue to pay attention to what you post on your Page unless you make the effort to engage them.

So how exactly do you hold your fans' attention on Facebook? The key is to make sure that what you're posting speaks to your audience's needs: It's not about what you want to say, but what they want to hear.

Try to put yourself in the minds of your fans, and think about what motivates them to click the Like button on your Page. What kind of information or entertainment are they hoping will show up in their News Feed once they've added your Page to the mix?

There are many different kinds of value that posts can deliver:

- **Useful or helpful information:** Maybe you've got breaking news or announcements that can be shared more quickly on your Facebook Page than anywhere else. If you're in the consulting or training field, share a little of your expertise on a regular basis to show it off.

- **Free ice cream:** Offer your fans goodies like rewards, tips, discounts, and giveaways. Some Pages post regular coupon codes that you can enter when placing online orders or visiting a business—a 10% discount on your next order, a free appetizer, and so forth. These posts are not only good motivators for your fans to stay tuned, they create good News Feed mojo because they're highly shareable: If what you're offering is good, customers will be motivated to hit the Share button to pass the info on to their friends. The Redbox DVD-rental company helped build a following for its Page by regularly posting codes that could be redeemed for a free one-night movie rental. And here in Chicago, the local Pockets restaurant chain let its fans know that they could get a 10% discount by entering a code word in the promo field for orders placed on its website.

- **Thought-provoking or inspiring ideas.** I'm not saying you should make the common mistake of posting a lot of recycled "inspirational" quotations on your Page. But if what you do genuinely involves ideas—because you're a writer, a designer, a nonprofit working to build schools in impoverished areas—then by all means discuss those ideas. Sometimes inspiration can be as appealing as ice cream (and more nutritious, too).

- **Entertainment value and humor.** Bringing personality to your Page is a big part of making it engaging. A little humor of the non-abrasive sort can be the spoonful of sugar that makes the medicine go down.

- **Opportunities for fans to express themselves.** Remember that the fans on your Page make up a community with something in common—the interest they share in whatever your Page represents. Your Wall is therefore a place where they can enjoy the camaraderie of Like-minded people, and express their enthusiasm among others who "get it." Give them questions to answer and plenty of fodder for discussion and sharing. The Stash Tea Company invites its Facebook fans to post haiku about tea every Friday—and fans not only respond prolifically with dozens of poems, they actually complain if the company neglects to post the Tea Haiku Friday thread.

■ **The inside scoop.** People often connect to Pages on Facebook in order to feel like they're joining the inner circle—the hardcore fans who are really wired in. Try to reward your followers with a little more info than you'd include in an official press release, on the assumption that they care a little more than most of the people who would read your press release. To put it in movie terms: Give your fans the kind of "bonus" info you'd put in the making-of/behind the scenes featurette on a DVD.

Putting the "Social" in Social Media: The Art of the Friendly Voice

Back in the *Communicating on Facebook* chapter, I pointed out that Facebook is primarily a social space, and compared it to a party where you should show up in something casual and a little fun instead of your navy-blue business suit. The vibe on Facebook is relaxed, friendly, and social. Which means that to enter into the spirit of the party, the voice you use to communicate with customers (and potential customers) on Facebook needs to *feel* friendly—rather than overly formal, pushy, or promotional.

So how do you achieve that social, friendly tone? Here are some useful dynamics to consider:

Cold	Warm
Formal	Informal
Distant	Congenial
"Written" style	"Spoken" style
Prerecorded	Live and spontaneous
Official	Confidential

In general, for social media, you want to steer toward the Warm side of the scale for the dynamics listed above.

- **Formal vs. Informal:** Even if you're in a more formal kind of business, on Facebook you can move the slider a little more toward the informal side of the scale than you might in your regular business communications. Be conversational, direct, and by all means use contractions. You don't have to get slangy or dumb things down—eloquence and proper English are never anything but a plus, at least in my book—but you want to sound like you're talking to your fans rather than declaiming to them.

- **Distant vs. Congenial:** Think of yourself as the host or hostess of your Page, and your fans as your guests. Be welcoming, supportive, and continually let them know that you're grateful for the enthusiasm and energy they bring to your Page. You want your fans to understand that there are real live people on the other side of that Facebook Wall, and that you're enjoying the process of connecting with your fans.

- **Written vs. Spoken Style:** This is closely related to the Formal/Informal dynamic mentioned above. The best social media writers, in my opinion, manage to create the feeling that they're speaking out loud to you as you read their writing. That brings energy and a sense of connectedness that's appropriate to the medium. Try saying your status update out loud—does it sound natural and conversational? If not, rewrite till it does.

- **Prerecorded vs. Live and Spontaneous:** Even if you're writing content for your Page days or weeks in advance so it can be pre-approved by a client or manager (a process I work with all the time for my corporate clients), it should be written to sound like it's as spontaneous, timely, and "in the moment" as possible.

- **Official vs. Confidential:** This ties in to what I discussed in the "Inside scoop" bullet point of the "Free Ice Cream" section earlier. Ideally, you want your fans to feel like you're lifting the veil just a little bit— confiding in them and giving them the real dish, so they get more out of their Facebook connection with you than they would just by reading your regular advertising or the official copy on your website. I wouldn't recommend actually typing "Pssst" at the beginning of all of your status updates—but if you imagine doing that, it might help you find the tone I'm talking about.

Using Landing Tabs Promotionally

Promotional Considerations
I've used the term *promoting* in a general sense in this chapter. But Facebook has special rules and guidelines for what it defines as promotions—specifically, anything that can be considered a "sweepstakes, contest, competition or other similar offering." It defines a sweepstakes as "a promotion that includes a prize and a winner selected on the basis of chance," and "a contest" or "competition" is "a promotion that includes a prize and a winner determined on the basis of skill (i.e., through judging based on specific criteria)." These kinds of promotions are subject not just to Facebook's rules, but legal restrictions that vary according to jurisdiction. If you're considering running any kind of promotion that meets these definitions, you'll want to take a careful look at Facebook's Promotions Guidelines, which you can find here: www.facebook.com/promotions_guidelines.php.

In the *Pages* chapter I mentioned that Pages give you the ability to choose a landing tab—the tab that visitors see first, by default, the first time they arrive at your Page. This gives you the ability to shape the first impression your Page makes, and make it function a little more promotionally by displaying exactly the content you want newcomers to see.

The key word here is *conversion:* persuading the people who visit your Page to click that Like button and become bona fide fans instead of just sightseers. Many social media marketers argue strongly that the most effective way to engage customers and increase conversion is to set a landing tab that explicitly encourages newcomers to click the Like button.

If you'd like to choose something other than the default Wall or the possibly somewhat lackluster Info tab as your first stop for visitors, there are basically two ways to go.

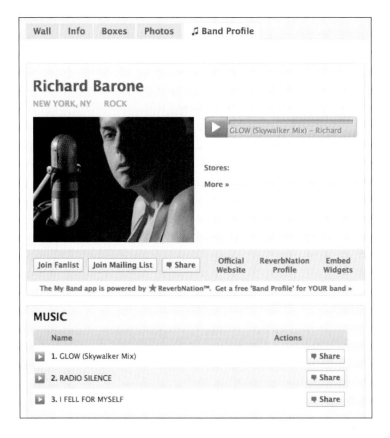

First, you can choose from a number of third-party applications that are designed to function as landing tabs. If you're a musician, for example, you might use the BandPage application by RootMusic, or the My Band application by ReverbNation (shown on the facing page). Both are designed to grab visitors' attention and get them listening to your music as soon as they arrive.

Of course, with an existing app, you're still limited to the options available in an application that was designed to serve the needs of many different users. So the other option is to have your own custom application developed—one that's tailored precisely to your specific needs. Doing so can give you complete control over what appears on your landing tab.

Here's an example of the landing tab for the Travelocity Page: a custom app called Travel Insider that lets you get started making travel plans right away, and also points out the Like button in no uncertain terms. (Also notice that Travelocity uses its gnome mascot to provide just enough humor to make this hard-sell approach palatable.)

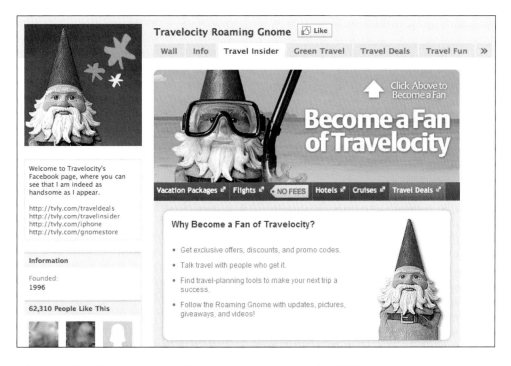

Of course, there's a downside to this approach: It requires the ability to develop a custom app using Facebook's FBML application or iframes. Application development is outside the scope of this book—if it's outside your skillset, too, your best bet is to track down and hire an experienced app developer.

click the like button and listen to some tracks from the forthcoming album from Vincent Minor on Facebook & come see him on tour!

Marc Felion and Dan Loughry like this.

👍 Like

Facebook's Social Ads tap the passive endorsement factor by pointing out when friends of yours have already Liked the subject of the ad.

💬 The Facebook Marketplace
One other method of advertising on Facebook that's worth a mention is Facebook's Marketplace application. You can think of Marketplace as Facebook's online classified ads section—or maybe the Facebook answer to Craigslist. Using Marketplace, you can create and browse listings for jobs, housing, vehicles, pets, services, and items for sale.

The advantage of using Marketplace, as compared with Craigslist or a newspaper, is that you can buy from, sell to, or connect with someone who belongs to your social network—a trusted friend, or a friend of a friend—instead of dealing with complete strangers. If you've got a great pair of concert tickets you can't use, for example, you might be happier knowing that your friends will get first crack at them. And if you're buying or selling a piece of furniture, you might be more comfortable arranging to meet someone with whom you share mutual friends.

If you don't see the bookmark for the Marketplace app on your Home page, you can find Marketplace easily by searching in the blue bar.

Using Facebook's Paid Ads

Once you've got a Page or Event to promote on Facebook, if you're willing to put a little cash in the game, Facebook's paid ads (aka Social Ads) can be a very effective way to pull traffic in your direction. These are the ads that appear in Facebook's right-hand column, and can be set up by just about any user with a credit card.

Facebook ads let you supply your own art and copy and choose the users you'd like to target based on factors like age, location, gender, and the Likes and interests found in their profiles—helping your ad to find its way to the Facebook members who are most likely to be interested in it.

For both kinds of ads, you can choose to pay for advertising on a per-click or per-impression basis. Facebook lets you specify how much you're willing to pay for each click or impression, and set a daily maximum amount to spend. At the end, when your ad is prepped and ready to go, you'll need to enter a valid credit card number for the billing process.

Facebook also reviews each ad to make sure that it's not spam, not obscene, and doesn't violate certain quality standards.

Once your ad is live, Facebook will provide you with regularly updated stats to show you how your ad is doing and which categories of Facebook users are clicking on it the most.

To learn more and begin the process, click the Advertising link in Facebook's footer. You'll find a step-by-step guide to planning and preparing your ad, with lots of guidance on what's allowed and what will be most effective in reaching your audience.

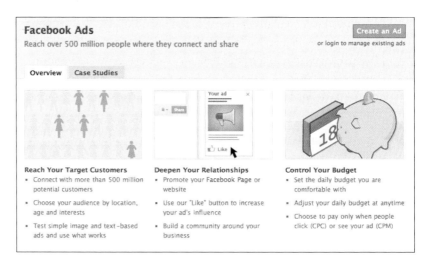

Facebook at Work

Finding a healthy relationship between work and one's personal life can be a tricky business, to put it mildly. So it's not surprising that the interface between Facebook and the nine-to-five world can be puzzling, too. Facebook is a fun, freewheeling, social kind of space, and work is, well—work.

So this chapter is about how to negotiate the boundaries between those two worlds. We'll start by tackling the ever-popular question of whether you should mix your social network with your work life, and whether it's even possible to keep them separate. We'll examine how Facebook can affect a job search in positive ways as well as negative ones. And we'll look at some guidelines for keeping your Facebook profile professional.

And finally, I'll give you a few tips for staying in touch with your Facebook network even when you're working in settings where access to Facebook is blocked.

Should You Friend Your Boss?
Facebook and Office Politics

In the media stories I read about Facebook, there's one head-scratcher that pops up again and again: Should you be Facebook friends with your boss?

Ah, life was so much less complicated in the old days, before social networking meant anything other than business cards at cocktail parties. Darrin Stephens never had to worry about Larry Tate poking around in his Facebook profile, reading bad jokes from Uncle Arthur and naughty comments from Serena.

Add to this the fact that everyone's work situation is different. Different career paths, industries, and workstyles with differing professional standards lead to diverse relationships with varying boss personality types. (And if you're self-employed like me, or in the corner suite at your company, you can simply substitute the word *client(s)* for *boss* throughout this essay.)

And yet, to this complicated modern question I'm going to give you a very simple answer: Yes. Yes, you should be Facebook friends with your boss.

Because even if your boss doesn't know Facebook from a hole in the nearest putting green, you should be behaving as if he or she already *is* in your Friends list. People who aren't on Facebook today have a way of suddenly showing up when you least expect it. It may take three months, or six months, but when you factor in Facebook's current rate of growth—especially among older people—the odds are pretty decent that sooner or later you'll see a friend request from your boss pop up on your screen.

And if and when that day arrives, it's hard to imagine a boss–employee relationship where clicking Ignore would be the smart or politic choice.

Which means that if your profile isn't already boss-friendly, you'll be frantically scrambling to clean up your Wall, photos, privacy settings, and so forth before clicking that Accept button. So why not get a jump on it?

Also factor in the possibility that prospective employers may ask to see your profile before hiring you; that someone you consider a friend could decide to snitch on you about something you post (which has happened to at least one friend of mine); and that if you work on-site and use the company's computer to access Facebook, your employer may have the means to snoop on your Facebook activity without your awareness.

For all of these reasons, I think the wisest course of action is to be proactive: Consider the professional standards that apply to your career—or the career you hope to have one day—and then apply them to your Facebook activity, now and going forward. If you keep your profile free of potential embarrassments as you go, then if the Facebook toothpaste does get out of the tube at some future date, you won't wind up with it smeared all over your résumé.

In some cases this may mean doing a little back-channel communication with your friends, via Inbox messages or other private means. If you have a friend who loves to post off-color jokes on your Wall, or photos you hoped were burned shortly after you graduated from college, it may help to take them aside and explain why you keep deleting and detagging what they post, and that it's nothing personal. (Well, unless it is.)

This line of thinking also applies to the related question of friending co-workers and colleagues. You may try to draw a thin beige line between your cubicle mates and your after-hours life—but if and when you start receiving friend requests from your co-workers, rejecting them could wind up lowering the temperature around the water cooler and in the meeting room. So it might save you some awkwardness in the long run to assume that your Facebook profile is an open book, and conduct yourself accordingly.

Additionally, if you shut your colleagues out of your Facebook Friends list, you may lose out on the remarkable professional networking opportunities that Facebook can deliver—including the ability to help you find jobs and gigs. (For more on that, see the sidebar "Putting Weak Ties to Work For You.")

Ultimately, you don't have to suck all the fun out of your Facebook life in order to make it career-friendly—just think of your profile as an extension of the same persona you already use to socialize with people in your profession. And if you have a wild and crazy alter ego that's only for your non-work pals to see, you can still express it using Facebook's private channels, such as Inbox messages and one-on-one chats—or by using Friend Lists to restrict who can see your postings.

Facebook and Job Hunting

Facebook has the potential to be both a help and a hindrance when you're looking for work. On the plus side is, well, the networking part of *social networking*. Facebook makes it easy to get the word out about your work search to your entire social network. You can use your status update to let your friends know you're looking—ask them to keep their eyes and ears open for you, and let you know if they've got any appropriate leads.

Facebook's public conversations can be useful, too. If you pay attention to your friends' Walls, status updates, and comment threads, someone might mention an opening at their company, remind you of a mutual colleague you should get in touch with, or provide other useful leads.

Facebook Groups are a good resource: You may be able to find Groups related to your profession, where you can make new connections and net-work with people who work in your field but are outside your social circle.

On the minus side? Well, as discussed in the *Privacy and Security* chapter, lots of companies scour the Facebook profiles of job candidates, looking for reasons to chuck them in the bad apple bin.

According to a survey of hiring managers conducted by CareerBuilder.com, the most common dealbreakers they found on Facebook profiles included references to drinking or using drugs; "provocative or inappropriate" photos; poor communication skills, including bad grammar and spelling; lying about qualifications; and derogatory remarks about race, gender, or religion.

Fortunately, it's a two-way street: The managers also said that Facebook profiles could work in candidates' favor if they demonstrated that a prospective employee was intelligent, articulate, and professional, with solid communication skills and a wide range of interests.

Many are also speculating that the time will soon draw to a close when an embarrassing photo or two can kill someone's job prospects. Younger people increasingly live their lives in the open online, and as the working popula-tion ages, it's going to get harder for employers to find employees who have perfectly blemish-free Internet lives.

Back in the '90s, there was a much-discussed moment in corporate culture when companies decided to start hiring the "tattooed and pierced." Hiring managers realized that limiting themselves to candidates with conventional appearances had backfired, by screening out some of the most talented and creative prospects. By the same token, smart managers will eventually figure out that blackballing anyone with a questionable photo in their past could leave their company stranded in the shallow end of the talent pool.

Putting Weak Ties to Work for You

Who do you think is more likely to help you find a great job or gig: a close friend, or a professional acquaintance you don't see or talk to very often? According to sociologist Mark Granovetter, the surprising answer is that the best leads often come from the people in our social network we barely know—distant connections, or as Granovetter calls them, *weak ties*.

Granovetter, whose work I first read about in Malcolm Gladwell's book *The Tipping Point*, conducted a groundbreaking study in 1974 that involved interviewing hundreds of professional and technical workers to find out how they landed their jobs. He discovered that the majority found their positions through a personal connection to someone else, and that most of those personal connections were weak ties—in fact, more than 70% were someone the respondent saw only "rarely" or "occasionally." By contrast, less than 17% of the connections who supplied winning leads were someone the respondent saw "often."

Granovetter's explanation for this phenomenon, which he called "the strength of weak ties," is that the people you see most often are likely to move in the same circles you do, and have similar sources of information. Whereas more distant connections go more places you don't go, know more people you don't know, and are therefore more likely to discover leads you wouldn't hear about on your own.

Granovetter conducted his study a couple of decades before the Internet began transforming the way people find work—but social media, it seems to me, makes the weak-tie effect exponentially stronger. Obviously, Facebook excels at keeping you in touch with the people in your network that you see "rarely" or "occasionally." And even better, Facebook provides tools that make it easy for those weak connections to share valuable job-hunting information with you—sometimes without even making a specific effort to do so.

So the next time you're on the fence about whether to add a professional contact to your Facebook Friends list, it might not hurt to consider what they could add to your collection of ties.

Keeping Your Profile Professional

Let's say you're willing to take my advice, and bring your Facebook profile in line with your professional identity so that you can comfortably open it up to colleagues, clients, and employers. What do you need to consider?

A lot depends on what line of work you're in, of course. But here are some general tips and guidelines. (Most of these points I've covered in other places throughout the book, but think of this as a checklist.)

- **Picture your entire audience.** Get in the habit of taking a moment, each and every time you click the Share button, to think about who'll be seeing the post—not just the people you do want to see it, but whether there's anyone in your Friends list you may *not* want to.

- **Consider posting to some of your friends rather than all of them.** Remember that you can use Friend Lists to control who sees what, so limiting specific posts to a certain segment of your Friends list is an option. (See the *Sharing Content on Facebook* chapter.)

- **Make use of private channels** (such as the Inbox or chat) for private communications.

- **When in doubt, don't post.** If something might cause problems for you at work, the safest approach is not to share it in the first place.

- **Remember the three D's: delete, detag, and discuss.** It's your Wall, after all, so ultimately you have the right to act as final editor of what does and doesn't appear there. If friends post inappropriate content on your Wall, don't be shy about deleting it or detagging it. If necessary you can follow up by discussing it with them to avoid any ruffled feathers.

- **Try to keep your Facebook persona on the upbeat side.** Some folks use their profiles as a dumping ground for negative energy, turning their Walls into endless lists of rants and grievances. Those who can do it in a witty or entertaining way may even win friends and fans for their tirades. But although venting on Facebook may be good therapy, overindulging in it can alienate the people you want to win over—after all, not many companies conduct extensive searches to fill the position of Office Crankypants. I'm not saying you need to slap up a smiley face as your profile pic and adopt a Pollyannaish tone for everything you post—but it can't hurt to stay cognizant of the fact that in just about every line of work, people respond favorably to positive energy, a can-do attitude, and a willingness to help others solve problems.

Facebook Fire Safety Tips: Avoiding Flame Wars

Getting drawn into a flame war on Facebook can cause (at least) two separate kinds of damage. Not only can it harm your relationship with the friend on the other side of the argument, but if you seriously lose your temper you may wind up diminishing yourself in the eyes of bystanders. If those bystanders are colleagues, clients, or employers, the smoke damage can affect your professional life as well as your personal life.

I'm not saying you can't have political debates on Facebook—in fact, depending on what you do, the ability to discuss topical issues intelligently may be an important part of your professional identity. But be aware of the pitfalls and slippery slopes that come with Internet debates, and how easily what starts out as a friendly conversation can turn into a heated argument.

Here are some tips to avoid letting flame wars make an ash out of you:

- **Avoid posting in anger.** If you find yourself getting hot under the collar when participating in a Facebook thread, take some cooling off time before you respond. Go for a walk or make some tea. If the conversation isn't time-sensitive, it might be a good idea to wait a full 24 hours. At that point, you may realize you don't need to reply at all, or at least can do so with a much cooler head.

- **Don't take it to round two.** If you post an opinion, and someone else strongly disagrees with you, the smartest approach is often to agree to disagree. Be satisfied with the fact that you've both expressed your viewpoints, and move on. If you post a counter-argument, you open the door to a back-and-forth debate that may spiral out of control.

- **Don't get personal.** Avoid ad hominem arguments, and if someone else crosses that line, don't take the bait—take the exit instead.

- **Get away from the audience.** If you absolutely need to hash out a contentious issue with someone, move the discussion to a one-on-one medium like the Inbox or e-mail. People often become more extreme in their rhetoric—and theatrical in their anger—when they know others are watching, because they want to persuade the audience.

Notes for Managers and Hirers

Now that we've addressed the importance of viewing one's own Facebook profile with a professional eye, let's look at this from the other table. If you're a manager or hirer and you find yourself in the position of judging employees or candidates on the basis of their Facebook profiles, it's important to make some allowances for the fact that Facebook is primarily a social space.

In a way, it's as if someone you work with has invited you to their home for a party. You're going to see a little more of their personality than you would around the office. But you're in their space now, not on work territory, so the standards are a little different.

- **Be careful of snap judgments.** Obviously, certain things are undeniably red flags (blatantly racist, sexist, or otherwise intolerant language, for example). But in general, context is critical—especially when looking at the profile of someone you don't know very well—because Facebook postings aren't always what they appear to be at first glance. That bizarre status update might turn out to be song lyrics, or a line from last night's episode of *30 Rock*.
- **Don't throw out the baby.** As discussed in the "Facebook and Job Hunting" section, some of the most talented potential hires may have an embarrassing photo or two lurking somewhere online.
- **Allow some margin for error.** Good written communication skills are important, but remember that everybody makes occasional typos now and then. Even professional writers who moonlight as copy editors, like myslef. (See what I did there?) And Facebook doesn't provide tools for easily correcting errors even when you do spot them—usually it's an unhappy choice between gritting your teeth and tolerating the mistake, or deleting the entire posting along with any comments and Likes it's already accumulated. (Ruefully commenting on one's own typos to show that you're aware of them is a time-honored strategy, of course.)
- **Don't assume people endorse everything their friends post.** Remember that people don't always immediately notice what gets posted on their Walls, or know how to remove offensive posts. So avoid judging Facebook members too harshly by what their friends have posted. (Of course, if the owner of the Wall chooses to Like or comment approvingly on a posting, that can reasonably be considered an endorsement.)

Checking Facebook—Without Actually Checking Facebook

It's a shame that Facebook is viewed with distrust by some workplaces—especially since Facebook can be a useful communication tool for work groups and project teams, a great way to get input and answers to questions, and of course an excellent forum for networking. Nonetheless, some companies see it as nothing but a time-waster and a drain on productivity, and block access to Facebook on their office networks.

If you find yourself working at a company where Facebook is blocked, you're probably not completely out of luck—because there are a number of ways to keep in touch with what's happening on Facebook without actually visiting the site.

E-Mail Notifications

As explained in the *Signing Up and Setting Up Your Profile* chapter, by default Facebook sends notifications to your primary e-mail address whenever someone writes on your Wall or sends you an Inbox message, among other actions. These e-mail notifications contain the full text of the messages they notify you about, so you can keep up with what your friends are saying to you just by checking your e-mail throughout the day. See the "Changing Notification Settings" section in that chapter for more info.

RSS Feeds

As discussed in the *Sharing Content on Facebook* chapter, you can subscribe to a feed for your Facebook notifications. You can then view the feed using your web browser or an RSS reader such as Google Reader.

TIP: In addition to the other methods on this page, you can access Facebook using most current mobile phones. In fact, that's what the next chapter, *Going Mobile*, is all about.

The Facebook Toolbar for Firefox

This one won't help you if the Facebook site is completely blocked. However, it can be useful in a situation where Facebook is accessible, but having a Facebook window open on your screen all day might create, shall we say, the wrong appearance. With the toolbar installed (as covered in the *Applications and Other Add-Ons* chapter), you'll be notified whenever anything important happens—such as a new Wall post or Inbox message. That should help you keep your visits to Facebook short and to the point during working hours.

Going Mobile

Have I mentioned yet that Facebook can be kind of addictive? Even when you're out and about, away from your computer, you may sometimes find yourself with the urge to check in with your friends, update your status, or upload a photo—especially if you just saw something interesting on Mulberry Street.

Fortunately, you can take a big chunk of the Facebook experience with you in your pocket. Armed with a reasonably up-to-date mobile phone and nothing else up your sleeve, you can update your status, read and write Wall posts and Inbox messages, check your invitations, respond to friend requests, upload photos and videos, and more.

This comes in especially handy if you're stuck on public transportation, languishing in a doctor's waiting room, or trapped in any other zone of enforced boredom.

Exactly what you can and can't do on Facebook with your phone depends on its specific level of functionality. In this chapter we'll run through the various options, from the more primitive

(Facebook via text message) to the more sophisticated (Facebook via mobile web browser, and Facebook apps for smartphones).

The Facebook Mobile Application

For best results, you should start your mobile Facebook life while you're still sitting at your desk—by accessing the Facebook Mobile application on your computer. The Facebook Mobile app gives you a central portal for instructions, settings, and features related to using your mobile phone with Facebook. If you don't already have the Facebook Mobile app bookmarked, simply point your browser to facebook.com/mobile.

Facebook by Text Message

The simplest and most no-frills way to access Facebook by mobile phone is via text message. If your phone is capable of sending and receiving SMS text messages, and uses one of Facebook's supported carriers, you can access a slew of basic Facebook features just by texting.

To get started, you'll need to activate Facebook Mobile on your computer. Go to the Facebook Mobile app and in the Facebook Texts area, click Sign Up for Facebook Text Messages.

Facebook Texts

Update your Status and receive your notifications via text messaging.

Sign Up for Facebook Text Messages

The Activate Texts dialog will open, and Facebook will take you through a three-step process to verify your mobile phone so you can use it to access your Facebook account. In Step 1, you'll need to select your country and your service provider from the menu of supported carriers. (If your service provider isn't listed, this method won't work for you, so you'll need to look at the other options in this chapter.)

In Step 2, Facebook will ask you to send a text message to 32665 (FBOOK), and then Facebook will text a confirmation code back to your phone. Once you get the code, you can enter it in the dialog for Step 3 to finish the process.

 TIP: To keep up with the latest news, tips, and updates on using Facebook with your mobile device, follow Facebook's official Using Facebook Mobile Page. Head to Facebook.com/UsingFacebookMobile and click the Like button.

Checking In with Facebook Places

Looking for info on Facebook's Places feature, which allows you to share your location with friends by checking in to places using your mobile phone? Visit the *Sharing Content on Facebook* chapter for all the 411.

Facebook Text Commands

So what exactly can you do with Facebook Mobile text commands? Well, just for starters, you can update your status, write on someone's Wall, send an Inbox message, poke someone, or post a Note. You can even have Facebook send you a friend's mobile phone number if you don't have it handy (subject to privacy settings, of course). For a complete list, including the necessary commands for each action, visit the Mobile Texts Demo page—where you can see a helpful onscreen demonstration of what each command does. You'll find it at www.facebook.com/mobile/?texts.

 TIP: You can choose to receive a particular friend's status updates as mobile text messages by visiting their profile and clicking the Subscribe via SMS link underneath their picture. (Repeat for each friend you'd like to subscribe to.)

NOTE: Facebook itself doesn't charge you anything for sending and receiving messages from your phone—but your carrier's standard rates will apply.

Do Mobile Phone Calls Want to Be Free?

As I write this, Vonage has just announced a new app for mobile phones, cleverly named Vonage Mobile, which works a little like Skype: It allows users who've installed the app on their phones to make "free" calls to anyone in their Facebook friends list who also has the app installed, over both cellular and Wi-Fi connections. "Free" in this case means that only data charges apply—so you won't use up any calling minutes. Visit the official Vonage Page on Facebook for more info.

Once you've activated your phone, you can manage all your settings related to Facebook Texts via the Mobile tab in your Account Settings.

Settings	Networks	Notifications	Mobile	Language	Payments	Facebook Ads

Go to Facebook Mobile »

Mobile Phones

You have activated Facebook Mobile. You can now receive friend requests, messages, wall posts, and status updates on your phone, or upload photos and videos on the go.*

Facebook via Mobile Web Browser

If your phone is equipped with a web browser, Facebook has a version of its site that's optimized for the smaller browsers found on handheld devices. The URL for the mobile site is http://m.facebook.com. (You can also type that address into your computer's web browser for a preview of what the mobile site looks like.)

If you're using an iPhone or other touchscreen device, you can navigate to http://touch.facebook.com for a touch-friendly version of the site.

TIP: Even if you point your phone's browser toward Facebook's regular URL, Facebook will most likely sniff out the fact that you're accessing it from a mobile device and redirect you toward the mobile version of the site.

Uploading Content from Mobile Phones

You can upload content—specifically photos, videos, and Notes—to Facebook from any phone that's capable of sending multimedia (MMS) messages to an e-mail address and is (optimally) using one of Facebook's supported carriers.

Facebook assigns you a dedicated, personalized e-mail address for this purpose. Anything you send to your upload address gets posted to Facebook. To find your upload address, make sure you're logged in to your account and go to the home page for the Facebook Mobile app. Your address will be displayed under the Upload via Email heading, as seen at right. (Note that this address is specific to your account, so don't share it!)

Upload via Email
Use a personalized upload email to post status updates or send photos and videos straight to your profile. Your personal email is:

●●●●●●●●@m.facebook.com

Find your personal upload e-mail address on the home page for the Facebook mobile app.

TIP: When uploading a photo, whatever you type for the subject line of your message will be the photo's caption on Facebook. When uploading a video, the subject line will become the video's title, and anything you type in the body of the message will appear as the video's description. When uploading a Note, the subject line of your message will become the title of the Note. If there's no other content included in your e-mail, the subject line will be posted as a status update.

Facebook Apps for Smartphones

There are special mobile phone apps available for a number of popular smartphones—including iPhone, BlackBerry, Android, Sidekick, and more. You can download these apps to your phone for a mobile Facebook interface that's custom designed for your specific device. To find out more about these apps, head to the home page for the Facebook Mobile app and choose your phone from the list.

Facebook for your phone
Download rich, interactive applications built for your phone. Available for:

iPhone	Nokia
Palm	Android
Sony Ericsson	Windows Mobile
INQ	Sidekick
Blackberry	

TIP: In addition to your personal profile, any Pages for which you're an admin are assigned their own upload addresses, too. So you can easily update your Pages from your mobile device. To find the upload address for a Page, click its Edit Page link, and then under the Mobile heading, click Settings.

NOTE: If you're not using one of Facebook's supported carriers, Facebook says that you "should" still be able to upload photos and videos—but it's not guaranteed.

TIP: Before you can upload videos to Facebook, you need to make sure you've added the Video application to your account. See the *Photos and Videos* chapter for details.

 Speed + Mobility = 0.Facebook.com
In addition to its regular and touch-friendly mobile sites, Facebook has recently launched another variation at 0.Facebook.com. This site includes all of Facebook's key features, but is specially designed to be both fast and free: It's optimized for speed, and can be accessed without incurring any data charges (hence the zero in the name). At startup, 0.Facebook.com was available only in a limited number of countries, from select carriers, but its availability is expected to continue expanding.

Index